Becca—
Christmas 2008
From Mommy & Daddy

Betty Crocker
Cookie Book

WILEY

Wiley Publishing, Inc.

Library of Congress Cataloging-in-Publication Data

Crocker, Betty
[Cookie Book]
Betty Crocker Cookie Book
p. cm.
Rev. ed of: Betty Crocker's Ultimate Cookie Book
Included index
ISBN 0-7645-3940-X
1. Cookies I. Crocker, Betty. Betty Crocker's ultimate cookie book. II. Title.
TX772.C69 1998   98-6404
641.8'654—dc21   CIP

GENERAL MILLS, INC.
Director, Book and Electronic Publishing: Kim Walter
Manager, Book Publishing: Lois L. Tlusty
Editor: Lori Fox
Recipe Development and Testing: Betty Crocker Kitchens
Food Stylists: Betty Crocker Kitchens
Photography: General Mills Photo Studios and General Mills Image Library
WILEY PUBLISHING, INC.
Publisher: Natalie Chapman
Executive Editor: Anne Ficklen
Editor: Emily Nolan
Cover Design: Holly Wittenberg and Jeff Faust
Interior Design: George J. McKeon
For consistent baking results, the Betty Crocker Kitchens recommend Gold Medal Flour.

Find more great ideas and shop for name-brand housewares at *BettyCrocker*.com

Manufactured in the United States of America
10 9 8 7 6 5 4

Cover photo: Magic Window Cookies (p.109); Lemon Bars (p.161), Russian Tea Cakes (p.179); Gingerbread Cookies (p.227)

I love Cookies. . .

Who doesn't like cookies. . .they're fun to eat, easily portable and always a crowd-pleaser. Whether they are chock-full of chocolate and nuts or sweet and buttery, everyone has their favorite. So, what better than to include everyone's favorite cookie within the pages of *Betty Crocker Cookie Book*! From the Most Requested Recipe, which begins each chapter, to tips and helpful hints throughout, this book is teeming with great cookie recipes. Learn the secret to making cookies all the same size (page xxii) and get tried-and-true advice for mailing those cookie care packages to ensure safe delivery (page xxvii).

Browse through the chapters of recipes and photos to find your favorite cookie, plus some new recipes to try. Learn about all the different ingredients that go into baking cookies (starts on page vi)—what you choose to use will have an effect on your cookies and bars. Discover some easy decorating ideas (pages 210–213) to spruce up your cookies without much effort, such as tinting granulated sugar or decorating with melted chocolate. Mmmmm.

With each chapter brimming with delicious recipes for every occasion, you will find this book indispensable. Whip up some classic drop cookies or explore the chapter on making cookies from cake mixes—you'll just need a few ingredients and a bit of time and get delicious results. And when time is really short, check out the no-bake recipes. They'll save time, and you'll still be rewarded with smiles. With food trends changing all the time, isn't it nice to know that cookies will always be a favorite? Enjoy!

Betty Crocker

Contents

Introduction **iii**

The "Doughs" and "Doughn'ts" of
Cookie Baking **vi**

CHAPTER 1
Easy Drop Cookies **1**

CHAPTER 2
Super Bars and Brownies **55**

CHAPTER 3
Kid Kookies **99**

CHAPTER 4
Fix em' with a Mix **137**

CHAPTER 5

Hand-Shaped and Pressed
Cookies **169**

CHAPTER 6

Rolling in Dough **207**

CHAPTER 7

Celebrate with Cookies **243**

CHAPTER 8

Special Cookies for Special
Diets **287**

Nutrition/Cooking/Metric Information **312–313**

Index **314**

The "Dough's" and "Doughn'ts" of Cookie Baking

This comprehensive guide will help ensure successful cookie baking every time. You will find information about ingredients, cookie baking equipment and specific tips and techniques for every aspect of making your cookies, such as measuring, mixing, shaping, baking and cooling. And finally, our question-and-answer section, "Cookie Cures," offers expert advice on common baking problems—why they happen and how to avoid them.

KNOW YOUR INGREDIENTS

Cookies and bars deliver such satisfaction for being in such a small, little package. To make each delicious bite count, use the best ingredients available. The information that follows will help you choose ingredients essential to baking cookies and bars.

Get the Scoop on Flour

Flour is just flour—anything will do, right? Wrong. Many types of flour are available, but some work better than others for baking cookies and bars. The main difference among types of flour is the amount of protein each flour has. The protein in the flour, when mixed with a liquid, creates gluten, which gives structure and texture to your baked goods. In some instances, you'll need more gluten (as in yeast breads); at other times, you'll need less (as in cakes and cookies). You may be surprised by the different results you can have, depending on which flour you choose.

Flour Facts

Here are some flour facts to help you pick the best type of flour for the cookies or bars you are baking:

Type	Description	Use in Cookies and Bars
All-Purpose Flour, Bleached	A blend of select hard and soft wheats, making it suitable for all types of baking. Bleaching agents are used in small amounts to whiten flour and improve baking results.	Most commonly used in cookies and bars, and makes the best cookies.

Flour Facts

Type	Description	Use in Cookies and Bars
All-Purpose Flour, Unbleached	All-purpose flour without the bleaching agents. Unbleached flour is not as white as all bleached flour, so light colored cookies and bars may have a creamy color.	Commonly used in cookies and bars and makes the best cookies.
Bread Flour	Unbleached flour made from a special blend of wheat higher in protein than those used in all-purpose flour. Protein produces gluten, which gives structure-building properties, particularly in baked goods made with yeast.	Suitable for cookies and bars, but the high protein content will result in slightly tougher cookies and bars.
Cake Flour	Milled from select soft wheat and is best suited for fine textured cakes, as well as biscuits and pastries	Cookies and bars made with this flour will be very delicate and fragile and may fall apart.
Quick Mixing Flour	A convenient all-purpose flour that mixes instantly in liquid. It is granular in texture, but works the same as regular all-purpose flour.	Some cookie doughs will look and feel different but the result will be the same. If dough seems dry at first, work with hands until dough holds together.
Self-Rising Flour	All-purpose flour with baking powder and salt added.	For best results, use a recipe developed for this flour.
Wheat Blend Flour	Specially formulated blend of 100 percent hard-wheat flour and wheat bran. The wheat bran gives the texture, taste and appearance common to wheat bread.	Wheat bran gives cookies a slightly coarse texture and mild nutty flavor. This flour can be directly substituted for all-purpose flour.
Whole Wheat Flour	Milled from the entire kernel of wheat, which includes the bran, germ and endosperm.	Produces satisfactory cookies. Many recipes call for part whole wheat flour and part all-purpose flour, giving cookies a nutty taste and coarser texture. If you want to use all whole wheat flour, stick to recipes developed for only whole wheat flour.

Note: Some recipes use cornstarch for a part of the flour, resulting in tender cookies that have a very fine and compact texture. Cornstarch and flour are not interchangeable cup for cup, so look for specific recipes that use cornstarch.

MEASURING FLOUR Today's flours are presifted, so sifting again isn't necessary. To measure flour correctly, spoon it lightly into a dry-ingredient measuring cup, then level with a metal spatula or straight-edged knife. Never dip the measuring cup into the flour or tap the measuring cup to settle the flour when measuring, or you'll get too much flour. Too much flour makes cookies tough, crumbly and dry. Measuring too little flour causes cookies to spread and lose their shape.

MEASURING FLOUR CORRECTLY

Lightly spoon flour into measuring cup.

Level with straight-edge spatula or knife.

STORING FLOUR Store all flours in airtight canisters in a cool, dry place. Use all-purpose (bleached and unbleached), bread, cake and quick-mixing flours within 15 months; self-rising within 9 months and wheat blend and whole wheat flours within 6 to 8 months. If keeping flour for an extended period, double-bag it in resealable plastic freezer bags and store in the refrigerator or freezer for up to 2 years; bring flour to room temperature before using. *Note: The oils in wheat blend and whole wheat flours can be become rancid, giving them a very strong, unpleasant flavor. To prevent this type of flour from becoming rancid, store in the refrigerator or freezer following the aforementioned guideline.*

Oats

Quick-cooking and old-fashioned rolled oats are interchangeable unless recipes call for a specific type. Instant oatmeal products are not the same as quick-cooking and should not be used for baking. Old-fashioned oats are larger than quick-cooking oats and don't absorb as much moisture. Because of this, cookies made with old-fashioned oats tend to be moist and chewy. Quick-cooking oats are smaller than old-fashioned oats and absorb moisture better.

These two factors make quick-cooking oats especially good for nonbaked cookies because they will hold together very well.

There are many ways to use oats, including toasting and grinding them. Toasting oats gives them a delicious, slightly nutty, rich flavor and a bit of extra crunch. When they're ground, they can be used for some of the flour in cookies, giving them great flavor and a chewy texture.

Toasting Oats

Toasted oats have a nutty flavor and slightly crunchy texture. To toast oats, heat oven to 350°. Spread 1 to 2 cups old-fashioned or quick-cooking oats in ungreased jelly roll pan, 15 1/2 × 10 1/2 × 1 inch, or on large cookie sheet. Toast 15 to 20 minutes, stirring once, until light golden brown. Toasted oats can be used cup for cup in cookie and bar recipes calling for oats. They're also great sprinkled on ice cream, yogurt and fruit.

Ground Oats

Ground oats add great texture and flavor to cookies. Place about 1 1/4 cups old-fashioned or quick-cooking oats in your blender or food processor. Cover and blend on medium speed about

1 minute, stopping occasionally to stir oats. You'll get about 1 cup of ground oats. Ground oats can be substituted for about one-third of the amount of flour called for in a cookie or bar recipe without causing major changes in the texture.

Fats and Oils

Fats add tenderness and flavor to cookies, but not all fats are created equal in texture and flavor. The type of fat you choose—butter, margarine, reduced-calorie or low-fat butter or margarine, vegetable-oil spreads or shortening—depends on the kind of cookie you want. The biggest difference among these fats is how much water they contain, which affects how cookies bake and their eating texture. Cookies made with fats that have a lot of water in them will be soft, puffy and tough and will dry out quickly. Check the list that follows for specific information on each type of fat.

BUTTER Available in sticks and whipped in tubs. Made from cream, butter must be 80 percent butterfat by USDA standards. *Use only sticks for baking cookies.* Many people stock up on butter for holiday baking. For more immediate use, store butter in the refrigerator (in the original package), and use on or before the expiration date printed on the package. Wrap partially used sticks of butter tightly in plastic wrap or aluminum foil to prevent it from absorbing refrigerator odors and drying out. For longer storage, store butter in freezer. Place the butter (in the original package) into resealable plastic freezer bags; label and freeze up to four months.

COOKIES MADE WITH BUTTER

- Spread more during baking
- Are more crisp
- Have a buttery flavor

SOFTENING BUTTER (OR MARGARINE)
Most cookie recipes call for softened butter or margarine. But how soft is it supposed to be, and how can you tell? Allow butter to soften at room temperature for 30 to 45 minutes; the time will vary, depending on the temperature of your kitchen. Perfectly softened butter should give gently to pressure (you should be able to leave a fingerprint and slight indentation on the stick) but shouldn't be soft in appearance. Butter that is too soft or is partially melted results in dough that is too soft, causing cookies to spread too much.

SOFTENED BUTTER

Perfectly softened butter

Butter too soft

Butter is partially melted

BUTTER-MARGARINE BLENDS Available in sticks and tubs, blends usually are a combination of 60 percent margarine and 40 percent butter and are interchangeable with butter or margarine. *Use only sticks for baking cookies.*

COOKIES MADE WITH BUTTER-MARGARINE BLENDS

- Spread more during baking
- Are more crisp
- Have a less buttery flavor than all-butter cookies

MARGARINE Available in sticks and tubs, this butter substitute must have at least 80 percent fat from vegetable oils to be legally labeled *margarine*. *Use only sticks for baking cookies.* Margarine is flavored with dairy products and can be used interchangeably with butter.

COOKIES MADE WITH MARGARINE

- Spread more during baking
- Are slightly less crisp than cookies made with butter
- Have a less buttery flavor than all-butter cookies

REDUCED-CALORIE OR LOW-FAT BUTTER OR MARGARINE Available in sticks and tubs and in whipped form, these products have water and air added and contain at least 20 percent less fat than regular butter or margarine. *Use only sticks containing at least 65 percent fat for baking cookies.* Some of these products have as much as 58 percent water, so read labels carefully.

COOKIES MADE WITH REDUCED-CALORIE OR LOW-FAT BUTTER OR MARGARINE

- Have a softer dough
- Spread much less or not at all
- Brown less

- Are cakelike rather than crisp
- Are tougher rather than tender
- Stick to the cookie sheet more easily
- Have a less buttery flavor than all-butter cookies
- Become hard and dry more quickly

VEGETABLE-OIL SPREADS Available in sticks, tubs and liquid squeeze bottles, these products have less than 80 percent fat (vegetable oil) by weight and are labeled "vegetable-oil spreads." *Use only sticks containing at least 65 percent fat for baking cookies.* Some of these products have as much as 58 percent water, so read labels carefully.

COOKIES MADE WITH VEGETABLE-OIL SPREADS*

- Have a softer dough
- Spread much less or not at all
- Brown less
- Are cakelike rather than crisp
- Are tougher rather than tender
- Stick to the cookie sheet more easily
- Have a less buttery flavor than all-butter cookies
- Become hard and dry more quickly

Special Note: We do not recommend that reduced-calorie and low-fat butter or margarine and vegetable-oil spreads with less than 65 percent fat be used for baking cookies and bars because results are usually very unsatisfactory. Products with less than 65 percent fat are made to be used as table spreads and for some cooking, but not for baking.

VEGETABLE OILS Vegetable oil is 100 percent fat. Use canola, corn, safflower and soybean oils for making cookies calling for oil. Olive and peanut oils have distinctive flavors that you might not like in cookies. Nut-flavored oils, such as walnut and pecan, however, can be used in place of vegetable oil. Vegetable oil cannot be substituted for a solid fat. Most recipes using oil call for half oil and half butter, margarine or shortening.

COOKIES MADE WITH PART VEGETABLE OIL AND PART BUTTER, MARGARINE OR SHORTENING

- Have no buttery taste
- Are flatter, chewier and crisper
- Have crackly or crinkled tops

COOKIES MADE WITH ALL VEGETABLE OIL

- Are crisp if recipe calls for no added liquids such as milk, juice or water
- Are soft and moist if liquids such as milk, juice or water are added to the recipe
- Are crispy cookies with crackly or crinkled tops

SHORTENING Available in cans and sticks and in regular and butter-flavored varieties, shortening is 100 percent fat. Butter flavored shortening and regular shortening can be used interchangeably. Shortening can be used interchangeably with butter or margarine.

COOKIES MADE WITH SHORTENING

- Have no buttery flavor unless the butter-flavored variety is used
- Spread less or not at all
- Are cakelike and softer
- Are crumbly and more dry

Sweeteners

Sweeteners not only add sweetness to cookies, but also aid in browning and affect the texture of cookies and bars. Most cookie and bar recipes call for granulated white sugar, brown sugar or both, but other types of sweeteners are frequently used. Types of sweeteners are discussed below.

BROWN SUGAR Brown sugar is a mixture of granulated white sugar and molasses, which is a by-product of making sugar. Brown sugar adds moistness, flavor and color to cookies. It comes in two varieties: light and dark . The dark variety contains more molasses and has a deeper, richer flavor. Light and dark brown sugars can be used interchangeably. To measure brown sugar correctly, spoon it into a dry-ingredient measuring cup and pack it down firmly until it's level with the top of the cup.

CORN SYRUP This thick liquid form of sugar comes in light and dark varieties. The dark syrup has a richer, brown-sugary flavor. The two can be used interchangeably unless one is specified in a recipe. Corn syrup adds moisture and makes cookies brown more quickly. To measure corn syrup correctly, spray the inside of a liquid measuring cup with cooking spray (allows sticky liquids to come out more easily). Pour syrup into cup. For an accurate amount, always read the measurement at eye level while the cup is on a flat surface.

GRANULATED WHITE SUGAR This is the variety of sugar we are most familiar with. It adds sweetness, tenderness, moisture, browning and contributes to spreading. Cookies with a higher ratio of sugar to flour will be more tender and crisp. To measure granulated sugar correctly, scoop the sugar into a dry-ingredient measuring cup, or dip the measuring cup into the sugar, and level with metal spatula or straight-edged knife.

HONEY The distinctive flavor of honey can be found in many recipes. Honey attracts moisture from the air, so cookies and bars made with honey will be soft after baking and may get even softer during storage. To measure honey correctly, spray the inside of a liquid measuring cup with cooking spray (allows sticky liquids to come out more easily). Pour honey into cup. For an accurate amount, always read the measurement at eye level while the cup is on a flat surface.

MOLASSES A thick and sweet by-product of making granulated white sugar, molasses is available in light, dark and blackstrap varieties. Light and dark molasses can be used interchangeably. Blackstrap molasses has a very strong, bitter flavor and is generally not used in baking. To measure molasses correctly, spray the inside of a liquid measuring cup with cooking spray (allows sticky liquids to come out more easily). Pour molasses into cup. For an accurate amount, always read the measurement at eye level while the cup is on a flat surface.

POWDERED SUGAR (CONFECTIONERS' SUGAR) This sugar actually is very finely ground granulated white sugar with a little cornstarch added to prevent it from clumping together. Although most often used in frostings and glazes, powdered sugar also is used in cookie and bar recipes. Powdered sugar, like cornstarch, produces a very fine, compact-textured and tender cookie. Powdered sugar and granulated sugar cannot be used interchangeably. To measure powdered sugar correctly, spoon it into a dry-ingredient measuring cup, then level with a metal spatula or straight-edged knife.

Leavening

Cookies usually call for one or two types of leavening, either baking soda or baking powder, which react with liquids to form a gas, causing the cookies to rise. Baking powder and baking soda are not interchangeable. You want your leaveners to be fresh, so always check the expiration dates on the containers. If the product is older than the date on the label, the leavening power is significantly decreased or completely gone, and cookies and bars will be flat and dense in texture.

BAKING SODA Because baking soda is alkaline, it needs to react with an acidic ingredient, such as buttermilk, brown sugar, lemon juice, chocolate or molasses, to create its leavening power. Less acidic doughs brown better. Because of this unique feature, baking soda often is added to an acidic dough not as a leavening, but to neutralize the dough's

acidity and create good browning, such as in chocolate chip cookies.

BAKING POWDER Unlike baking soda, baking powder does not need an acidic ingredient to react. Baking powder contains baking soda and just the right amount of acid to produce its leavening power. Since baking powder does not react with or neutralize any acids in the dough, doughs made with baking powder spread less, bake more quickly and do not brown very well. That's why sometimes baking soda is added to doughs that use baking powder as their leavener to produce a better-browning cookie.

Eggs

Eggs add richness, moisture and structure to cookies. Yet, too many eggs can make cookies crumbly. All the recipes in this book have been tested with large eggs. Egg product substitutes, made of egg whites, can be used in place of whole eggs, but cookies may be drier.

Can't break the habit of nibbling on raw cookie dough? A word of caution: Salmonella, a very serious and potentially fatal food poisoning, can be contracted by eating raw whole eggs. The solution? Don't eat unbaked dough made with raw whole eggs. Or make your cookies with *pasteurized raw whole eggs* or *egg product substitutes* (both are perfectly safe to eat raw). We happen to know that some cookie dough never gets baked, because you like to nibble on it while baking cookies. With these options, you can have your cookie dough and eat it, too—safely, that is!

Liquids

Liquids such as water, fruit juice, cream and milk tend to make cookies crisper by causing them to spread more. Add only as much liquid as your recipe calls for. Buttermilk can be substituted for regular milk, but beware. Buttermilk is an acid ingredient; if the recipe you're using doesn't have 1/4 teaspoon of baking soda already in it, please add this to your dough with the flour. The reason? Without the baking soda, the leavening won't work very well.

Chocolate

BAKING COCOA When a recipe calls for baking cocoa, use the unsweetened kind; do not use instant cocoa mix. Two types of baking cocoa are available: nonalkalized (regular) and alkalized ("Dutched" or European). Alkalized cocoa goes through a "Dutching" process to neutralize the natural acids found in cocoa. The result is a darker cocoa with a more mellow chocolate flavor than regular cocoa. The two types of cocoa can be used interchangeably, but you will notice differences in color and flavor. Baked goods made with Dutched cocoa will be darker in color and a bit milder in flavor.

BITTERSWEET CHOCOLATE Similar to semisweet chocolate in its makeup, but has more chocolate flavor and is slightly less sweet. Bittersweet can be used interchangeably with semisweet chocolate. Usually available in eating bars or squares.

CHOCOLATE-FLAVORED SYRUP A mixture of cocoa or chocolate liquor, sugar, water, salt and sometimes other flavorings such as vanilla.

CHOCOLATE FUDGE TOPPING Similar to chocolate syrup but with the addition of milk, cream or butter.

COMPOUND CHOCOLATE A term used for products in which most of the cocoa butter has been removed and replaced by another vegetable fat. It can be purchased as chocolate- and vanilla-flavored candy coating, confectioners' coating or summer coating. It is available in dark, white or pastel colors. It is almost never used in baked cookies and bars but is frequently used in unbaked candylike mixtures.

MILK CHOCOLATE A combination of chocolate liquor, additional cocoa butter, sugar and milk or cream. It must contain at least 10 percent chocolate liquor. It is commonly available in candy bars, other types of candies and chips.

PREMELTED UNSWEETENED CHOCOLATE A mixture of cocoa and vegetable oils in 1-ounce foil packets or plastic envelopes. It can be used in place of melted unsweetened chocolate squares.

SEMISWEET CHOCOLATE A combination of chocolate liquor, additional cocoa butter and sugar. It contains at least 35 percent chocolate liquor. It is usually in the form of chips or squares.

SWEET CHOCOLATE A combination of chocolate liquor, additional cocoa butter and sugar. It must contain at least 15 percent chocolate liquor, and it has more sugar than semisweet chocolate. This is the type of chocolate called for in German chocolate cake recipes.

UNSWEETENED CHOCOLATE Sometimes referred to as baking, cooking or bitter chocolate. It is chocolate liquor that has been molded and cooled. It doesn't contain sugar and is too bitter for eating by itself.

WHITE CHOCOLATE Not a true chocolate because it doesn't contain chocolate liquor. Still, the term "white chocolate" has stuck, and the flavor is featured in many desserts. White chocolate should contain cocoa butter as a portion or all of the fat. It should be ivory or cream colored, not pure white. Terms for white chocolate include white baking bar, vanilla milk (white) chips and deluxe white baking pieces. White chocolate can scorch or burn easily while melting.

Melting Chocolate

Melting any type of chocolate must be done carefully because chocolate burns easily. When you are melting chocolate, you are not trying to cook it. Never heat dark chocolate above 120°F or white or milk chocolate above 110°F. If you are melting bars or squares of chocolate, chop it first; the smaller pieces will melt faster and there is less chance of burning.

STOVE-TOP METHOD Melt chocolate in a heavy saucepan directly over the lowest possible heat. Melt the chocolate slowly, and stir frequently; remove it from the heat just before it is completely melted. Stir the chocolate until it is completely melted.

MICROWAVE METHOD When melted in the microwave, most forms of chocolate will not change their shape (except for unsweetened chocolate), but the surface will become shiny. Place chocolate in a microwavable measuring cup or deep bowl. Stir after half the time and again at the minimum total time. Any small lumps will melt while chocolate is stirred.

Melting Chocolate in the Microwave

Amount	Power Level	Time
Bittersweet (1-ounce square)	High (100%)	1 to 2 minutes; stir halfway through heating time (the square will retain some of its original shape). Remove from microwave; stir until completely melted. Add 10 seconds for each additional square.
Semi-sweet or milk chocolate chips (1 cup)	High (100%)	3 to 4 minutes, stir halfway through heating time (chips will retain some of their original shape). Remove from microwave; stir until completely melted. If needed, microwave at additional 10 to 20 second intervals, stirring until smooth.
Unsweetened semisweet square (1-ounce)	High (100%)	1 to 2 minutes or until almost melted; stir halfway through heating time. Remove from microwave; stir until completely melted. Add 10 seconds for each additional square.
White baking bar (1-ounce square) or **Vanilla milk (white) chips** (1 cup)	Medium (70%)	1 minute; stir. Microwave an additional 10- to 20-second intervals, stirring until smooth.

Helpful Chocolate Information

SEIZING is the term used when any moisture (even the smallest amount) causes chocolate to become thick, lumpy and grainy during melting. To prevent seizing, be sure all utensils, saucepans and bowls are completely dry and that no moisture gets into the chocolate when melting. If this happens, here's an easy solution: Stir about 1 tablespoon of solid shortening or vegetable oil into every 6 ounces of chocolate. If vegetable oil is used, the chocolate will take longer to set or harden.

BLOOM is the term for the grayish-white color or film that forms on chocolate that has been stored at temperatures that vary from hot to cold. In this process, cocoa butter melts and rises to the surface of the chocolate. Bloom does not affect the flavor or quality of the chocolate.

SUBSTITUTES FOR CHOCOLATE See page xviii.

Chocolate Storage

Store chocolate properly to maintain its quality. It is important to store it in a cool, dry place, between 60° and 75°. Chocolate can be stored in the refrigerator if tightly wrapped to keep out moisture and odors. Keeping chocolate in the refrigerator does not allow you to store it any longer than if it is kept at room temperature. Refrigerated chocolate usually will "bloom," (see above). Cold chocolate becomes hard and brittle, so remove it from the refrigerator and let stand at room temperature before using. Unsweetened, bittersweet, semisweet and sweet chocolate can be stored for up to 2 years, and white chocolate up to 15 months. If the temperature is higher than 75° or the humidity is above 50 percent, wrap chocolate in plastic wrap or place in resealable plastic bags.

Cocoa is less sensitive to temperature and humidity than chocolate. It is best to store cocoa in a tightly covered container in a cool, dry place. Cocoa will keep indefinitely.

Nuts and Peanuts

Most cookie recipes call for walnuts, pecans, almonds or peanuts. Hazelnuts, cashews and macadamia nuts are also used. When nuts are called for in a recipe, you can use any variety of nut or peanuts instead. Nuts can easily become rancid. Rancid nuts have a very unpleasant, strong flavor that can ruin the taste of your cookies. To prevent rancidity, store nuts and peanuts tightly covered in your refrigerator or freezer for up to 2 years. Cashews should not be frozen because they can become soggy. Before using nuts or peanuts in a recipe, do a little taste test. If they don't taste fresh, throw them out.

Note: Almond brickle baking chips can also become rancid. To prevent rancidity, store in the refrigerator or freezer up to 6 months. Do a taste test before using.

Cookie Ingredient Equivalents

Ingredient	Amount You Have	Will Equal
Apricots (dried)	1 pound	3 cups
Butter, margarine, shortening	1 pound	2 cups
Cherries, maraschino cherries	10-ounce jar	About 33
Chocolate, baking (bittersweet, sweetened and unsweetened)	8-ounce package	8 squares
Chocolate chips	6-ounce bag	1 cup
Cocoa, baking	8-ounce container	About 3 cups
Coconut, shredded or flaked	7-ounce bag	2 2/3 cups
Corn syrup, light or dark	16-ounce bottle	2 cups
Cranberries, dried	6-ounce package	About 2 cups
Cranberries, fresh	1 pound	4 cups
Cream cheese	8-ounce package 3-ounce package	1 cup 1/3 cup
Dates (pitted), chopped	1 pound	2 1/2 cups
Egg product substitute	1/4 cup	1 whole large egg
Figs (dried), chopped	1 pound	2 2/3 cups
Flour, all-purpose	1 pound 5 pounds	3 1/3 cups 17 cups
Flour, whole wheat	1 pound 5 pounds	3 1/2 cups 17 cups
Honey	16-ounce jar	About 1 1/4 cups
Jam or jelly	12-ounce jar	1 cup
Lemon juice (freshly squeezed)	1 medium lemon	2 to 3 tablespoons
Lemon peel, grated	1 medium lemon	1 1/2 to 3 teaspoons

Ingredient	Amount You Have	Will Equal
Marshmallows, large	10-ounce bag 5 marshmallows 1 large marshmallow	40 marshmallows 1/2 cup 10 miniature
Marshmallows, miniature	10 1/2-ounce bag 1/2 cup 10 miniature	5 cups 45 marshmallows 1 large marshmallow
Milk, evaporated	12-ounce can	1 1/3 cups
Milk, sweetened condensed	14-ounce can	1 1/3 cups
Molasses, light or dark	12-ounce bottle	1 1/3 cups
Nuts, shelled		
Almonds (whole)	1 pound	3 1/2 cups
Peanuts (whole)	1 pound	3 cups
Pecans (halves)	1 pound	4 cups
Walnuts (halves)	1 pound	6 1/4 cups
Oats	18-ounce container	About 6 1/3 cups
Orange juice (freshly squeezed)	1 medium orange	1/4 to 1/3 cup
Orange peel, grated	1 medium orange	1 to 2 tablespoons
Peanut butter	18-ounce jar	2 cups
Prunes (pitted), whole	1 pound	2 1/4 cups
Pumpkin, canned (solid pack)	15-ounce can	About 2 cups
Raisins	1 pound	2 3/4 cups
Sour cream	8-ounce container	1 cup
Sugar, brown	2 pounds	About 5 cups packed
Sugar, granulated	1 pound 5 pounds	2 1/4 cups About 12 cups
Sugar, powdered	2 pounds	About 7 1/2 cups

Baker's Substitutions

Using the ingredients recommended in the recipe is best. But if you have to substitute, try the following:

Ingredient	Substitution
Baking powder, 1 teaspoon	1/2 teaspoon cream of tartar plus 1/4 teaspoon baking soda
Brown sugar, 1 cup packed	1 cup granulated sugar mixed with 2 tablespoons molasses or dark corn syrup
Buttermilk, 1 cup	1 tablespoon cider vinegar, white vinegar or lemon juice plus enough milk to equal 1 cup (let stand 5 minutes); or use 1 cup plain yogurt
Cinnamon (ground), 1 teaspoon	1 teaspoon pumpkin or apple pie spice
Chocolate, Bittersweet and Semisweet, 1 ounce	1 ounce unsweetened baking chocolate plus 1 tablespoon sugar
Semisweet chips, 1 cup	6 ounces semisweet chocolate, chopped
Sweet baking, 4 ounces	1/4 cup baking cocoa plus 1/3 cup granulated sugar and 3 tablespoons shortening
Unsweetened baking, 1 ounce	3 tablespoons baking cocoa plus 1 tablespoon vegetable oil or melted shortening
White baking bar, 1 ounce	1 ounce white almond bark or candy coating
Corn Syrup, Light, 1 cup	1 1/4 cups granulated sugar plus 1/4 cup water (mix together before using)
Dark, 1 cup	1 cup light corn syrup; 3/4 cup light corn syrup plus 1/4 cup molasses; 1 cup maple-flavored syrup
Egg (large), 1 whole	2 egg whites; 2 egg yolks plus 1 tablespoon water; 1/4 cup egg product substitute

Ingredient	Substitution
Flour	See page vi for specifics on using different types of flour for baking cookies and bars.
Gingerroot (grated or finely chopped), 1 teaspoon	1/4 teaspoon ground ginger
Milk, sweetened condensed	Pour 1/3 cup plus 2 tablespoons boiling water into blender or food processor. Add 1 cup nonfat dry milk, 2/3 cup sugar, 1/4 cup melted margarine or butter and 1/8 teaspoon vanilla. Cover and blend on high speed 30 seconds or until smooth. Remove from blender. Store covered in refrigerator. Makes about 1 1/4 cups milk (equivalent to a 14-ounce can of sweetened condensed milk).
Molasses, 1 cup	1 cup dark corn syrup or honey
Nuts (any amount)	Almonds, hazelnuts, peanuts, pecans and walnuts are interchangeable in recipes. For nut allergies, substitute an equal amount of wheat germ nuts snack.
Pumpkin or apple pie spice, 1 teaspoon	Mix 1/2 teaspoon ground cinnamon, 1/4 teaspoon ground ginger, 1/8 teaspoon ground allspice and 1/8 teaspoon ground nutmeg.
Raisins, 1/2 cup	1/2 cup currants, dried cherries, dried cranberries, chopped dates or chopped prunes
Sour cream, 1 cup	1 cup plain yogurt

Cookie Sheet Facts

Type	Baking Results	Hints for Success
Shiny Aluminum	Consistent shape, color, diameter and eating quality	If cookie sheets are thin, put 2 sheets together (one on top of the other) for added insulation.
Insulated (also called cushioned or double layered)	Cookies take longer to bake. Bottoms of cookies are light colored. Cookies may not brown as much as indicated in recipe doneness test. May be difficult to remove from cookie sheet because bottom of cookie is more tender.	Do a touch test to see if cookies are set
Dark Nonstick	Diameter of cookies may be smaller. Cookie shape may be more rounded. Tops and bottoms are more browned, especially the bottoms. Bottoms of cookies may be hard.	No need to grease pans. Reduce oven temperature by 25°. Rotate cookie sheet during baking for even browning.
Black Surface	Cookies bake faster because black color absorbs heat. Diameter of cookies may be smaller. Cookie shape may be more rounded.	Reduce oven temperature by 25°. Check cookies before minimum doneness time given in the recipe. Tops of cookies are more browned. Bottoms of cookies may get too dark or burn and be hard.

COOKIE-MAKING EQUIPMENT

Cookies are an all-time favorite to make and to eat! To make sure you get the best results every time you bake, we suggest starting out by using the right equipment for the job. The information that follows will help you select the best equipment.

Cookie Sheets

There are many types of cookie sheets to choose from, including shiny aluminum, insulated, dark nonstick and black surface. Have at least three or four cookie sheets, so as you bake one sheet, you can get another one ready to go. Use cookie sheets that are at least 2 inches narrower and shorter than the inside dimensions of your oven, so the heat will circulate around them. In a pinch, the aluminum cover for a 13×9×2-inch baking pan will work too. Check the chart above for specifics on cookie sheets.

Reusable Cookie Sheet Liners

In last few years, a number of reusable cookie sheet liners have become available. These are placed on cookie sheets to make cleaning the sheet easier. Although the liners work as intended, they themselves are a mess to clean. We don't recommend going to the bother of using the liners when the surface of the cookie sheets works just fine for baking cookies.

Baking Pans for Bars

Use the exact size of pan called for in the recipe. Shiny metal pans are preferred for baking bars. They reflect the heat away from the bars, preventing the crust from getting too brown and hard. Dark nonstick and glass baking pans should be used following the manufacturer's directions. These pans absorb heat easily; reducing the oven heat by 25° or checking for doneness 3 to 5 minutes before the minimum time given is usually recommended. Bars baked in pans that are too big become hard and overcooked, and those baked in pans that are too small can be doughy in the center and hard on the edges. Be careful when cutting bars baked in nonstick pans, or you may scratch the surface. Try using a plastic knife to avoid this problem. In fact, a plastic knife works best for cutting brownies and soft, sticky bars such as lemon bars.

Liquid Measuring Cups

Glass cups come in 1-, 2-, 4- and 8-cup sizes. These cups measure liquids accurately, whereas nested, or dry-ingredient measuring cups, do not. For the accurate amount of liquid, always read the measurement line at eye level while the cup is on a flat surface. Before measuring sticky liquids, such as corn syrup, honey and molasses, spray the cup with cooking spray or coat it very lightly with vegetable oil—the sticky liquid will come out more easily.

Dry-Ingredient Measuring Cups

Also called nested measuring cups, these metal or plastic cups range from 1/4 to 1 cup. Some sets include 1/8 cup, 2/3 cup and 3/4 cup. These cups are used to measure all dry ingredients and solid fats, such as butter, margarine and shortening. See specific ingredients for how to measure correctly.

Graduated Measuring Spoons

Made of metal or plastic, these spoons are hooked together by a ring and range in size from 1/4 teaspoon to 1 tablespoon. Some sets have 1/8 teaspoon and 3/4 teaspoon. These spoons are used to measure dry ingredients or small amounts of liquid ingredients. The ingredients measured should be level with the top edge of the spoon.

Wooden Spoons

Wooden spoons are great for making cookie dough because they're so sturdy, and the handles are more comfortable to hold when mixing stiffer doughs.

Hand or Stand Mixers

Electric mixers make the job of mixing ingredients easy and fast. Mixers are used to beat butter, cream cheese, fats and sugar and to mix in eggs and flavorings. Flour and other dry ingredients are almost always stirred in by hand to avoid overmixing the dough, which can result in tougher cookies.

Food Processors

None of the recipes in this book were tested using a food processor. However, this appliance method would work best when the dough can be made from start to finish in the processor. Recipes that have extra ingredients stirred in, such as chips, nuts or dried fruits, would require a separate bowl, making the processor much less convenient to use. Check manufacturers' directions for making cookie dough in food processors. However, a food processor is a great tool to have around when you're baking because it makes quick work of chopping nuts and dried fruits, or shredding carrots.

Pancake Turners

Pancake turners, which may also be called cookie turners, are made of metal or plastic. The turner part should be as wide or wider than the baked cookie you're removing from cookie sheets to prevent breakage and keep softer cookies from drooping over the sides of the turner. The thinner the turner, the easier it is to slide under cookies, especially thin, delicate and fragile cookies.

Wire Cooling Racks

Cooling racks are definitely a cookie baker's necessity. Look for racks that rise at least 1/2 inch above the surface of your countertop, so air can circulate around the cookies better. Also, look for racks with the metal wires placed closely together, so softer, more delicate or very small cookies won't drop through the spaces between the wires. If the wires are spaced too far apart, try this trick: Place one rack on the counter, then top with a second rack with the wires in the opposite direction. If you run out of space on your racks before you're done baking, you can place your cookies on waxed paper, brown wrapping paper, baking parchment paper or paper towels.

MIX IT UP

An electric mixer or spoon can be used for making the dough in most of the recipes in this book. The sugars, fats and liquids usually are mixed together first until well combined. Flour and other dry ingredients are almost always stirred in by hand to avoid overmixing the dough, which can result in tougher cookies. When testing these recipes, we didn't notice significant differences in the baked appearance or eating texture of cookies in which the sugars, fats and liquids were mixed with a mixer versus a spoon.

MIXING SUGAR AND FAT

Proper appearance of sugar and butter when recipe states to beat sugar and butter with an electric mixer until fluffy.

GET IT INTO SHAPE

Drop Cookies

Spoon dough with a flatware teaspoon or tablespoon unless a level graduated measuring teaspoon or tablespoon is specified in the recipe. Push dough onto cookie sheet with another spoon or a rubber spatula.

MEASURING COOKIE DOUGH

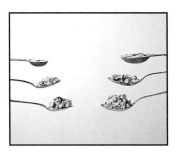

Level teaspoon   *Level tablespoon*

Rounded teaspoon   *Rounded tablespoon*

Heaping teaspoon   *Heaping tablespoon*

A trick we use in the Betty Crocker Kitchens to make drop cookies the same size and shape is to use a spring-handled cookie or ice-cream scoop. Scoops come in various sizes and are referred to by number. Because not all manufacturers' sizes are the same, be sure to measure the volume of the scoop with water first. (The number corresponds to the number of level scoops per quart of ice cream; the larger the number, the smaller the scoop.) Use the size scoop that drops the amount of dough called for in the recipe. Some common scoop sizes are:

> 1 level tablespoon = #70 scoop
> 1/4 cup = #16 scoop

Rolled Cookies

Many recipes call for rolling dough on a floured surface to prevent sticking. If a recipe calls for using a pastry cloth and stockinet- or cloth-covered rolling pin, rub a small amount of flour into the cloth before rolling. Cookies tend to be more tender when rolled this way, because less flour becomes incorporated into the dough. Pastry cloths and stockinets (elasticized fabric rolling-pin covers) are available in cake decorating, kitchen specialty or large department stores. If you can't find pastry cloths in your area, dough also can be rolled between two sheets of waxed paper, or you can use a very tightly woven, nonterry cotton towel. To keep the pastry cloth or towel on your counter and to keep it from wrinkling, either tape the edges down on the counter with wide, sturdy tape or wrap the cloth around a large cutting board, and tape to secure it. Wash both the pastry cloth and stockinet after every use.

When rolling dough, use light pressure on the rolling pin, and roll evenly from the center to edges, lifting the pin off at the edges. There are several tools to help you roll dough evenly:

ADJUSTABLE ROLLING PINS These can be adjusted for various thickness.

ROLLING PIN RINGS These are rubberized rings that fit over your rolling pin, allowing you to roll dough to various thickness.

FLAT WOODEN OR PLASTIC RULERS Place dough between the rulers, then roll the rolling pin over the rulers; the dough will roll out to the thickness of the rulers or about 1/8 inch thick.

ROLLING DOUGH EVENLY

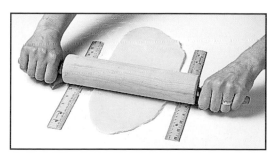

Place dough between flat wooden or plastic rulers that are about 1/8 inch thick. Roll the rolling pin over the rulers until dough is even. Stack two sets of rulers for rolling dough 1/4 inch thick.

When rolling a chilled dough, roll only part of the dough at one time and keep the rest of it in the refrigerator so it doesn't become too warm and sticky to roll out. Dip cookie cutters into flour or powdered sugar and shake off excess before cutting. Try dipping cutters in baking cocoa for chocolate doughs. Cut cookies very close together to avoid rerolling (rerolled dough will be a little tougher). When using a cookie cutter that has one wide end and one narrow end, alternate the direction of the cookie cutter each time you press it into the dough. In other words, the first cookie you cut has the wide end toward you, and the next cookie is cut with the narrow end toward you. This way, you can cut out more cookies. To save space on your wire cooling racks, do the same thing, alternating the direction of each cookie. Lift cut dough to the cookie sheet with a turner at least as wide as the cookie to prevent stretching, which results in misshapen cookies.

ALTERNATING ROLLED CUT-OUT COOKIES

Alternate direction of cut-outs in cookie dough; alternate placement of baked cookies on wire cooling racks.

Refrigerator Cookies

Take the time to make the cookies the same size, so they will not only look nice but also bake evenly. If the dough is too soft to work with, cover and refrigerate it about one hour or until firm. Chill wrapped rolls of refrigerator cookie dough until firm enough to slice easily with a sharp knife. Or place a piece of dental floss or heavy thread under the roll. Bring ends of floss up and crisscross at top of roll, then pull strings in the opposite direction to slice the dough. Cut slices into the thickness specified in the recipe. If cut too thin, the cookies will be overbaked and hard; if cut too thick, they will not be done.

Place a piece of dental floss or heavy thread under roll. Bring ends of floss up and crisscross at top of roll. Pull strings in opposite direction to slice.

Stay in Shape

To keep rolls of refrigerator dough a nicely round shape, try this easy trick: Wrap rolls of dough in plastic wrap, aluminum foil or waxed paper. Insert each wrapped roll in a tall, round drinking glass that has been placed on its side, or make a lengthwise cut on a cardboard cylinder from a roll of paper towels and place the roll inside the cylinder. Refrigerate rolls in glasses or cylinders on their sides until the dough is firm. The rolls won't flatten on the bottom from lying on a flat refrigerator shelf!

Pressed Cookies

Several types of cookie presses are available. For best results, follow the manufacturer's directions. Do not refrigerate dough for pressed cookies unless specified in the recipe, or it will become too stiff to push through the press. Test the dough for the proper stiffness before adding all the flour. Place a small amount of dough in the cookie press and squeeze out. The dough should be soft and pliable but not crumbly. If the dough is too stiff, add one egg yolk. If it's too soft, add flour, one tablespoon at a time, until it's the right stiffness. When forming cookies, hold the press so it rests on the cookie sheet (unless

using the ribbon plate). Squeeze gently, and raise the press from the cookie sheet after enough dough has come out to form a whole cookie. For the ribbon plate, hold the press at an angle to the cookie sheet, and press out enough dough to form the length desired.

Bars and Brownies

Spread or press the dough for bars and brownies evenly to the sides of the pan. There are several ways to do this: If the dough is sticky, use wet hands or spray hands with cooking spray. Another method is to place a piece of plastic wrap directly on top of the dough, and smooth out the top of the dough with your hands. Placing your hands in plastic bags also works. Use the exact size of pan called for in the recipe. Bars baked in a pan that is too large will overbake and be hard. Those baked in a pan too small can be doughy in the center and hard on the edges.

Line pans with aluminum foil for super-quick cleanup and to help cut bars and brownies evenly. Turn the pan upside down. Tear off a piece of foil longer than pan and shape the foil around the pan (it doesn't matter whether the shiny side of the foil is up or down); carefully remove foil and set aside. Turn the pan over and gently fit the shaped foil into the pan with the longer ends serving as "handles" (grease the foil if the recipe calls for a greased pan). When the bars or brownies are cool, just lift them out of the pan by the "handles," peel back the foil and cut the bars as directed.

Turn pan upside down. Tear off a piece of foil longer than pan and shape the foil around the pan; carefully remove foil and set aside. Flip the pan over and gently fit the shaped foil into the pan.

GREASING COOKIE SHEETS AND BAKING PANS

Use shortening or cooking spray to grease cookie sheets and baking pans. Do not use butter, margarine or vegetable oil for greasing; the area between the cookies will burn during baking and will be almost impossible to clean. Grease only if the recipe tells you to. Nonstick cookie sheets shouldn't need to be greased even if the recipe calls for greasing; cookies may spread too much if greasing isn't necessary. Regrease sheets as needed during baking if cookies are sticking to the sheets. Baking parchment paper can be used in place of shortening or cooking spray. It comes in rolls and can be found in stores near the waxed paper, aluminum foil and plastic wrap. Some stores may stock it in the baking ingredient aisle, too. If baking parchment paper is used to line cookie sheets instead of greasing them—just tear off the length of parchment you need to cover your cookie sheet.

Although nonstick cookie sheets shouldn't need to be greased, you may want to bake a test cookie just to be sure. Also, as nonstick surfaces age, they lose some of their ability to prevent sticking. Finally, some recipes give you only the option of using baking parchment paper. This is usually done for cookies that are tender and fragile, and the parchment paper works best for removing cookies from the sheet.

LET'S START BAKING

The first step for baking is to heat your oven; this usually takes up to 10 minutes.

Test Cookie

Bake one "test" cookie by putting the cookie dough on a greased or ungreased cookie sheet as directed in the recipe. If the cookie spreads too much, add 1 to 2 tablespoons of flour to the dough, or chill the dough 1 to 2 hours before baking. If the cookie comes out too dry, add 1 to 2 tablespoons of milk to the dough. By testing the cookie dough, you can see if any adjustments need to be made to your dough before a whole sheet of cookies that you're disappointed with are baked.

Cool Cookie Sheets

Always put cookie dough on completely cooled cookie sheets. Cookies will spread too much if put on a hot, or even a warm, cookie sheet. You can cool cookie sheets quickly by popping them in the refrigerator or freezer or by running cold water over them (dry completely and grease again if needed). If you have more than one cookie sheet to work with, you can let the hot sheet cool while another sheet of cookies is baking. A cookie sheet doesn't take long to cool to room temperature.

Size It Up

Make all cookies on each cookie sheet the same size so they bake evenly. Cookies that are smaller than the others will become too brown or burn, and cookies that are bigger than the others won't be done in the center.

Which Oven Rack?

Always bake cookies on the middle oven rack.

One Sheet at a Time

For even baking, bake one cookie sheet at a time. If you decide to bake two sheets at once, switch the placement of the sheets halfway through baking to help the cookies bake more evenly. Also, when baking two sheets at once, position the oven racks as close to the middle as possible. If racks are too close to the top of the oven, the tops of the cookies may become too brown or burn; if racks are too close to the bottom, the bottoms of the cookies may become too brown or burn.

ARE THEY DONE YET?

How can you tell when your cookies are done? Each recipe gives you two ways to determine when cookies are done: a bake time and a doneness test. Check cookies at the minimum bake time listed in the recipe. Watch cookies carefully while they bake because even one minute can make a difference. The longer cookies bake, the more brown, crisp or hard they become. Sometimes the color of the cookie is the best test for doneness; for example, when the cookie is light brown, or until its edges begin to brown. If the dough is dark, color changes are hard to see. Then the test may be until cookies are set or until almost no indentation remains when touched in center. After baking one or two sheets, you should have a feel for just the right baking time. Use that time for your first doneness check, but always use the doneness test as your final check.

THE BIG COOL-DOWN

Thinner cookies that are rolled or sliced, as well as dense or very sturdy cookies, generally should be removed from cookie sheets immediately after baking to prevent sticking. Drop and soft cookies generally need to cool 1 to 2 minutes before being removed to allow them time to set; otherwise, they may fall apart while being transferred to a cooling rack. Always use a pancake turner to remove cookies from a cookie sheet. The larger the cookie, the longer the cooling time on the cookie sheet.

Always cool cookies on wire cooling racks to allow air to flow around the cookies, which will prevent them from becoming soggy. Cool pans of bars and brownies in the pan on a wire cooling rack.

Uh-oh! The cookies were left to cool too long on the cookie sheet, and you're having trouble getting them off without breaking them. Here's what you do: Put the cookies back in the oven for about 1 to 2 minutes to warm them, and then remove them; they should come off the sheet easily. Cool cookies and bars completely before frosting them unless the recipe tells you to frost them while they're warm.

CUTTING BARS AND BROWNIES

Check out our bar-cutting guide on page 58 for a visual reference. The guide not only shows you the cutting lines for all of the pan sizes and bar yields in this book but also shows a few of the other most

popular cuts. Follow recipe directions for when to cut bars. Most bars are cut when completely cooled to avoid crumbling, but some bars are best cut when warm.

In general, a sharp knife works best for cutting most bars. Brownies, very moist or sticky bars or bars baked in a nonstick pan cut best with a plastic knife. Use a wet knife for cutting meringue-topped or cheesecake bars, wiping off crumbs after each cut. To keep your pan firmly in place while cutting, place a damp paper towel, dishcloth, or even an extra computer mouse pad under it before starting.

STORING

Refrigerating Unbaked Cookie Dough

Store unbaked cookie dough tightly covered in the refrigerator for up to 24 hours.

Freezing Unbaked Cookie Dough

Freeze batches of unbaked cookie dough wrapped in waxed paper, plastic wrap or aluminum foil and placed in resealable plastic freezer bags or freezer containers. Dough also can be formed into rolls, rectangles or individual cookies before freezing. Freeze rolls and rectangles wrapped as stated earlier. Freeze individual drops of cookie dough on cookie sheets; when dough is completely frozen, place individual pieces in a resealable plastic freezer bag or freezer container. Label and freeze up to six months. Before baking, thaw frozen dough in the refrigerator at least 8 hours. If the thawed dough is too stiff to work with, let it stand at room temperature until it's workable.

Which Unbaked Doughs Can't Be Frozen?

Do not freeze meringue, macaroon mixtures, or any other cookie doughs using whipped egg whites because the egg whites break down during freezing and the cookies will not bake properly.

Storing Crisp Baked Cookies

Keep cookies crisp by storing them in a loosely covered container, such as a cookie jar without a sealed gasket (rubber ring around inside of lid) or screw-on lid. Allow frosted or decorated cookies to set or harden before storing; store between layers of waxed paper, plastic wrap or aluminum foil. If cookies soften, heat them on a cookie sheet at 300° for 3 to 5 minutes to re-crisp. Cool them on a wire cooling rack. Store different flavors and varieties of cookies in separate containers, or they will pick up the flavors of the other cookies. Your butter cookies may end up tasting like the mint cookies stored with them. To keep longer, freeze cookies tightly wrapped and labeled up to six months. Do not freeze meringue, custard- or cream-filled cookies.

Storing Chewy and Soft Baked Cookies

Keep cookies chewy and soft by storing them tightly covered. Resealable plastic bags, plastic food containers with tight-fitting lids, metal tins and cookie jars with screw-on lids or sealed gasket lids (rubber ring around inside of lid) work best. Allow frosted or decorated cookies to set or harden before storing; store between layers of waxed paper, plastic wrap or aluminum foil. Store different kinds of cookies in separate containers, or your chocolate cookies may end up tasting like the spice drop cookies stored with them. To keep longer, freeze cookies tightly wrapped and labeled up to six months. Do not freeze meringues, custard- or cream-filled cookies.

IT'S IN THE MAIL!

A care package of homemade cookies, bars or brownies sent to college students, military bases or out-of-town grandparents are always welcome. Here are handy mailing tips to help prevent someone from opening a box of crumbs:

- Firm, moist, sturdy drop cookies, molded cookies and refrigerator cookies are best for mailing.

Dense, sturdy unfrosted bars and brownies are great to send, too. Thin, fragile and very crisp cookies tend to break during shipping.

- Wrap cookies in pairs, back-to-back, and place them flat or on end in a can, firm-sided cardboard box or metal or plastic container. Before adding cookies, line container with waxed paper, plastic wrap or aluminum foil to prevent cookies from absorbing odors.

- Fill each container as full as practical, padding the top with crumpled waxed paper or packing material to prevent shaking and breakage.

- Pack containers in a corrugated cardboard or fiberboard packing box. For fill, use crumpled newspaper, shredded paper, packing peanuts or other packing material. Be sure to pack several inches of fill in the bottom of the packing box and between the items, so the containers cannot move easily inside of the packing box.

- Seal the packing box with shipping tape, and cover the address label with transparent tape for protection. Label the package "perishable" to encourage careful handling.

COOKIE CURES

Cookies and bars are easy to make, but we sometimes end up frustrated. Most problems are due to improper measurement of ingredients, so be sure to follow recipes accurately. In a nutshell, dry and hard cookies are caused by overmeasurement of flour and other dry ingredients, such as rolled oats. Overbaking also will make them hard and dry, so be careful to check for doneness at the minimum bake time stated in the recipe. If you consistently have problems with overbaking, your oven may actually be hotter than the temperature the dial reads. In that case, shave off a few minutes from the minimum bake time given in recipes. You may also want to purchase an oven thermometer to keep in your oven to test for temperature accuracy.

Soft and doughy results are caused by undermeasurement of flour, using butter or margarine that is too soft or partially melted in cookies calling for softened butter or margarine, overmeasuring liquid ingredients and underbaking. Though other factors may be involved, those listed above are the primary culprits.

CURES TO COMMON PROBLEMS

WHAT HAPPENED?: Cookie dough is dry and crumbly.

HOW TO FIX IT: Work in 1 to 2 tablespoons milk, water or another liquid called for in the recipe.

WHAT HAPPENED?: Cookie dough is soft and sticky.

HOW TO FIX IT: If the dough is still too soft after chilling for 2 hours, mix in flour, 1 tablespoon at a time, just until dough is easy to work with.

WHAT HAPPENED?: Cookies bake together on the cookie sheet.

HOW TO FIX IT: Space dough 2 inches apart. Place cookie dough only on cool cookie sheets.

WHAT HAPPENED?: Second and third sheets of cookies spread more than the first sheet.

HOW TO FIX IT: As the dough stands out on the counter, it becomes warmer, causing the fat to melt sooner in the oven, which results in more spreading. To avoid this, keep cookie dough refrigerated between baking each sheet of cookies.

WHAT HAPPENED?: Cookies are very thin and flat.

HOW TO FIX IT: Place cookie dough only on cool cookie sheets. Don't use butter or margarine that is too soft or partially melted if the recipe calls for softened butter or margarine. If this always happens with any cookie recipe, you may be measuring your flour too lightly. When making your next batch of cookies, add 2 additional tablespoons of flour to the dough, and bake a test cookie. If it still spreads too much, add flour, 1 tablespoon at a time, to remaining dough. Bake a test cookie each time you add another tablespoon of flour until you like the results. For future cookie baking, you'll know how much additional flour to add to recipes to get the cookie you want. You may also want to try chilling the dough until it's firm—but not too firm to handle—before shaping and baking.

WHAT HAPPENED?: Cookies are dry and hard after baking

HOW TO FIX IT: Don't pack, tap or shake flour into measuring cup, or you'll get too much flour. Instead, lightly spoon flour into measuring cup, and level with a straight-edged knife or spatula.

WHAT HAPPENED?: Crisp cookies became soft.

HOW TO FIX IT: Store loosely covered. To recrisp cookies, put them on a cookie sheet and heat them in a 300° oven for 5 minutes. Immediately remove to wire cooling racks; cool completely.

WHAT HAPPENED?: Soft cookies became crisp or hard.

HOW TO FIX IT: Store tightly covered. To soften, put a slice of bread in the storage container with the cookies, and let stand for a day or two. The moisture from the bread will be drawn into the cookies, and they will soften.

WHAT HAPPENED?: Bars crumbled when cut.

HOW TO FIX IT: Cool completely before cutting. Brownies and soft and sticky bars cut better with a plastic knife.

WHAT HAPPENED?: Bars are dry and hard.

HOW TO FIX IT: Use the exact pan size called for. Make sure your oven temperature isn't too hot, and check for doneness at the minimum bake time given in the recipe. Don't pack, tap or shake flour into measuring cup, or you'll get too much flour. Instead, lightly spoon flour into measuring cup, and level with a straight-edged knife or spatula. Be sure to spread dough evenly in the pan. If using a dark nonstick pan or glass baking dish, reduce the oven temperature by 25°, or check for doneness 3 to 5 minutes before the minimum bake time given in the recipe.

Sidebar Key

Cookie Tips

Tips for preparation, special techniques or cookie trivia.

Ingredient

Information about an ingredient in the recipe.

"I Don't Have That"

Provides a substitution for a specific recipe ingredient.

Make It Your Way

Easy ideas for serving, adding a special touch to make it festive or easy recipe variations.

CHAPTER 1

The Ultimate Oatmeal Cookie *2*
The Ultimate Chocolate Chip Cookie *4*
Giant Toffee–Chocolate Chip Cookies *5*
Deluxe Chocolate Chip Cookies *6*
Chocolate Chip Sandwich Cookies *8*
Sour Cream–Milk Chocolate Chip Cookies *9*
Fresh Mint–Chocolate Chip Cookies *10*
Inside-Out Chocolate Chip Cookies *12*
Chocolate-Covered Peanut-Chocolate Chip Cookies *14*
Outrageous Double Chocolate–White Chocolate Chunk Cookies *15*
White Chocolate Chunk-Macadamia Cookies *16*
Toasted Oatmeal Cookies *17*
Double Oat Cookies *18*
Oatmeal Lacies *20*
Frosted Banana Oaties *21*
Giant Honey and Oat Cookies *22*
Chocolate-Oatmeal Chewies *24*
Chocolate Drop Cookies *25*

Chocolate-Mint Cookies *26*
Fudgy Macadamia Cookies *27*
Chocolate–Peanut Butter No-Bakes *28*
Frosted Cinnamon-Mocha Cookies *29*
Double Peanut Cookies *30*
Whole Wheat–Honey Cookies *32*
Whole Wheat–Fruit Drops *34*
Whole Wheat Rounds *35*
Brown Sugar Drops *36*
Soft Molasses Cookies *37*
Sour Cream Cookies *38*
Spicy Pumpkin-Date Cookies *39*
Old-Fashioned Date Drop Cookies *40*
Old-Fashioned Rum-Raisin Cookies *41*
Brandied Fruit Drops *42*
Pineapple Puffs *43*
Lemon-Lime Cookies *44*
Applesauce-Granola Cookies *46*
Banana-Ginger Jumbles *47*
Pastel Mint Drops *48*
Coconut Meringue Cookies *49*
Ginger-Pecan Chews *50*
Cornmeal Crispies *52*
Poppy Drop Cookies *53*

Easy Drop Cookies

Outrageous Double Chocolate–White Chocolate Chunk Cookies (page 15),
White Chocolate Chunk-Macadamia Cookies (page 16)

It's not always the fancy recipes that people ask for the most because oatmeal cookies continue to be an all-time favorite.

The Ultimate Oatmeal Cookie

BAKE: 9 to 11 min per sheet ● YIELD: About 3 dozen cookies

Cookie Tips

Oats can be measured either by pouring them into a measuring cup or by dipping the measuring cup into the oats container.

Make It Your Way

Kids love **Oatmeal–Chocolate Chip Cookies.** To make them, just omit the cinnamon and stir in a 12-ounce package of semisweet or milk chocolate chips with the oats and flour.

1 1/4 cups packed brown sugar

1 cup butter or margarine, softened

1 teaspoon baking soda

1 teaspoon ground cinnamon

1 teaspoon vanilla

1/2 teaspoon salt

2 eggs

3 cups quick-cooking or old-fashioned oats

1 1/3 cups all-purpose flour

1 cup raisins, if desired

Heat oven to 350°. Beat all ingredients except oats, flour and raisins in large bowl with electric mixer on medium speed, or mix with spoon. Stir in oats, flour and raisins.

Drop dough by rounded tablespoonfuls about 2 inches apart onto ungreased cookie sheet. Bake 9 to 11 minutes or until light brown. Immediately remove from cookie sheet to wire rack.

1 Cookie: Calories 120 (Calories from Fat 55); Fat 6g (Saturated 1g); Cholesterol 10mg; Sodium 110mg; Carbohydrate 15g (Dietary Fiber 0g); Protein 2g.

Ultimate Oatmeal Cookies, Chocolate-Oatmeal Chewies (page 24),
Frosted Banana Oaties (page 21)

The Ultimate Chocolate Chip Cookie

BAKE: 13 to 15 min per sheet ● YIELD: About 3 1/2 dozen cookies

1 1/2 cups butter or margarine, softened

1 1/4 cups granulated sugar

1 1/4 cups packed brown sugar

1 tablespoon vanilla

2 eggs

4 cups all-purpose flour

2 teaspoons baking soda

1/2 teaspoon salt

2 cups coarsely chopped nuts, if desired

1 package (24 ounces) semisweet chocolate chips (4 cups)

Heat oven to 375°. Beat butter, sugars, vanilla and eggs in large bowl with electric mixer on medium speed, or mix with spoon. Stir in flour, baking soda and salt (dough will be stiff). Stir in nuts and chocolate chips.

Drop dough by level 1/4 cupfuls or #16 cookie/ice-cream scoop about 2 inches apart onto ungreased cookie sheet. Flatten slightly with fork. Bake 13 to 15 minutes or until light brown (centers will be soft). Cool 1 to 2 minutes; remove from cookie sheet to wire rack.

1 Cookie: Calories 240 (Calories from Fat 110); Fat 12g (Saturated 4g); Cholesterol 15mg; Sodium 170mg; Carbohydrate 32g (Dietary Fiber 1g); Protein 2g.

Giant Toffee–Chocolate Chip Cookies

BAKE: 12 to 14 min per sheet ● YIELD: About 1 1/2 dozen cookies

1 cup packed brown sugar

1/2 cup butter or margarine, softened

1/2 cup shortening

1/4 cup honey

1 egg

2 cups all-purpose flour

1 teaspoon baking soda

1/2 teaspoon baking powder

1/4 teaspoon salt

1 package (12 ounces) miniature semisweet chocolate chips (2 cups)

1 package (7 1/2 ounces) almond brickle chips (1 cup)

Heat oven to 350°. Beat brown sugar, butter, shortening, honey and egg in large bowl with electric mixer on medium speed, or mix with spoon. Stir in flour, baking soda, baking powder and salt. Stir in chocolate chips and brickle chips.

Drop dough by level 1/4 cupfuls or #16 cookie/ice-cream scoop about 2 inches apart onto ungreased cookie sheet. Bake 12 to 14 minutes or until edges are golden brown (centers will be soft). Cool 3 to 4 minutes; remove from cookie sheet to wire rack.

1 Cookie: Calories 365 (Calories from Fat 180); Fat 20g (Saturated 8g); Cholesterol 15mg; Sodium 220mg; Carbohydrate 44g (Dietary Fiber 1g); Protein 3g.

Cookie Tips

Save your cookies from the rancor of rancidity! Almond brickle chips can become rancid, which would spoil the taste of your cookies. Do a taste test of the brickle chips before adding them to your recipe to be sure they taste fresh. Refrigerate or freeze the brickle chips to help prevent rancidity.

"I Don't Have That"

Maple-flavored syrup can be used instead of honey.

Deluxe Chocolate Chip Cookies

BAKE: 11 to 14 min per sheet ● YIELD: About 2 dozen

Cookie Tips

Just as vanilla ice cream is America's favorite ice-cream flavor, the chocolate chip cookie takes the blue ribbon for also being an American favorite.

"I Don't Have That"

Vanilla extract isn't the only great flavoring to add to these cookies. If you're out of vanilla, maple-flavored extract is a great substitute.

1 cup packed brown sugar

3/4 cup granulated sugar

1 cup butter or margarine, softened

1 teaspoon vanilla

2 eggs

2 1/2 cups all-purpose flour

3/4 teaspoon baking soda

3/4 teaspoon salt

1 cup chopped walnuts

12 ounces semisweet or milk chocolate, coarsely chopped, or
    1 package (12 ounces) semisweet chocolate chips (2 cups) or
    1 package (11 1/2 ounces) large semisweet chocolate chips

Heat oven to 375°. Beat sugars and butter in large bowl with electric mixer on medium speed about 3 minutes or until fluffy, or mix with spoon. Beat in vanilla and eggs. Stir in flour, baking soda and salt. Stir in walnuts and chocolate.

Drop dough by level 1/4 cupfuls or #16 cookie/ice-cream scoop about 2 inches apart onto ungreased cookie sheet. Flatten slightly with fork. Bake 11 to 14 minutes or until edges are light brown (centers will be soft). Cool 3 to 4 minutes; remove from cookie sheet to wire rack.

1 Cookie: Calories 315 (Calories from Fat 155); Fat 17g (Saturated 5g); Cholesterol 20mg; Sodium 230mg; Carbohydrate 38g (Dietary Fiber 1g); Protein 4g.

Deluxe Chocolate Chip Cookies,
Chocolate-Orange—Chocolate Chip Cookies (page 178),
Sour Cream—Milk Chocolate Chip Cookies (page 9)

Chocolate Chip Sandwich Cookies

BAKE: 8 to 10 min per sheet ● YIELD: About 4 dozen cookies

Cookie Tips

These little sandwich cookies will get soft during storage due to the moisture in the frosting.

"I Don't Have That"

About 1 cup of canned frosting can be used if you don't feel like making the frosting from scratch.

1 1/4 cups packed brown sugar

1/2 cup butter or margarine, softened

1 egg

1 1/4 cups all-purpose flour

1/4 teaspoon baking soda

1/8 teaspoon salt

1 cup miniature semisweet chocolate chips

Chocolate Frosting (page 25)

Heat oven to 350°. Lightly grease cookie sheet. Beat brown sugar, butter and egg in large bowl with electric mixer on medium speed, or mix with spoon. Stir in flour, baking soda and salt. Stir in chocolate chips.

Drop dough by level teaspoonfuls about 2 inches apart onto cookie sheet (dough will flatten and spread). Bake 8 to 10 minutes or until golden brown. Cool 1 to 2 minutes; remove from cookie sheet to wire rack. Cool completely. Spread 1 teaspoon Chocolate Frosting between bottoms of pairs of cookies.

1 Cookie: Calories 95 (Calories from Fat 35); Fat 4g (Saturated 1g); Cholesterol 5mg; Sodium 50mg; Carbohydrate 14g (Dietary Fiber 0g); Protein 1g.

Sour Cream– Milk Chocolate Chip Cookies

BAKE: 12 to 14 min per sheet ● YIELD: About 3 1/2 dozen cookies

1 1/2 cups sugar

1/2 cup sour cream

1/4 cup butter or margarine, softened

1/4 cup shortening

1 teaspoon vanilla

1 egg

2 1/4 cups all-purpose flour

1/2 teaspoon baking soda

1/4 teaspoon salt

1 package (11 1/2 ounces) milk chocolate chips (2 cups)

Make It Your Way

For white-on-white cookies, try Sour Cream–Vanilla Milk Chip Cookies; just substitute vanilla milk (white) chips for the milk chocolate chips.

"I Don't Have That"

Substitute regular plain yogurt for the sour cream.

Heat oven to 350°. Beat sugar, sour cream, butter, shortening, vanilla and egg in large bowl with electric mixer on medium speed, or mix with spoon. Stir in flour, baking soda and salt. Stir in chocolate chips.

Drop dough by rounded tablespoonfuls about 2 inches apart onto ungreased cookie sheet. Bake 12 to 14 minutes or until set and just beginning to brown. Cool 1 to 2 minutes; remove from cookie sheet to wire rack.

1 Cookie: Calories 115 (Calories from Fat 45); Fat 5g (Saturated 2g); Cholesterol 10mg; Sodium 50mg; Carbohydrate 17g (Dietary Fiber 0g); Protein 1g.

Fresh Mint–
Chocolate Chip Cookies

BAKE: 11 to 13 min per sheet ● YIELD: About 3 1/2 dozen cookies

Cookie Tips

Fresh mint makes these cookies very cool and refreshing. They would be great served with iced or hot tea.

"I Don't Have That"

1/4 teaspoon mint extract can be substituted for the chopped mint leaves.

1 1/3 cups sugar

3/4 cup butter or margarine, softened

1 tablespoon finely chopped mint leaves

1 egg

2 cups all-purpose flour

1 teaspoon baking soda

1/2 teaspoon salt

1 package (10 ounces) mint-chocolate chips (1 1/2 cups)

Heat oven to 350°. Beat sugar, butter, mint leaves and egg in large bowl with electric mixer on medium speed, or mix with spoon. Stir in flour, baking soda and salt. Stir in chocolate chips.

Drop dough by rounded tablespoonfuls about 2 inches apart onto ungreased cookie sheet. Bake 11 to 13 minutes or until golden brown. Cool 1 to 2 minutes; remove from cookie sheet to wire rack.

1 Cookie: Calories 110 (Calories from Fat 45); Fat 5g (Saturated 2g); Cholesterol 5mg; Sodium 100mg; Carbohydrate 15g (Dietary Fiber 0g); Protein 1g.

Fresh Mint–Chocolate Chip Cookies

Inside-Out Chocolate Chip Cookies

BAKE: 10 to 12 min per sheet ● YIELD: About 4 1/2 dozen cookies

Cookie Tips

Measure shortening by spooning and pressing it into a dry measuring cup. Pressing it with the back of the spoon does away with any air pockets.

Make It Your Way

If you believe there is no such thing as too much chocolate, up the ante with **Double Chocolate–Chocolate Chip Cookies**. Substitute 1 1/2 cups semisweet or milk chocolate chips for the vanilla milk chips.

1 cup granulated sugar

3/4 cup packed brown sugar

3/4 cup butter or margarine, softened

1/2 cup shortening

1 teaspoon vanilla

2 eggs

2 1/2 cups all-purpose flour

1/2 cup baking cocoa

1 teaspoon baking soda

1/4 teaspoon salt

1 1/2 cups vanilla milk (white) chips

1 cup chopped nuts

Heat oven to 350°. Beat sugars, butter, shortening, vanilla and eggs in large bowl with electric mixer on medium speed, or mix with spoon. Stir in flour, cocoa, baking soda and salt. Stir in vanilla milk chips and nuts.

Drop dough by rounded tablespoonfuls about 2 inches apart onto ungreased cookie sheet. Bake 10 to 12 minutes or until set. Cool 1 to 2 minutes; remove from cookie sheet to wire rack.

1 Cookie: Calories 140 (Calories from Fat 70); Fat 8g (Saturated 2g); Cholesterol 10mg; Sodium 70mg; Carbohydrate 15g (Dietary Fiber 0g); Protein 2g.

Inside-Out Chocolate Chip Cookies

Chocolate-Covered Peanut-Chocolate Chip Cookies

BAKE: 10 to 12 min per sheet ● YIELD: About 3 1/2 dozen cookies

Cookie Tips

If you oversoften butter or margarine, especially if it's been microwaved to the point of it being almost melted, your cookies will spread a lot and be flat.

Make It Your Way

How about giving **Chocolate-Covered Raisin-Chocolate Chip Cookies** a whirl? Just substitute chocolate-covered raisins for the chocolate-covered peanuts.

1 cup sugar

1/2 cup butter or margarine, softened

1/2 cup shortening

1 teaspoon vanilla

1 egg

1 3/4 cups all-purpose flour

1/2 teaspoon baking soda

1/4 teaspoon salt

1 cup chocolate-covered peanuts

1 cup milk chocolate chips

Heat oven to 375°. Beat sugar, butter, shortening, vanilla and egg in large bowl with electric mixer on medium speed, or mix with spoon. Stir in flour, baking soda and salt. Stir in peanuts and chocolate chips.

Drop dough by rounded tablespoonfuls about 2 inches apart onto ungreased cookie sheet. Bake 10 to 12 minutes or until edges are golden brown (centers will be soft). Cool 1 to 2 minutes; remove from cookie sheet to wire rack.

1 Cookie: Calories 120 (Calories from Fat 65); Fat 7g (Saturated 2g); Cholesterol 5mg; Sodium 60mg; Carbohydrate 13g (Dietary Fiber 0g); Protein 1g.

Outrageous Double Chocolate– White Chocolate Chunk Cookies

BAKE: 11 to 14 min per sheet ● YIELD: About 2 dozen cookies

1 package (24 ounces) semisweet chocolate chips (4 cups)

1 cup butter or margarine, softened

1 cup packed brown sugar

1 teaspoon vanilla

2 eggs

2 1/2 cups all-purpose flour

1 1/2 teaspoons baking soda

1/2 teaspoon salt

1 package (6 ounces) white baking bars, cut into 1/4- to 1/2-inch chunks

1 cup pecan or walnut halves

Heat oven to 350°. Heat 1 1/2 cups of the chocolate chips in 1-quart saucepan over low heat, stirring constantly, until melted. Cool to room temperature, but do not allow chocolate to become firm.

Beat butter, brown sugar and vanilla in large bowl with electric mixer on medium speed until light and fluffy. Beat in eggs and melted chocolate until light and fluffy. Stir in flour, baking soda and salt. Stir in remaining 2 1/2 cups chocolate chips, the white baking bar chunks and pecan halves.

Drop dough by level 1/4 cupfuls or #16 cookie/ice-cream scoop about 2 inches apart onto ungreased cookie sheet. Bake 12 to 14 minutes or until set (centers will appear soft and moist). Cool 1 to 2 minutes; remove from cookie sheet to wire rack.

1 Cookie: Calories 375 (Calories from Fat 200); Fat 22g (Saturated 12g); Cholesterol 40mg; Sodium 200mg; Carbohydrate 42g (Dietary Fiber 2g); Protein 4g.

Cookie Tips

These gourmet cookies are great to give as a gift in a decorative tin. If you don't have a tin, just stack about 6 to 8 cookies and wrap in colored or clear plastic wrap and tie the top with a pretty ribbon or bow.

"I Don't Have That"

If you don't have any pecan or walnuts, you can leave them out or use a cup of dried cherries, raisins or chocolate chips instead.

White Chocolate Chunk– Macadamia Cookies

BAKE: 10 to 12 min per sheet ● YIELD: About 2 1/2 dozen cookies

1 cup packed brown sugar

1/2 cup granulated sugar

1/2 cup butter or margarine, softened

1/2 cup shortening

1 teaspoon vanilla

1 egg

2 1/4 cups all-purpose flour

1 teaspoon baking soda

1/4 teaspoon salt

1 package (6 ounces) white baking bars, cut into 1/4- to 1/2-inch chunks

1 jar (3 1/2 ounces) macadamia nuts, coarsely chopped

Heat oven to 350°. Beat sugars, butter, shortening, vanilla and egg in large bowl with electric mixer on medium speed until light and fluffy, or mix with spoon. Stir in flour, baking soda and salt (dough will be stiff). Stir in white baking bar chunks and nuts.

Drop dough by rounded tablespoonfuls about 2 inches apart onto ungreased cookie sheet. Bake 10 to 12 minutes or until light brown. Cool 1 to 2 minutes; remove from cookie sheet to wire rack.

1 Cookie: Calories 190 (Calories from Fat 100); Fat 11g (Saturated 5g); Cholesterol 15mg; Sodium 90mg; Carbohydrate 21g (Dietary Fiber 0g); Protein 2g.

Toasted Oatmeal Cookies

TOAST: 15 to 20 min ● BAKE: 8 to 10 min ● YIELD: About 3 1/2 dozen cookies

2 1/2 cups quick-cooking or old-fashioned oats

1 cup chopped walnuts

1 1/2 cups packed brown sugar

1 cup butter or margarine, softened

1 teaspoon vanilla

1 egg

1 cup all-purpose flour

1 teaspoon baking soda

1/4 teaspoon salt

Heat oven to 350°. Spread oats and walnuts in ungreased jelly roll pan, 15 1/2 × 10 1/2 × 1 inch. Bake 15 to 20 minutes, stirring occasionally, until light brown; cool.

Beat brown sugar, butter, vanilla and egg in large bowl with electric mixer on medium speed, or mix with spoon. Stir in oat mixture and remaining ingredients.

Drop dough by rounded tablespoonfuls about 2 inches apart onto ungreased cookie sheet. Bake 8 to 10 minutes or until golden brown. Cool 1 to 2 minutes; remove from cookie sheet to wire rack.

1 Cookie. Calories 125 (Calories from Fat 65); Fat 7g (Saturated 1g); Cholesterol 5mg; Sodium 100mg; Carbohydrate 14g (Dietary Fiber 0g); Protein 2g.

Cookie Tips

Toasting the oatmeal gives it a nutty flavor and slightly crunchy texture. Toasted oats are much lower in calories and fat than nuts and can be used in place of nuts in recipes such as no-bake and drop cookies.

Make It Your Way

Vanilla-Frosted Toasted Oatmeal Cookies would taste so good with a hot cup of coffee or hot chocolate. Make and bake cookies as directed. When completely cool, frost with Vanilla Frosting on page 21.

Double Oat Cookies

BAKE: 10 to 12 min per sheet ● YIELD: About 3 dozen cookies

Oat Bran

The bran is the outermost layer of the oat and is a good source of fiber. You can find oat bran in the hot cereal or health food section of most large supermarkets.

"I Don't Have That"

Try using wheat germ instead of the oat bran. If you do, the cookies will have a coarser texture and nuttier flavor.

1 cup butter or margarine, softened
1 cup packed brown sugar
1 teaspoon vanilla
1 egg white
1 1/4 cups all-purpose flour
1 cup quick-cooking or old-fashioned oats
1 cup oat bran
1/2 teaspoon ground cinnamon
1/4 teaspoon salt
1/4 teaspoon baking powder

Heat oven to 350°. Beat butter, brown sugar, vanilla and egg white in large bowl with electric mixer on medium speed, or mix with spoon. Stir in remaining ingredients.

Drop dough by rounded tablespoonfuls about 2 inches apart onto ungreased cookie sheet. Bake 10 to 12 minutes or until golden brown. Cool 1 to 2 minutes; remove from cookie sheet to wire rack.

1 Cookie: Calories 100 (Calories from Fat 45); Fat 5g (Saturated 1g); Cholesterol 0mg; Sodium 85mg; Carbohydrate 13g (Dietary Fiber 0g); Protein 1g.

Double Oat Cookies, Toasted Oatmeal Cookies (page 17)

Oatmeal Lacies

BAKE: 8 to 10 min per sheet ● YIELD: About 2 1/2 dozen cookies

Cookie Tips

These cookies spread quite a bit, so don't be alarmed when they are paper-thin and look like lace. The texture of the baked cookie is delicate and crisp with a wonderful buttery, brown sugar flavor.

Make It Your Way

Chocolate Oatmeal Lacies look elegant and sophisticated. To make them, drizzle tops of cookies with 1/2 cup melted semisweet chocolate. An easy way to drizzle chocolate is to put the melted chocolate in a small, resealable plastic bag. Snip off a tiny bit of one corner and gently squeeze the chocolate out through the hole. Or you can dip a fork or spoon in the melted chocolate and drizzle a pattern on the cookies.

1 1/2 cups quick-cooking oats

2/3 cup packed brown sugar

1/3 cup butter or margarine, melted

1/4 cup milk

2 tablespoons all-purpose flour

1 teaspoon baking powder

1/8 teaspoon salt

1 egg

Heat oven to 350°. Grease and flour cookie sheet.* Beat all ingredients in large bowl with electric mixer on medium speed, or mix with spoon.

Drop dough by level tablespoonfuls about 3 inches apart onto cookie sheet. Bake 8 to 10 minutes or until edges are golden brown. Cool 1 to 2 minutes; remove from cookie sheet to wire rack, using wide, thin-bladed pancake turner.

1 Cookie: Calories 55 (Calories from Fat 20); Fat 2g (Saturated 1g); Cholesterol 5mg; Sodium 55mg; Carbohydrate 8g (Dietary Fiber 0g); Protein 1g.

Or cover cookie sheet with baking parchment paper. Peel away parchment paper from cookies when they are cool.

Frosted Banana Oaties

BAKE: 10 to 12 min per sheet ● YIELD: About 3 1/2 dozen cookies

1 cup sugar

1 cup mashed very ripe bananas (2 medium)

3/4 cup butter or margarine, softened

1 egg

2 1/2 cups quick-cooking or old-fashioned oats

1 cup all-purpose flour

1/2 teaspoon salt

1/2 teaspoon baking soda

1/2 teaspoon ground cinnamon

1/4 teaspoon ground allspice

Vanilla Frosting (below)

Heat oven to 350°. Grease cookie sheet. Beat sugar, bananas, butter and egg in large bowl with electric mixer on medium speed, or mix with spoon. Stir in remaining ingredients except Vanilla Frosting.

Drop dough by rounded tablespoonfuls about 2 inches apart onto cookie sheet. Bake 10 to 12 minutes or until edges are golden brown and almost no indentation remains when touched in center. Cool 1 to 2 minutes; remove from cookie sheet to wire rack. Cool completely. Frost with Vanilla Frosting.

Vanilla Frosting

3 cups powdered sugar

1/3 cup butter or margarine, softened

1 1/2 teaspoons vanilla

2 to 3 tablespoons milk

Mix all ingredients until smooth and spreadable.

1 Cookie: Calories 130 (Calories from Fat 45); Fat 5g (Saturated 1g); Cholesterol 5mg; Sodium 100mg; Carbohydrate 20g (Dietary Fiber 0g); Protein 1g.

Cookie Tips

Fully ripened bananas—yep, the ones on your counter that are turning brown with some black spots—are the ones you want to use for this recipe. They are much more flavorful and add more moistness to baked goods than bananas that are tinged green or have just turned bright yellow.

"I Don't Have That"

Contrary to popular belief, allspice is not a combination of spices, but is a single spice. If you don't have allspice, use ground cloves or nutmeg.

Giant Honey and Oat Cookies

BAKE: 11 to 14 min per sheet ● YIELD: About 1 1/2 dozen cookies

Cookie Tips

Using honey in cookie dough makes a softer baked cookie. Why is that? Honey is like a sponge; it absorbs moisture from the air, which will make your cookies soft, even during storage.

Make It Your Way

Try **Giant Honey-Roasted Peanut and Oat Cookies** by stirring 1 cup of honey-roasted peanuts in with the oats, flour, soda and salt.

1 1/2 cups sugar

3/4 cup butter or margarine, softened

2/3 cup honey

3 egg whites

4 cups quick-cooking or old-fashioned oats

2 cups all-purpose flour

1 teaspoon baking soda

1/2 teaspoon salt

Heat oven to 350°. Grease cookie sheet. Beat sugar, butter, honey and egg whites in large bowl with electric mixer on medium speed, or mix with spoon. Stir in remaining ingredients.

Drop dough by level 1/4 cupfuls or #16 cookie/ice-cream scoop about 3 inches apart onto cookie sheet. Bake 11 to 14 minutes or until edges are light brown (centers will be soft). Cool 3 to 4 minutes; remove from cookie sheet to wire rack.

1 Cookie: Calories 295 (Calories from Fat 80); Fat 9g (Saturated 2g); Cholesterol 0mg; Sodium 230mg; Carbohydrate 50g (Dietary Fiber 2g); Protein 5g.

Giant Honey and Oat Cookies, Chocolate Drop Cookies (page 25)

Chocolate-Oatmeal Chewies

BAKE: 10 to 12 min per sheet ● YIELD: About 3 1/2 dozen cookies

Make It Your Way

This variation was the result of the unexpected results we saw during recipe testing. We ended up liking our "mistake" so much, we decided to stick with it and offer it as a recipe variation! To make **Hazelnut-Oatmeal Lacies,** substitute 1/2 cup hazelnut-flavored instant coffee (dry) for the cocoa. Unlike the original recipe above, these cookies will be very flat, but still very chewy!

"I Don't Have That"

Sometimes we run out of such staples as milk. The same amount of melted vanilla ice cream or even yogurt will work as a substitute or, in a pinch, just use water.

1 1/2 cups sugar

1 cup butter or margarine, softened

1/4 cup milk

1 egg

2 2/3 cups quick-cooking or old-fashioned oats

1 cup all-purpose flour

1/2 cup baking cocoa

1/2 teaspoon salt

1/2 teaspoon baking soda

Heat oven to 350°. Beat sugar, butter, milk and egg in large bowl with electric mixer on medium speed, or mix with spoon. Stir in remaining ingredients.

Drop dough by rounded tablespoonfuls about 2 inches apart onto ungreased cookie sheet. Bake 10 to 12 minutes or until almost no indentation remains when touched in center. Cool 1 to 2 minutes; remove from cookie sheet to wire rack.

1 Cookie: Calories 105 (Calories from Fat 45); Fat 5g (Saturated 1g); Cholesterol 5mg; Sodium 95mg; Carbohydrate 14g (Dietary Fiber 1g); Protein 2g.

Chocolate Drop Cookies

BAKE: 8 to 10 min per sheet • YIELD: About 3 dozen cookies

1 cup sugar

1/2 cup butter or margarine, softened

1/3 cup buttermilk

1 teaspoon vanilla

2 ounces unsweetened baking chocolate, melted and cooled

1 egg

1 3/4 cups all-purpose flour

1/2 teaspoon baking soda

1/2 teaspoon salt

1 cup chopped nuts

Chocolate Frosting (below)

Heat oven to 375°. Grease cookie sheet. Beat sugar, butter, buttermilk, vanilla, chocolate and egg in large bowl with electric mixer on medium speed, or mix with spoon. Stir in flour, baking soda and salt. Stir in nuts.

Drop dough by rounded tablespoonfuls about 2 inches apart onto cookie sheet. Bake 8 to 10 minutes or until almost no indentation remains when touched in center. Immediately remove from cookie sheet to wire rack. Cool completely. Frost with Chocolate Frosting.

Chocolate Frosting

2 ounces unsweetened baking chocolate

2 tablespoons butter or margarine

2 cups powdered sugar

3 tablespoons hot water

Melt chocolate and butter in 2-quart saucepan over low heat, stirring occasionally; remove from heat. Stir in powdered sugar and hot water until smooth and spreadable. (If frosting is too thick, add more water. If frosting is too thin, add more powdered sugar.)

1 Cookie: Calories 145 (Calories from Fat 65); Fat 7g (Saturated 2g); Cholesterol 5mg; Sodium 90mg; Carbohydrate 18g (Dietary Fiber 0g); Protein 2g.

Cookie Tips

This very old-fashioned cookie is a time-tested classic. It bakes up into a tender, cakelike cookie adorned with an incredibly fudgy chocolate frosting.

Make It Your Way

If you love chocolate-covered raisins, add them to this cookie to make **Raisin-Filled Chocolate Drops.** Stir in 1 cup semisweet- or milk chocolate-covered raisins with the nuts. Serve with a cup of rich, full-bodied coffee or a glass of ice cold milk.

Chocolate-Mint Cookies

BAKE: 8 min per sheet ● YIELD: About 3 dozen cookies

Cookie Tips

To easily crush peppermint candies, place in resealable plastic freezer bag. Seal bag and pound with rolling pin or meat mallet to crush.

Make It Your Way

If you want to try another flavor combination, we suggest **Chocolate-Orange Cookies.** To make these, substitute orange extract for the peppermint extract in the frosting. If you would like, crush orange-flavored hard candies to sprinkle on top of the cookies in place of the peppermint candies. This orange variation would make a fun Halloween treat.

1 cup sugar

1/2 cup butter or margarine, softened

1 teaspoon vanilla

1 egg

2 squares (1 ounce each) unsweetened chocolate, melted and cooled

1 cup all-purpose flour

1/2 teaspoon salt

Peppermint Frosting (below)

1/4 cup butter or margarine

2 tablespoons corn syrup

1 package (6 ounces) semisweet chocolate chips

Crushed hard peppermint candies, if desired

Heat oven to 375°. Beat sugar, 1/2 cup butter, the vanilla, egg and unsweetened chocolate in large bowl with electric mixer on medium speed, or mix with spoon. Stir in flour and salt.

Drop dough by rounded teaspoonfuls about 2 inches apart onto ungreased cookie sheet. Flatten cookies with greased bottom of glass dipped in sugar. Bake until set, about 8 minutes. Cool 1 to 2 minutes; remove from cookie sheet to wire rack. Cool cookies completely.

Spread Peppermint Frosting over each cookie to within 1/4 inch of edge. Melt 1/4 cup butter, the corn syrup and chocolate chips over low heat, stirring constantly, until smooth. Spoon or drizzle mixture over each cookie; sprinkle with crushed candies.

Peppermint Frosting

2 1/2 cups powdered sugar

1/4 cup butter or margarine, softened

3 tablespoons milk

1/2 teaspoon peppermint extract

Mix all ingredients until smooth and of spreading consistency.

1 Cookie: 160 Calories (Calories from Fat 70); Fat 8g (Saturated 5g); Cholesterol 20mg; Sodium 70mg; Carbohydrate 21g (Dietary Fiber 0g); Protein 1g.

Fudgy Macadamia Cookies

BAKE: 9 to 11 min per sheet ● YIELD: About 2 dozen cookies

1 cup sugar

1/2 cup butter or margarine, softened

1 teaspoon vanilla

2 ounces unsweetened baking chocolate, melted and cooled

1 egg

1 cup all-purpose flour

1/2 teaspoon baking powder

1/2 teaspoon salt

1 cup chopped macadamia nuts

Heat oven to 350°. Beat sugar, butter, vanilla, chocolate and egg in large bowl with electric mixer on medium speed, or mix with spoon. Stir in flour, baking powder and salt. Stir in nuts.

Drop dough by rounded tablespoonfuls about 2 inches apart onto ungreased cookie sheet. Bake 9 to 11 minutes or until almost no indentation remains when touched in center. Cool 1 to 2 minutes; remove from cookie sheet to wire rack.

1 Cookie: Calories 135 (Calories from Fat 80); Fat 9g (Saturated 2g); Cholesterol 10mg; Sodium 120mg; Carbohydrate 14g (Dietary Fiber 1g); Protein 1g.

Macadamia Nuts

These buttery-rich, slightly sweet nuts are from the macadamia tree, a native of Australia. Macadamia trees are also grown in Hawaii and California. Their shells are extremely hard; that's why they are always sold already shelled.

"I Don't Have That"

Macadamia nuts are definitely expensive, but oh so delicious when you decide to indulge! You don't have to use macadamias though; use any nut you like instead.

Chocolate–Peanut Butter No-Bakes

PREP: 12 min ● CHILL: 1 hr ● YIELD: About 2 dozen cookies

1 package (6 ounces) semisweet chocolate chips (1 cup)

1/4 cup light corn syrup

1/4 cup peanut butter

2 tablespoons milk

1 teaspoon vanilla

2 cups quick-cooking oats

1 cup peanuts

Cover cookie sheet with waxed paper. Heat chocolate chips, corn syrup, peanut butter, milk and vanilla in 3-quart saucepan over medium heat, stirring constantly, until chocolate is melted and mixture is smooth; remove from heat. Stir in oats and peanuts until well coated.

Drop mixture by rounded tablespoonfuls onto waxed paper. Refrigerate uncovered about 1 hour or until firm. Store covered in refrigerator.

1 Cookie: Calories 125 (Calories from Fat 65); Fat 7g (Saturated 2g); Cholesterol 0mg; Sodium 20mg; Carbohydrate 13g (Dietary Fiber 1g); Protein 4g.

Frosted Cinnamon-Mocha Cookies

BAKE: 10 to 12 min per sheet ● YIELD: About 2 1/2 dozen cookies

1 cup sugar

1/2 cup butter or margarine, softened

2 teaspoons instant coffee (dry)

1 egg

3 ounces unsweetened baking chocolate, melted and cooled

1 1/4 cups all-purpose flour

1/4 cup milk

1 teaspoon ground cinnamon

1/2 teaspoon baking soda

1/4 teaspoon salt

Mocha Frosting (below)

Heat oven to 350°. Beat sugar, butter, coffee and egg in large bowl with electric mixer on medium speed, or mix with spoon. Stir in chocolate. Stir in remaining ingredients except Mocha Frosting.

Drop dough by rounded tablespoonfuls about 2 inches apart onto ungreased cookie sheet. Bake 10 to 12 minutes or until almost no indentation remains when touched in center. Remove from cookie sheet to wire rack. Cool completely. Frost with Mocha Frosting.

Mocha Frosting

1 teaspoon instant coffee (dry)

3 tablespoons hot water

2 ounces unsweetened baking chocolate

2 tablespoons butter or margarine

2 cups powdered sugar

2 to 3 teaspoons water

Dissolve coffee in 3 tablespoons hot water; set aside. Melt chocolate and butter in 2-quart saucepan over low heat, stirring frequently; remove from heat. Stir in powdered sugar, coffee mixture and 2 to 3 teaspoons water until smooth and spreadable.

1 Cookie: Calories 145 (Calories from Fat 65); Fat 7g (Saturated 2g); Cholesterol 5mg; Sodium 90mg; Carbohydrate 20g (Dietary Fiber 1g); Protein 1g.

Double Peanut Cookies

BAKE: 8 to 10 min per sheet ● YIELD: About 4 1/2 dozen cookies

Cookie Tips

Creamy peanut butter works best in these cookies because it's so easy to work with.

Reduced-fat peanut butter spread will work, too, but the cookies will be a little drier and bit tougher.

For a richer, more butter-scotch-like flavor, use all brown sugar.

1 cup creamy peanut butter

3/4 cup granulated sugar

3/4 cup packed brown sugar

1/2 cup butter or margarine, softened

2 eggs

1 1/2 cups all-purpose flour

1 teaspoon baking soda

1 1/2 cups chopped unsalted dry-roasted peanuts

Heat oven to 375°. Beat peanut butter, sugars, butter and eggs in large bowl with electric mixer on medium speed, or mix with spoon. Stir in flour and baking soda. Stir in peanuts (dough will be stiff).

Drop dough by rounded tablespoonfuls about 2 inches apart onto ungreased cookie sheet. Bake 8 to 10 minutes or until light brown. Cool 1 to 2 minutes; remove from cookie sheet to wire rack.

1 Cookie: Calories 105 (Calories from Fat 55); Fat 6g (Saturated 1g); Cholesterol 10mg; Sodium 70mg; Carbohydrate 10g (Dietary Fiber 0g); Protein 3g.

Double Peanut Cookies

Whole Wheat–Honey Cookies

BAKE: 9 to 11 min per sheet ● YIELD: About 2 dozen cookies

Cookie Tips

Whole wheat flour contains the wheat germ, which is oily. The oil can become rancid, so it's best to store whole wheat flour in the refrigerator or freezer. It's a good idea to let the flour come to room temperature before using it for baking.

Make It Your Way

If you love the taste of cinnamon-flavored graham crackers, try our cookie version called **Honey-Cinnamon Cookies**. To make them, stir in 1/2 teaspoon ground cinnamon with the flour. Mix 2 tablespoons granulated sugar and 1/2 teaspoon ground cinnamon; sprinkle over cookies immediately after you take them out of the oven.

1/2 cup packed brown sugar

1/2 cup butter or margarine, softened

1/2 cup honey

1/2 teaspoon vanilla

1 egg

2 cups whole wheat flour

1/2 teaspoon salt

1/2 teaspoon baking soda

Heat oven to 375°. Beat brown sugar, butter, honey, vanilla and egg in large bowl with electric mixer on medium speed, or mix with spoon. Stir in remaining ingredients.

Drop dough by rounded tablespoonfuls about 2 inches apart onto ungreased cookie sheet. Bake 9 to 11 minutes or until edges are light brown. Remove from cookie sheet to wire rack.

1 Cookie: Calories 110 (Calories from Fat 35); Fat 4g (Saturated 1g); Cholesterol 10mg; Sodium 125mg; Carbohydrate 18g (Dietary Fiber 1g); Protein 2g.

Whole Wheat–Honey Cookies, Whole Wheat Rounds (page 35)

Whole Wheat–Fruit Drops

BAKE: 11 to 13 min per sheet ● YIELD: About 2 1/2 dozen cookies

Cookie Tips

An easy way to dice dried fruits is to spray your knife periodically with cooking spray.

Make It Your Way

The nutty taste of whole wheat flour goes great with dates. To make **Whole Wheat–Date Cookies**, decrease the brown sugar to 1/2 cup and substitute an 8-ounce package of chopped dates for the diced dried fruits and raisins.

3/4 cup packed brown sugar

1/2 cup plain yogurt

1/4 cup butter or margarine, softened

1 tablespoon grated orange peel

1/2 teaspoon vanilla

1 egg

1 1/2 cups whole wheat flour

1/2 teaspoon baking soda

1/4 teaspoon baking powder

1 package (6 ounces) diced dried fruits and raisins (about 1 1/4 cups)

Heat oven to 375°. Beat brown sugar, yogurt, butter, orange peel, vanilla and egg in large bowl with electric mixer on medium speed, or mix with spoon. Stir in flour, baking soda and baking powder. Stir in dried fruits.

Drop dough by rounded tablespoonfuls about 2 inches apart onto ungreased cookie sheet. Bake 11 to 13 minutes or until light brown. Remove from cookie sheet to wire rack.

1 Cookie: Calories 75 (Calories from Fat 20); Fat 2g (Saturated 0g); Cholesterol 10mg; Sodium 50mg; Carbohydrate 14g (Dietary Fiber 1g); Protein 1g.

Whole Wheat Rounds

BAKE: 12 to 15 min per sheet ● YIELD: About 2 dozen cookies

1 cup butter or margarine, softened

1 cup powdered sugar

2 teaspoons vanilla

1 cup all-purpose flour

3/4 cup whole wheat flour

1/4 teaspoon salt

Powdered sugar

Cookie Tips

The very, tender texture of this cookie comes from the powdered sugar mixed in the dough, and it's what makes them melt in your mouth when you eat them.

Heat oven to 375°. Beat butter, 1 cup powdered sugar and vanilla in large bowl with electric mixer on medium speed, or mix with spoon. Stir in flours and salt.

Drop dough by rounded tablespoonfuls about 2 inches apart onto ungreased cookie sheet. Bake 12 to 15 minutes or until almost no indentation remains when touched in center. Cool 1 to 2 minutes; remove from cookie sheet to wire rack. Cool completely. Sprinkle lightly with additional powdered sugar.

1 Cookie: Calories 125 (Calories from Fat 70); Fat 8g (Saturated 2g); Cholesterol 0mg; Sodium 115mg; Carbohydrate 12g (Dietary Fiber 0g); Protein 1g.

Brown Sugar Drops

BAKE: 9 to 11 min per sheet ● YIELD: About 5 dozen cookies

Make It Your Way

We've got three more ways we think you'll enjoy to make this cookie. How about **Applesauce–Brown Sugar Drops**? Simply substitute 1 cup applesauce for the 1/2 cup milk. Then stir in 1 1/2 teaspoons ground cinnamon, 1/4 teaspoon ground cloves and 1 cup raisins.

Or try **Cherry–Brown Sugar Drops**. Stir in 1 cup chopped, well-drained maraschino cherries. Press an additional cherry half in each cookie before baking, if desired. Omit the glaze. This version makes about 6 dozen cookies.

Finally, there's **Whole Wheat–Brown Sugar Drops**. Substitute 2 cups whole wheat flour for 2 cups of the all-purpose flour. Stir in 1 cup chopped pecans. Press a pecan half in each cookie before baking, if desired. Omit the glaze.

2 cups packed brown sugar

1/2 cup butter or margarine, softened

1/2 cup shortening

1/2 cup milk

2 eggs

3 1/2 cups all-purpose flour

1 teaspoon baking soda

1/2 teaspoon salt

Light Brown Glaze (below)

Heat oven to 400°. Beat brown sugar, butter, shortening, milk and eggs in large bowl with electric mixer on medium speed, or mix with spoon. Stir in flour, baking soda and salt.

Drop dough by rounded tablespoonfuls about 2 inches apart onto ungreased cookie sheet. Bake 9 to 11 minutes or until almost no indentation remains when touched in center. Cool 1 to 2 minutes; remove from cookie sheet to wire rack. Cool completely. Spread with Light Brown Glaze.

Light Brown Glaze

4 cups powdered sugar

1/2 cup butter or margarine, melted

2 teaspoons vanilla

2 to 4 tablespoons milk

Mix all ingredients until smooth and spreadable.

1 Cookie: Calories 135 (Calories from Fat 45); Fat 5g (Saturated 1g); Cholesterol 10mg; Sodium 80mg; Carbohydrate 21g (Dietary Fiber 0g); Protein 1g.

Soft Molasses Cookies

BAKE: 9 to 11 min per sheet ● YIELD: About 4 dozen cookies

1 cup sugar

1/2 cup butter or margarine, softened

1/2 cup shortening

3/4 cup sour cream

1/2 cup light or dark molasses

1 egg

3 cups all-purpose flour

1 1/2 teaspoons baking soda

1 teaspoon ground ginger

1 teaspoon ground cinnamon

1/2 teaspoon salt

Sugar, if desired

Heat oven to 375°. Beat 1 cup sugar, the butter, shortening, sour cream, molasses and egg in large bowl with electric mixer on medium speed, or mix with spoon. Stir in remaining ingredients except sugar.

Drop dough by rounded tablespoonfuls about 2 inches apart onto ungreased cookie sheet. Bake 9 to 11 minutes or until almost no indentation remains when touched in center. Cool 1 to 2 minutes; remove from cookie sheet to wire rack. Sprinkle sugar over cookies while still warm.

1 Cookie: Calories 100 (Calories from Fat 45); Fat 5g (Saturated 1g); Cholesterol 5mg; Sodium 90mg; Carbohydrate 13g (Dietary Fiber 0g); Protein 1g.

Cookie Tips

Before measuring the molasses, spray the measuring cup with cooking spray; the molasses will come out of the cup much easier.

Make It Your Way

Childhood memories may capture a soft, puffy molasses cookie covered in a creamy white frosting. Make **Frosted Soft Molasses Cookies** by frosting them with the Vanilla Frosting on page 21, instead of sprinkling them with sugar.

Sour Cream Cookies

BAKE: 8 to 10 min per sheet ● YIELD: About 6 dozen cookies

Make It Your Way

For apples and spice and everything nice, try **Applesauce Cookies**. Substitute 3/4 cup applesauce for sour cream. Stir in 1 teaspoon ground cinnamon, 1/4 teaspoon ground cloves and 1 cup raisins with the flour.

Warm-up to tropical flavor with **Coconut–Sour Cream Cookies**. All you do is substitute shredded coconut for the pecans.

You can't work for peanuts, but you can put them in your cookies! **Salted Peanut–Sour Cream Cookies** are easy to make, just substitute salted peanuts for the pecans.

Old-fashioned flavor can be found in **Spice–Sour Cream Cookies**. Mix 1/2 cup granulated sugar, 1 teaspoon ground cinnamon and 1/4 teaspoon ground cloves; sprinkle over cookies before baking. Omit glaze.

1 1/2 cups packed brown sugar

1 cup sour cream

1/2 cup shortening

1 teaspoon vanilla

2 eggs

2 3/4 cups all-purpose flour

1/2 teaspoon baking soda

1/2 teaspoon salt

1 cup chopped pecans, if desired

Browned Butter Glaze (below)

Heat oven to 375°. Beat brown sugar, sour cream, shortening, vanilla and eggs in large bowl with electric mixer on medium speed, or mix with spoon. Stir in flour, baking soda and salt. Stir in pecans.

Drop dough by rounded teaspoonfuls about 2 inches apart onto ungreased cookie sheet. Bake 8 to 10 minutes or until almost no indentation remains when touched in center. Cool 1 to 2 minutes; remove from cookie sheet to wire rack. Cool completely. Spread with Browned Butter Glaze.

Browned Butter Glaze

1/3 cup butter or margarine

2 cups powdered sugar

1 1/2 teaspoons vanilla

2 to 3 tablespoons hot water

Heat butter in 1-quart saucepan over low heat, stirring occasionally, until golden brown; remove from heat. Stir in remaining ingredients until smooth and spreadable.

1 Cookie: Calories 80 (Calories from Fat 25); Fat 3g (Saturated 1g); Cholesterol 10mg; Sodium 40mg; Carbohydrate 12g (Dietary Fiber 0g); Protein 1g.

Spicy Pumpkin-Date Cookies

BAKE: 8 to 10 min per sheet ● YIELD: About 4 dozen cookies

1 cup sugar

1/2 cup butter or margarine, softened

1 cup canned pumpkin

2 eggs

2 cups all-purpose flour

2 teaspoons baking powder

2 teaspoons ground cinnamon

1/2 teaspoon ground nutmeg

1/2 teaspoon ground ginger

1/4 teaspoon ground cloves

1 cup chopped dates

1/2 cup chopped walnuts

Heat oven to 375°. Beat sugar and butter in large bowl with electric mixer on medium speed until light and fluffy, or mix with spoon. Beat in pumpkin and eggs. Stir in remaining ingredients except dates and walnuts. Stir in dates and walnuts.

Drop dough by rounded teaspoonfuls about 2 inches apart onto ungreased cookie sheet. Bake 8 to 10 minutes or until edges are set. Immediately remove from cookie sheet to wire rack.

1 Cookie: Calories 80 (Calories from Fat 25); Fat 3g (Saturated 1g); Cholesterol 10mg; Sodium 45mg; Carbohydrate 12g (Dietary Fiber 0g); Protein 1g.

Nutmeg

Nutmeg was popular throughout the world from the fifteenth to the nineteenth century. Nutmeg is a seed from the nutmeg tree. Whole nutmeg can be grated or you can buy ground nutmeg. The nutmeg seed also gives us a second spice called mace. The mace comes from a lacy membrane surrounding the seed. Mace is more pungent tasting than nutmeg but can be used interchangeably.

Make It Your Way

To make **Spicy Pumpkin-Date Cookies with Cream Cheese Frosting,** use the Cream Cheese Frosting recipe on page 78.

Old-Fashioned Date Drop Cookies

BAKE: 8 to 10 min per sheet ● YIELD: About 6 dozen cookies

Cookie Tips

For convenience, you can buy dried orange peel, which you can find in the spice section of your supermarket. Or grate several fresh oranges (use just the orange peel; the white part, called pith, is bitter) and freeze the peels in plastic freezer bags for up to 6 months.

Nuts stay fresh much longer if you store them in the freezer. Keep nuts in an airtight container with a lid or in resealable plastic freezer bags.

1 1/2 cups packed brown sugar

1 cup butter or margarine, softened

1 tablespoon grated orange peel

1 teaspoon vanilla

2 eggs

2 cups all-purpose flour

1 cup quick-cooking or old-fashioned oats

1 teaspoon baking soda

1/4 teaspoon salt

1 package (8 ounces) chopped dates

1/2 cup chopped pecans

Heat oven to 350°. Grease cookie sheet. Beat brown sugar, butter, orange peel, vanilla and eggs in large bowl with electric mixer on medium speed, or mix with spoon. Stir in flour, oats, baking soda and salt. Stir in dates and pecans.

Drop dough by rounded teaspoonfuls about 2 inches apart onto cookie sheet. Bake 8 to 10 minutes or until light brown. Remove from cookie sheet to wire rack.

1 Cookie: Calories 70 (Calories from Fat 25); Fat 3g (Saturated 1g); Cholesterol 5mg; Sodium 60mg; Carbohydrate 10g (Dietary Fiber 0g); Protein 1g.

Old-Fashioned Rum-Raisin Cookies

BAKE: 9 to 11 min per sheet ● YIELD: About 2 1/2 dozen cookies

1 cup raisins

1/2 cup water

1/4 cup rum

3/4 cup sugar

1/2 cup butter or margarine, softened

1 egg

1 3/4 cups all-purpose flour

1/2 teaspoon baking soda

1/2 teaspoon baking powder

1/4 teaspoon salt

Heat raisins, water and rum to boiling in 1-quart saucepan; reduce heat. Simmer uncovered 20 to 30 minutes or until raisins are plump and liquid has evaporated. Cool raisins 30 minutes.

Heat oven to 375°. Beat sugar and butter in large bowl with electric mixer on medium speed about 3 minutes or until fluffy, or mix with spoon. Beat in egg. Stir in remaining ingredients. Stir in raisins.

Drop dough by rounded tablespoonfuls about 2 inches apart onto ungreased cookie sheet. Bake 9 to 11 minutes or until light brown. Remove from cookie sheet to wire rack.

1 Cookie: Calories 90 (Calories from Fat 25); Fat 3g (Saturated 1g); Cholesterol 5mg; Sodium 85mg; Carbohydrate 15g (Dietary Fiber 0g); Protein 1g.

Rum

Rum is made from fermented sugar-cane juice or molasses. Most rum comes from the Caribbean. It is available in light and dark varieties. Light rum is light in both color and flavor, whereas dark rum is richer in color and flavor. Either variety can be used in this recipe.

"I Don't Have That"

1 teaspoon rum extract mixed with 1/4 cup water can be substituted for the rum.

Brandied Fruit Drops

BAKE: 9 to 11 min per sheet ● YIELD: About 5 dozen cookies

3/4 cup packed brown sugar

1/2 cup butter or margarine, softened

1/3 cup brandy

2 eggs

2 cups all-purpose flour

2 teaspoons baking powder

1 teaspoon ground cardamom

1/2 teaspoon ground cinnamon

1/2 teaspoon ground nutmeg

1 cup chopped pecans

1 cup dried apricots, chopped

1/2 cup currants

1/2 cup golden raisins

Heat oven to 350°. Grease cookie sheet. Beat brown sugar, butter, brandy and eggs in large bowl with electric mixer on medium speed, or mix with spoon. Stir in flour, baking powder, cardamom, cinnamon and nutmeg. Stir in remaining ingredients.

Drop dough by rounded teaspoonfuls about 2 inches apart onto cookie sheet. Bake 9 to 11 minutes or until light brown. Remove from cookie sheet to wire rack.

1 Cookie: Calories 70 (Calories from Fat 25); Fat 3g (Saturated 0g); Cholesterol 5mg; Sodium 40mg; Carbohydrate 10g (Dietary Fiber 0g); Protein 1g.

Pineapple Puffs

BAKE: 8 to 10 min per sheet ● YIELD: About 6 1/2 dozen cookies

1 1/2 cups sugar

1/2 cup butter or margarine, softened

1/2 cup sour cream or plain yogurt

1 egg

1 can (8 ounces) crushed pineapple in juice, undrained

3 1/2 cups all-purpose flour

1 teaspoon baking soda

1 teaspoon vanilla

1/2 teaspoon salt

1/2 cup chopped almonds

Vanilla Glaze (below)

Heat oven to 375°. Beat sugar, butter, sour cream, egg and pineapple in large bowl with electric mixer on medium speed, or mix with spoon. Stir in flour, baking soda, vanilla and salt. Stir in almonds.

Drop dough by rounded teaspoonfuls about 2 inches apart onto ungreased cookie sheet. Bake 8 to 10 minutes or until almost no indentation remains when touched in center. Immediately remove from cookie sheet to wire rack. Cool completely. Spread with Vanilla Glaze.

Vanilla Glaze

2 cups powdered sugar

1 teaspoon vanilla

2 to 3 tablespoons milk

Mix all ingredients until smooth and spreadable.

1 Cookie: Calories 70 (Calories from Fat 20); Fat 2g (Saturated 0g); Cholesterol 5mg; Sodium 45mg; Carbohydrate 12g (Dietary Fiber 0g); Protein 1g.

Cookie Tips

White glazes and frosting that call for milk will look whiter and less translucent if you use whole milk, half-and-half or cream.

Make It Your Way

To make **Coconut Pineapple Puffs,** substitute 1/2 cup coconut for the almonds in the cookie dough. To add to the tropical flavor, substitute rum extract for the vanilla in both the cookie and glaze.

Lemon-Lime Cookies

BAKE: 11 to 13 min per sheet ● YIELD: About 2 dozen cookies

Cookie Tips

Serve these sweet, tart cookies for a summer wedding or baby shower with lemonade or iced tea. They would look very pretty arranged on a doily-lined serving plate.

Make It Your Way

If you love the flavor of orange, create some sunshine with **Orange Cookies**. Substitute 2 tablespoons grated orange peel for the lemon and lime peels and 1/4 cup orange juice for the lemon and lime juices in the cookie dough. Substitute 1 teaspoon grated orange peel for the lime peel and about 2 tablespoons orange juice for the lemon juice and water in the frosting.

1 cup sugar

2/3 cup shortening

1 tablespoon grated lemon peel

2 tablespoons lemon juice

2 teaspoons grated lime peel

1 tablespoon lime juice

1 egg

1 3/4 cups all-purpose flour

1/2 teaspoon baking powder

1/2 teaspoon baking soda

1/2 teaspoon salt

Lemon-Lime Frosting (below)

Heat oven to 375°. Beat sugar, shortening, lemon peel, lemon juice, lime peel, lime juice and egg in large bowl with electric mixer on medium speed, or mix with spoon. Stir in flour, baking powder, baking soda and salt.

Drop dough by rounded tablespoonfuls about 2 inches apart onto ungreased cookie sheet. Bake 11 to 13 minutes or until edges are golden brown. Cool 1 to 2 minutes; remove from cookie sheet to wire rack. Cool completely. Frost with Lemon-Lime Frosting.

Lemon-Lime Frosting

2 cups powdered sugar

2 tablespoons butter or margarine, softened

1 teaspoon grated lime peel

1 tablespoon lemon juice

2 to 3 teaspoons water

Mix all ingredients until smooth and spreadable.

1 Cookie: Calories 170 (Calories from Fat 65); Fat 7g (Saturated 2g); Cholesterol 10mg; Sodium 100mg; Carbohydrate 26g (Dietary Fiber 0g); Protein 1g.

Lemon-Lime Cookies, Pineapple Puffs (page 43)

Applesauce-Granola Cookies

BAKE: 11 to 13 min per sheet ● YIELD: About 3 1/2 dozen cookies

Cookie Tips

Use either sweetened or unsweetened applesauce in these cookies. Sweetened applesauce will give you a sweeter cookie.

1 cup packed brown sugar

1/2 cup shortening

1 teaspoon vanilla

1 egg

1/2 cup applesauce

2 cups all-purpose flour

2 cups granola

1/2 teaspoon baking soda

1/2 teaspoon salt

Heat oven to 375°. Beat brown sugar, shortening, vanilla and egg in large bowl with electric mixer on medium speed, or mix with spoon. Stir in applesauce. Stir in remaining ingredients.

Drop dough by rounded tablespoonfuls about 2 inches apart onto ungreased cookie sheet. Bake 11 to 13 minutes or until almost no indentation remains when touched in center. Cool 1 to 2 minutes; remove from cookie sheet to wire rack.

1 Cookie: Calories 90 (Calories from Fat 35); Fat 4g (Saturated 1g); Cholesterol 5mg; Sodium 50mg; Carbohydrate 13g (Dietary Fiber 0g); Protein 1g.

Banana-Ginger Jumbles

BAKE: 9 to 11 min per sheet ● YIELD: About 3 1/2 dozen cookies

1 cup packed brown sugar

1/2 cup butter or margarine, softened

1/2 cup shortening

1 tablespoon grated gingerroot or 1 teaspoon ground ginger*

2 eggs

1 cup mashed very ripe bananas (2 medium)

1/4 cup milk

3 cups all-purpose flour

1 teaspoon baking powder

3/4 teaspoon salt

Powdered sugar, if desired

Heat oven to 375°. Beat brown sugar, butter, shortening, gingerroot and eggs in large bowl with electric mixer on medium speed, or mix with spoon. Stir in bananas and milk. Stir in flour, baking powder and salt.

Drop dough by rounded tablespoonfuls about 2 inches apart onto ungreased cookie sheet. Bake 9 to 11 minutes or until almost no indentation remains when touched in center. Remove from cookie sheet to wire rack. Sprinkle with powdered sugar while warm.

1 Cookie: Calories 100 (Calories from Fat 45); Fat 5g (Saturated 1g); Cholesterol 10mg; Sodium 85mg; Carbohydrate 13g (Dietary Fiber 0g); Protein 1g.

*If using ground ginger, stir in with the flour.

Make It Your Way

Wholesome goodness is just an ingredient away with **Whole Wheat–Banana-Ginger Cookies**. Substitute 2 3/4 cups whole wheat flour for the all-purpose flour.

Check out the new, super-moist and plump baking raisins. You'll find them in the baking aisle in the supermarket. Give them a try in **Banana-Raisin Cookies**. Omit gingerroot and stir in 1 cup golden raisins with flour.

Pastel Mint Drops

BAKE: 8 to 10 min per sheet • YIELD: About 5 dozen cookies

Cookie Tips

Pastel mint candies are those little pillow-shaped mints that come in very light, pastel shades of pink, yellow and green. They are commonly served at bridal and baby showers and weddings along with mixed nuts. Look for them in the candy aisle in your supermarket.

Chop the mints quickly by using a food processor, or place mints in a resealable plastic bag and pound gently with a rolling pin until they look coarsely chopped.

3/4 cup sugar

1/2 cup vegetable oil

2 eggs

1 teaspoon vanilla

2 cups all-purpose flour

2 teaspoons baking powder

1/2 teaspoon salt

1/2 cup chopped party mints (pastel mint candies)

Heat oven to 375°. Beat sugar, oil, eggs and vanilla in large bowl with electric mixer on medium speed, or mix with spoon. Stir in flour, baking powder and salt. Stir in candies.

Drop dough by rounded teaspoonfuls about 2 inches apart onto ungreased cookie sheet. Bake 8 to 10 minutes or until edges are light brown. Remove from cookie sheet to wire rack.

1 Cookie: Calories 50 (Calories from Fat 20); Fat 2g (Saturated 0g); Cholesterol 5mg; Sodium 40mg; Carbohydrate 7g (Dietary Fiber 0g); Protein 1g.

Coconut Meringue Cookies

BAKE: 15 to 20 min per sheet • YIELD: About 3 dozen cookies

4 egg whites (1/2 cup)
1 1/4 cups sugar
1/4 teaspoon salt
1/2 teaspoon vanilla
2 1/2 cups shredded or flaked coconut

Heat oven to 325°. Lightly grease cookie sheet, or cover with baking parchment paper. Beat egg whites in large bowl with electric mixer on high speed until foamy. Beat in sugar, 1 tablespoon at a time; continue beating until stiff and glossy (do not underbeat). Stir in salt, vanilla and coconut.

Drop mixture by heaping teaspoonfuls about 2 inches apart onto cookie sheet. Bake 15 to 20 minutes or until set and light brown. Cool 5 minutes; carefully remove from cookie sheet to wire rack.

1 Cookie: Calories 60 (Calories from Fat 20); Fat 2g (Saturated 2g); Cholesterol 0mg; Sodium 40mg; Carbohydrate 10g (Dietary Fiber 0g); Protein 1g.

Cookie Tips

Egg whites beat much better if they're at room temperature. It's safe to allow your egg whites to stand on your counter for about 30 minutes. To warm them more quickly, place whites in a small metal bowl and place the bowl in hot water for 10 to 15 minutes.

Make It Your Way

Some people are crazy about the taste of nuts. Well here's your chance to get lots of nut flavor into a little macaroon. To make **Nut Meringue Cookies**, substitute 2 cups finely chopped nuts for the coconut.

Ginger-Pecan Chews

BAKE: 12 to 14 min per sheet ● YIELD: About 2 1/2 cookies

Cookie Tips

If you don't want to chop the crystallized ginger with a knife, use kitchen scissors sprayed with cooking spray and snip the ginger into pieces.

Crystallized Ginger

Crystallized ginger, also called "candied ginger," can be a bit pricy, but it has a flavor that ground ginger can't really replace. It's made by cooking fresh gingerroot in a sugar syrup until it soaks into the ginger through and through. It's then coated with granulated sugar. Crystallized ginger has a chewy texture.

1/2 cup sugar

1/2 cup butter or margarine, softened

1/2 cup molasses

1 egg

1 jar (2 ounces) crystallized ginger, chopped (about 1/3 cup)

2 cups all-purpose flour

1 teaspoon ground ginger

1/2 teaspoon baking soda

1/2 teaspoon salt

1/2 cup chopped pecans

Pecan halves, if desired

Heat oven to 375°. Beat sugar, butter, molasses, egg and crystallized ginger in large bowl with electric mixer on medium speed, or mix with spoon. Stir in flour, ground ginger, baking soda and salt. Stir in chopped pecans.

Drop dough by rounded tablespoonfuls about 2 inches apart onto ungreased cookie sheet. Press pecan half onto each cookie. Bake 12 to 14 minutes or until almost no indentation remains when touched near center. Immediately remove from cookie sheet to wire rack.

1 Cookie: Calories 110 (Calories from Fat 45); Fat 5g (Saturated 1g); Cholesterol 5mg; Sodium 100mg; Carbohydrate 15g (Dietary Fiber 0g); Protein 1g.

Ginger-Pecan Chews

Cornmeal Crispies

BAKE: 10 to 12 min per sheet ● YIELD: About 5 dozen cookies

Cookie Tips

Yellow and white cornmeal are interchangeable in this recipe, so use what you have on hand. The cornmeal adds a rustic texture and great crunch to these cookies. For fun, use blue cornmeal in these cookies; the baked color will be bluish purple. How many blue cookies have you ever seen?

Make It Your Way

If you just want a straight-away, buttery-tasting, crisp cookie, just leave out the lemon peel. And if you're a real adventure-seeker at heart, take two of these cookies and spread about a teaspoon of red or green jalapeño jelly between the cookies to make jalapeño jelly sandwich cookies. Our recipe tasters just loved them!

3/4 cup sugar

1 cup butter or margarine, softened

1 egg

1 1/4 cups all-purpose flour

1 cup yellow cornmeal

1 teaspoon baking powder

1 teaspoon grated lemon peel

1/2 teaspoon salt

Heat oven to 350°. Beat sugar, butter and egg in large bowl with electric mixer on medium speed, or mix with spoon. Stir in remaining ingredients.

Drop dough by rounded teaspoonfuls about 2 inches apart onto ungreased cookie sheet. Bake 10 to 12 minutes or until edges are light brown. Cool 1 to 2 minutes; remove from cookie sheet to wire rack.

1 Cookie: Calories 55 (Calories from Fat 25); Fat 3g (Saturated 1g); Cholesterol 5mg; Sodium 65mg; Carbohydrate 6g (Dietary Fiber 0g); Protein 1g.

Poppy Drop Cookies

BAKE: 10 to 12 min per sheet ● YIELD: About 2 dozen cookies

1 cup sugar

1 cup butter or margarine, softened

1 egg

1 3/4 cups all-purpose flour

2 tablespoons poppy seed

1 teaspoon baking powder

1/4 teaspoon salt

Poppy Seed Glaze (below)

Heat oven to 375°. Beat sugar, butter and egg in large bowl with electric mixer on medium speed, or mix with spoon. Stir in flour, poppy seed, baking powder and salt.

Drop dough by rounded tablespoonfuls about 2 inches apart onto ungreased cookie sheet. Bake 10 to 12 minutes or until edges are golden brown. Cool 1 to 2 minutes; remove from cookie sheet to wire rack. Cool completely. Drizzle with Poppy Seed Glaze.

Poppy Seed Glaze

1 1/2 cups powdered sugar

2 tablespoons milk

1 teaspoon poppy seed

1/2 teaspoon vanilla

Mix all ingredients until smooth.

1 Cookie: Calories 170 (Calories from Fat 70); Fat 8g (Saturated 2g); Cholesterol 10mg; Sodium 135mg; Carbohydrate 23g (Dietary Fiber 0g); Protein 1g.

Cookie Tips

If you're not wild about poppy seeds, just leave them out of the cookie dough and glaze. What you will have then is a nice little butter cookie with a vanilla glaze.

Poppy Seed

When you use poppy seeds in a recipe, you might find it interesting to know that it takes about 900,000 seeds to equal 1 pound! The tiny seeds come from the poppy plant.

CHAPTER 2

The Ultimate Brownie 56
Bars and Brownies Cutting
    Guide 58
Fudgy Saucepan Brownies 60
Milk Chocolate–Malt
    Brownies 61
Cocoa Brownies 62
Amaretto Brownies 64
Vanilla Brownies 65
Mocha Brownies 66
German Chocolate
    Brownies 68
Cream Cheese Brownies 70
Peanut Butter Swirl
    Brownies 71
The Ultimate Date Bars 72
Linzer Torte Bars 74
Lemon Squares 75
Cherry-Almond Bars 76

Zucchini Bars 77
Banana-Nut Bars 78
Double Apple Bars 80
Pumpkin Spice Bars 81
Cinnamon-Coffee Bars 82
Fudgy Layer Squares 83
Toffee Bars 84
Mousse Bars 85
Tiramisu Cheesecake Bars 86
Dream Bars 87
Lemon Cream Oat Bars 88
Caramel Candy Bars 90
Mixed Nut Bars 91
Pecan Pie Squares 92
No-Bake Peanut Butter
    Squares 94
No-Bake Honey-Oat Bars 96
Coconut Macaroon Bars 97

Super Bars and Brownies

Cherry Cream Cheese Brownies (variation, page 70),
Tiramisu Cheesecake Bars (page 86)

Chocolate, chocolate, chocolate! It often wins hands down as a top choice, and this moist, fudgy brownie fills the bill.

The Ultimate Brownie

BAKE: 40 to 45 min per pan ● YIELD: 24 brownies

Cookie Tips

Be sure not to overbake brownies because the edges will get hard and dry.

Make It Your Way

To make **Triple Chocolate Brownies**, stir in a 6-ounce bag of semisweet chocolate chips with the nuts and then spread with Chocolate Frosting (page 25).

5 ounces unsweetened baking chocolate

2/3 cup butter or margarine

1 3/4 cups sugar

2 teaspoons vanilla

3 eggs

1 cup all-purpose flour

1 cup chopped nuts

Heat oven to 350°. Grease square pan, 9×9×2 inches. Melt chocolate and butter over low heat, stirring frequently; remove from heat. Cool slightly.

Beat sugar, vanilla and eggs in large bowl with electric mixer on high speed 5 minutes. Beat in chocolate mixture on low speed. Beat in flour just until blended. Stir in nuts.

Spread batter in pan. Bake 40 to 45 minutes or just until brownies begin to pull away from sides of pan. Cool completely. Cut into 6 rows by 4 rows.

1 Brownie: Calories 200 (Calories from Fat 110); Fat 12g (Saturated 3g); Cholesterol 25mg; Sodium 70mg; Carbohydrate 21g (Dietary Fiber 1g); Protein 3g

The Ultimate Brownie, Milk Chocolate–Malt Brownies (page 61)

Bars and Brownies Cutting Guide

To help make cutting easier, we've created a series of grids showing how to cut bars and brownies into various yields from a variety of pan sizes. To make the cutting directions even easier, each of our recipes tells you the number of rows to cut.

To cut triangle shapes, cut squares diagonally in half.

To cut diamond shapes, first cut straight parallel lines 1 or 1 1/2 inches apart down the length of the pan. Second, cut diagonal lines 1 or 1 1/2 inches apart across the straight cuts. You will find irregularly shaped pieces in the corners and at the ends of the pan—consider those extra little treats for snacking!

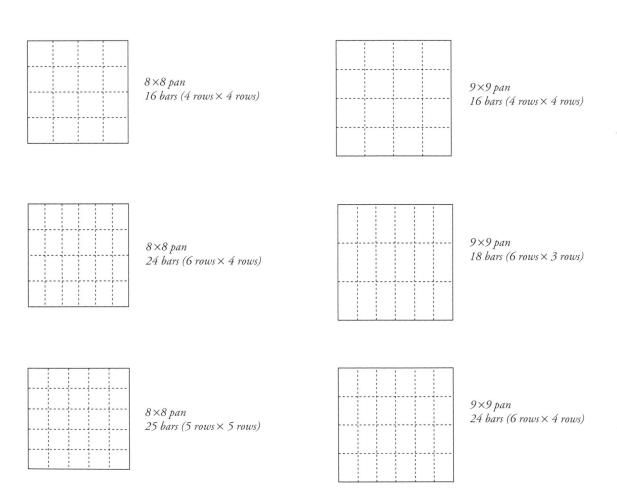

8×8 pan
16 bars (4 rows × 4 rows)

9×9 pan
16 bars (4 rows × 4 rows)

8×8 pan
24 bars (6 rows × 4 rows)

9×9 pan
18 bars (6 rows × 3 rows)

8×8 pan
25 bars (5 rows × 5 rows)

9×9 pan
24 bars (6 rows × 4 rows)

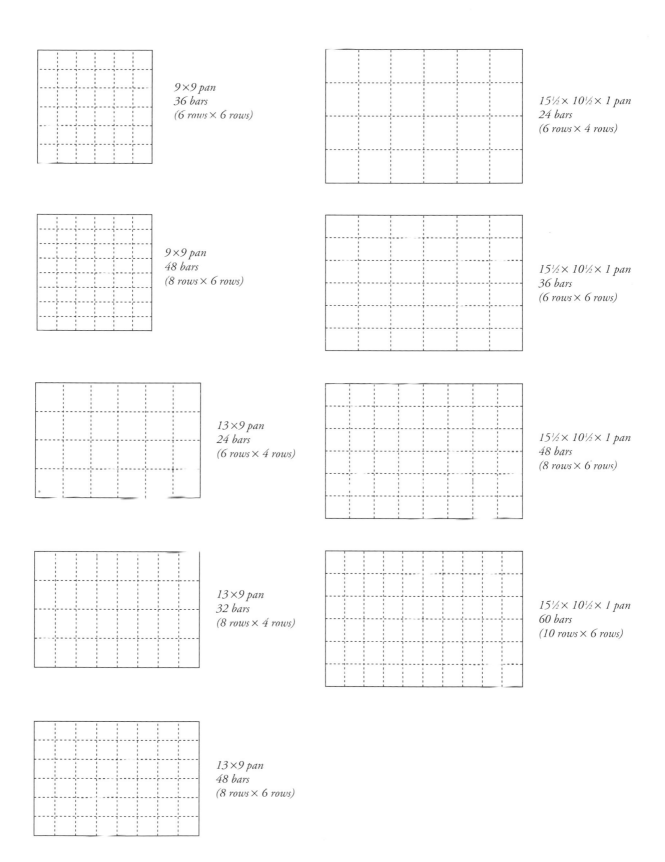

9×9 pan
36 bars
(6 rows × 6 rows)

15½ × 10½ × 1 pan
24 bars
(6 rows × 4 rows)

9×9 pan
48 bars
(8 rows × 6 rows)

15½ × 10½ × 1 pan
36 bars
(6 rows × 6 rows)

13×9 pan
24 bars
(6 rows × 4 rows)

15½ × 10½ × 1 pan
48 bars
(8 rows × 6 rows)

13×9 pan
32 bars
(8 rows × 4 rows)

15½ × 10½ × 1 pan
60 bars
(10 rows × 6 rows)

13×9 pan
48 bars
(8 rows × 6 rows)

Super Bars and Brownies **59**

Fudgy Saucepan Brownies

BAKE: 25 to 30 min per pan ● YIELD: 32 brownies

Cookie Tips

We call for chopped nuts, which allows you to pick your favorite. Although all types of nuts will work in this recipe, chocolate and walnuts seem to be a blue ribbon combination. It's always a good idea to sample a few nuts before adding them to your recipe to make sure they aren't rancid.

Make a festive dessert by cutting the brownies into 16 bars. Top with sweetened whipped cream and sprinkle with cocoa. Add a stemmed maraschino cherry for that special touch.

1 package (12 ounces) semisweet chocolate chips (2 cups)
1/2 cup butter or margarine
1 cup sugar
1 1/4 cups all-purpose flour
1 teaspoon vanilla
1/2 teaspoon baking powder
1/2 teaspoon salt
3 eggs, beaten
1 cup chopped nuts, if desired

Heat oven to 350°. Heat chocolate chips and butter in 3-quart saucepan over low heat, stirring frequently, until smooth; remove from heat. Stir in remaining ingredients except nuts. Stir in nuts.

Spread batter in ungreased rectangular pan, 13×9×2 inches. Bake 25 to 30 minutes or until center is set. Cool completely. Cut into 8 rows by 4 rows.

1 Brownie: Calories 155 (Calories from Fat 65); Fat 7g (Saturated 3g); Cholesterol 20mg; Sodium 85mg; Carbohydrate 21g (Dietary Fiber 0g); Protein 2g.

Milk Chocolate–Malt Brownies

BAKE: 30 to 35 min per pan ● YIELD: 48 brownies

1 package (11 1/2 ounces) milk chocolate chips (2 cups)

1/2 cup butter or margarine

3/4 cup sugar

1 teaspoon vanilla

3 eggs

1 3/4 cups all-purpose flour

1/2 cup natural- or chocolate-flavor malted milk powder

1/2 teaspoon baking powder

1/4 teaspoon salt

1 cup malted milk balls, coarsely chopped

Heat oven to 350°. Grease rectangular pan, 13×9×2 inches. Melt chocolate chips and butter in 3-quart saucepan over low heat, stirring frequently, until smooth; remove from heat. Cool slightly. Beat in sugar, vanilla and eggs with spoon. Stir in remaining ingredients except malted milk balls.

Spread batter in pan. Sprinkle with malted milk balls. Bake 30 to 35 minutes or until toothpick inserted in center comes out clean. Cool completely. Cut into 8 rows by 6 rows.

1 Brownie: Calories 100 (Calories from Fat 45); Fat 5g (Saturated 2g); Cholesterol 15mg; Sodium 55mg; Carbohydrate 12g (Dietary Fiber 0g); Protein 2g.

Cookie Tips

This luscious brownie is almost a candy confection and sure to please those who love the flavor of malted milk.

Malted Milk

Malted milk powder is made from dehydrated milk and malted cereals. You can find it with the ice-cream toppings in the supermarket.

Cocoa Brownies

BAKE: 20 to 25 min per pan ● YIELD: 16 brownies

Cookie Tips

This is the one for people who like cakelike, tender brownies.

Make It Your Way

To indulge in **Caramel-Pecan Brownies**, sprinkle 1/2 cup coarsely chopped pecans over the batter before you bake it. To make the ooey-gooey part, heat 12 vanilla caramels and 1 tablespoon milk over low heat, and stir until everything is melted and smooth. Drizzle caramel over warm brownies. Even though it's hard to do, cool the brownies completely before cutting and serving them.

1 cup sugar

1/2 cup butter or margarine, softened

1 teaspoon vanilla

2 eggs

2/3 cup all-purpose flour

1/2 cup baking cocoa

1/2 teaspoon baking powder

1/4 teaspoon salt

1/2 cup chopped walnuts, if desired

Heat oven to 350°. Grease square pan, 9×9×2 inches. Beat sugar, butter, vanilla and eggs in large bowl with electric mixer on medium speed, or mix with spoon. Stir in remaining ingredients except walnuts. Stir in walnuts.

Spread batter evenly in pan. Bake 20 to 25 minutes or until toothpick inserted in center comes out clean. Cool completely. Cut into 4 rows by 4 rows.

1 Brownie: Calories 140 (Calories from Fat 65); Fat 7g (Saturated 2g); Cholesterol 25mg; Sodium 60mg; Carbohydrate 18g (Dietary Fiber 1g); Protein 2g.

Caramel-Pecan Brownies (variation)

Amaretto Brownies

BAKE: 22 to 27 min per pan ● YIELD: 32 brownies

2/3 cup slivered almonds, toasted
8 ounces semisweet baking chocolate
1/3 cup butter or margarine
1 1/4 cups all-purpose flour
1 cup sugar
2 tablespoons Amaretto
1 teaspoon baking powder
1/2 teaspoon salt
2 eggs
Amaretto Frosting (below)

Heat oven to 350°. Grease rectangular pan, 13×9×2 inches. Place 1/3 cup of the almonds in food processor. Cover and process, using quick on-and-off motions, until almonds are ground. Chop remaining almonds; set aside.

Melt chocolate and butter in 3-quart saucepan over low heat, stirring frequently, until smooth; remove from heat. Stir in remaining ground almonds, flour, sugar, Amaretto, baking powder, salt and eggs.

Spread batter in pan. Bake 22 to 27 minutes or until toothpick inserted in center comes out clean. Cool completely. Frost with Amaretto Frosting. Sprinkle with chopped almonds. Cut into 8 rows by 4 rows.

Amaretto Frosting

2 cups powdered sugar
3 tablespoons butter or margarine, softened
1 tablespoon Amaretto
1 to 2 tablespoons milk

Mix all ingredients until smooth and spreadable.

1 Brownie: Calories 165 (Calories from Fat 65); Fat 7g (Saturated 2g); Cholesterol 15mg; Sodium 90mg; Carbohydrate 23g (Dietary Fiber 0g); Protein 2g.

Cookie Tips

To toast nuts, bake uncovered in ungreased shallow pan in 350° oven about 10 minutes, stirring occasionally, until golden brown. Or cook in ungreased heavy skillet over medium-low heat 5 to 7 minutes, stirring frequently until browning begins, then stirring constantly until golden brown.

"I Don't Have That"

1/4 teaspoon almond extract and 1 tablespoon maraschino cherry juice mixed with 1 tablespoon water can be substituted for the 2 tablespoons Amaretto in the brownies.

1/8 teaspoon almond extract and 1 1/2 teaspoons maraschino cherry juice mixed with 1 1/2 teaspoons water can be substituted for the 1 tablespoon Amaretto in the frosting.

Vanilla Brownies

BAKE: 30 to 35 min per pan ● YIELD: 32 brownies

1 package (10 ounces) vanilla milk (white) chips (1 2/3 cups)

1/2 cup butter or margarine

1 1/4 cups all-purpose flour

3/4 cup sugar

1 teaspoon vanilla

1/4 teaspoon salt

3 eggs

1/2 cup chopped nuts

Creamy Vanilla Frosting (below)

Heat oven to 350°. Grease and flour rectangular pan, 13 × 9 × 2 inches. Heat vanilla milk chips and butter in heavy 2-quart saucepan over low heat, stirring frequently, just until melted (mixture may appear curdled). Remove from heat; cool. Stir in flour, sugar, vanilla, salt and eggs. Stir in nuts.

Spread batter in pan. Bake 30 to 35 minutes or until toothpick inserted in center comes out clean. Cool completely. Spread with Creamy Vanilla Frosting. Cut into 8 rows by 4 rows.

Creamy Vanilla Frosting

1 1/2 cups powdered sugar

3 tablespoons butter or margarine, softened

1/2 teaspoon vanilla

1 to 2 tablespoons milk

Mix all ingredients until smooth and spreadable.

1 Brownie: Calories 160 (Calories from Fat 70); Fat 8g (Saturated 3g); Cholesterol 20mg; Sodium 80mg; Carbohydrate 20g (Dietary Fiber 0g); Protein 2g.

Vanilla Milk Chips

Vanilla milk chips and white baking chocolate bars can burn easily, so it's important to melt them over low heat while stirring frequently. Don't confuse vanilla milk chips or white baking chocolate bars with white candy coating. White candy coating is also called almond bark, compound white chocolate and confectionery or summer coating. Candy coating contains oil versus cocoa butter, more sugar and lacks the rich vanilla and dairy flavor of the baking bars or chips.

Vanilla Sugar

Add even more to the flavor of these cookies by using vanilla sugar. Make your own by placing a piece of vanilla bean in an airtight container of granulated sugar for 3 to 4 days.

Mocha Brownies

BAKE: 18 to 22 min per pan ● YIELD: 16 brownies

Cookie Tips

A wonderfully sophisticated blend of coffee and chocolate, these brownies are rich and chocolaty.

Make It Your Way

To make **Coconut Brownies**, omit instant coffee from brownies and omit Coffee Frosting. Mix together 1 1/2 cups powdered sugar, 1/2 cup shredded or flaked coconut, 2 tablespoons softened margarine and 2 tablespoons milk. Continue as directed, using coconut frosting.

To make **Raspberry Brownies**, omit instant coffee and add 1/4 teaspoon almond extract to brownies. Omit Coffee Frosting. Spread 1/4 cup red raspberry preserves over cooled brownies. Drizzle with glaze made with chocolate or vanilla milk chips.

2 ounces unsweetened baking chocolate

1/2 cup butter or margarine

3/4 cup all-purpose flour

3/4 cup sugar

1 tablespoon instant coffee (dry)

2 tablespoons milk

1/2 teaspoon baking powder

1/4 teaspoon salt

2 eggs

Coffee Frosting (below)

Easy Chocolate Glaze (below)

Heat oven to 350°. Grease square pan, 8×8×2 inches. Melt chocolate and butter in 2-quart saucepan over low heat, stirring frequently, until smooth; remove from heat. Stir in remaining ingredients except Coffee Frosting and Easy Chocolate Glaze.

Spread batter in pan. Bake 18 to 22 minutes or until toothpick inserted in center comes out clean. Cool completely. Frost with Coffee Frosting. Drizzle with Easy Chocolate Glaze. Cut into 4 rows by 4 rows.

Coffee Frosting

2 teaspoons instant coffee

1 tablespoon very hot water

2 cups powdered sugar

2 tablespoons butter or margarine, softened

2 to 3 teaspoons water

Dissolve coffee in very hot water in medium bowl. Stir in remaining ingredients until smooth.

Easy Chocolate Glaze

1/4 cup semisweet chocolate chips

1 teaspoon shortening

Melt ingredients in a 1-quart saucepan over low heat, stirring constantly, until smooth.

1 Brownie: Calories 230 (Calories from Fat 100); Fat 11g (Saturated 3g); Cholesterol 25mg; Sodium 150mg; Carbohydrate 32g (Dietary Fiber 1g); Protein 2g.

Mocha Brownies, Coconut Brownies (variation), Raspberry Brownies (variation)

German Chocolate Brownies

BAKE: 20 to 25 min per pan ● YIELD: 32 brownies

Cookie Tips

Did you know that there are different types of coconut at the grocery store? Look closely and notice there is flaked and shredded coconut. The flaked coconut is cut into small pieces and is much drier than shredded coconut. In fact, you could squeeze a handful of shredded coconut and it would stick together a bit, but flaked coconut is dry, like uncooked rice kernels. Either works, but shredded coconut will give you more moistness and chewiness.

"I Don't Have That"

Out of nuts? Don't fret! Just use 1 2/3 cups of coconut in the frosting instead of nuts and coconut.

2 packages (4 ounces each) sweet baking chocolate
1/2 cup butter or margarine
1 1/2 cups all-purpose flour
1 cup sugar
1/2 teaspoon baking powder
1/2 teaspoon vanilla
1/4 teaspoon salt
2 eggs
Coconut-Pecan Frosting (below)

Heat oven to 350°. Grease rectangular pan, 13×9×2 inches. Melt chocolate and butter in 3-quart saucepan over low heat, stirring frequently, until smooth; remove from heat. Stir in remaining ingredients except Coconut-Pecan Frosting.

Spread batter in pan. Bake 20 to 25 minutes or until toothpick inserted in center comes out clean. Cool completely. Frost with Coconut-Pecan Frosting. Cut into 8 rows by 4 rows.

Coconut-Pecan Frosting

1/2 cup sugar
1/4 cup butter or margarine
1/3 cup evaporated milk
1/2 teaspoon vanilla
2 egg yolks
1 cup flaked coconut
2/3 cup chopped pecans

Cook sugar, butter, milk, vanilla and egg yolks in 1 1/2-quart saucepan over medium heat about 12 minutes, stirring frequently, until thickened. Stir in coconut and pecans. Refrigerate about 1 hour or until spreadable.

1 Brownie: Calories 175 (Calories from Fat 100); Fat 11g (Saturated 4g); Cholesterol 25mg; Sodium 90mg; Carbohydrate 18g (Dietary Fiber 1g); Protein 2g.

German Chocolate Brownies, Cream Cheese Brownies (page 70),
Vanilla Brownies (page 65)

BAKE SALE

Cream Cheese Brownies

BAKE: 45 to 50 min per pan ● YIELD: 48 brownies

Cookie Tips

Swirl the two different batters together if you don't want three distinct layers. Once all of the batter is in the pan, take a knife and swirl it through all of the layers to create a marbled effect.

To customize the color of the Cream Cheese Filling, add desired food coloring, a drop at a time until you like the shade and bake as usual. Once colored, swirl the filling with the chocolate batter.

Make It Your Way

Make **Mint Cream Cheese Brownies**. Substitute 1 teaspoon peppermint extract for the vanilla in the Cream Cheese Filling and stir in 1/4 teaspoon green food coloring.

To make **Cherry Cream Cheese Brownies**, substitute 2 teaspoons maraschino cherry juice for the vanilla in the Cream Cheese Filling. Stir in 1/2 cup chopped maraschino cherries.

4 ounces unsweetened baking chocolate

1 cup butter or margarine

Cream Cheese Filling (below)

2 cups sugar

2 teaspoons vanilla

4 eggs

1 1/2 cups all-purpose flour

1/2 teaspoon salt

1 cup coarsely chopped nuts

Heat oven to 350°. Grease rectangular pan, 13×9×2 inches. Melt chocolate and butter over low heat, stirring frequently, until smooth; remove from heat. Cool 5 minutes. Meanwhile, prepare Cream Cheese Filling; set aside.

Beat chocolate mixture, sugar, vanilla and eggs in large bowl with electric mixer on medium speed 1 minute, scraping bowl occasionally. Beat in flour and salt on low speed 30 seconds, scraping bowl occasionally. Beat on medium speed 1 minute. Stir in nuts.

Spread half of the batter (about 2 1/2 cups) in pan. Spread Cream Cheese Filling over batter. Carefully spread remaining batter over filling. Bake 45 to 50 minutes or until toothpick inserted in center comes out clean. Cool completely. Cut into 8 rows by 6 rows. Store covered in refrigerator.

Cream Cheese Filling

2 packages (8 ounces each) cream cheese, softened

1/2 cup sugar

2 teaspoons vanilla

1 egg

Beat all ingredients with spoon until smooth.

1 Brownie: Calories 165 (Calories from Fat 100); Fat 11g (Saturated 4g); Cholesterol 35mg; Sodium 105mg; Carbohydrate 15g (Dietary Fiber 0g); Protein 2g.

Peanut Butter Swirl Brownies

BAKE: 30 to 35 min per pan ● YIELD: 16 brownies

2/3 cup granulated sugar

1/2 cup packed brown sugar

1/2 cup butter or margarine, softened

2 tablespoons milk

2 eggs

3/4 cup all-purpose flour

1/2 teaspoon baking powder

1/4 teaspoon salt

1/4 cup creamy peanut butter

1/3 cup peanut butter chips

1/3 cup baking cocoa

1/3 cup semisweet chocolate chips

Cookie Tips

The "hills" created when the knife is drawn through the batter to make a swirl effect level off while the brownies bake.

"I Don't Have That"

No peanut butter chips on hand? Butterscotch will work just as well and taste great too.

Heat oven to 350°. Grease square pan, 9×9×2 inches. Beat sugars, butter, milk and eggs in large bowl with electric mixer on medium speed, or mix with spoon. Stir in flour, baking powder and salt. Divide batter in half (about 1 cup plus 2 tablespoons for each half). Stir peanut butter and peanut butter chips into one half. Stir cocoa and chocolate chips into remaining half.

Spoon chocolate batter into pan in 8 mounds in checkerboard pattern. Spoon peanut butter batter between mounds of chocolate batter. Gently swirl through batters with knife for marbled design.

Bake 30 to 35 minutes or until toothpick inserted in center comes out clean. Cool completely. Cut into 4 rows by 4 rows.

1 Brownie: Calories 180 (Calories from Fat 100); Fat 11g (Saturated 3g); Cholesterol 25mg; Sodium 150mg; Carbohydrate 18g (Dietary Fiber 1g); Protein 3g.

The Ultimate Date Bars

BAKE: 25 to 30 min per pan ● YIELD: 32 bars

Cookie Tips

In a hurry? Use the chopped dates, which are lightly coated with sugar to prevent sticking. If you choose to chop your own whole dates, try one of these methods to help prevent sticking: Spray your knife with cooking spray several times during chopping, run your knife under cold water several times during chopping or cut-up dates using kitchen shears sprayed with cooking spray.

Make It Your Way

Add some tang with the tart flavor of dried apricots. For **Date-Apricot Bars**, skip the Date Filling. In its place mix an 8-ounce box of chopped dates, 1 1/2 cups chopped dried apricots (8 ounces), 1/2 cup sugar and 1 1/2 cups water in saucepan. Cook over medium-low heat about 10 minutes, stirring constantly, until thickened. Cool and continue as directed.

Date Filling (below)
1 cup butter or margarine, softened
1 cup packed brown sugar
1 3/4 cups all-purpose flour
1 1/2 cups quick-cooking or old-fashioned oats
1/2 teaspoon baking soda
1/2 teaspoon salt

Prepare Date Filling; cool.

Heat oven to 400°. Mix butter and brown sugar in large bowl with spoon. Stir in remaining ingredients. Press half of the oat mixture in ungreased rectangular pan, 13×9×2 inches. Spread with filling. Top with remaining oat mixture; press gently into filling.

Bake 25 to 30 minutes or until light brown. Cool 30 minutes. Cut into 8 rows by 4 rows while warm.

Date Filling

2 packages (8 ounces each) pitted dates, chopped
1/4 cup sugar
1 1/2 cups water

Mix all ingredients in 2-quart saucepan. Cook over low heat 10 minutes, stirring constantly, until thickened.

1 Bar: Calories 160 (Calories from Fat 55); Fat 6g (Saturated 1g); Cholesterol 0mg; Sodium 125mg; Carbohydrate 26g (Dietary Fiber 1g); Protein 2g.

Ultimate Date Bars, Lemon Squares (page 75), Cherry-Almond Bars (page 76)

Linzer Torte Bars

BAKE: 20 to 25 min per pan ● YIELD: 48 bars

Cookie Tips

The flavors in this bar were inspired by *linzertorte,* a classic European dessert originating in Linz, Austria. Ground nuts, spices and raspberry preserves are quintessential to the namesake.

It's easy to cut bars into triangles. First cut into squares, then cut each square diagonally in half.

Make It Your Way

Make **Apricot Linzer Bars** by substituting ground almonds for the ground walnuts and apricot preserves for the raspberry preserves.

1 cup all-purpose flour

1 cup powdered sugar

1 cup ground walnuts

1/2 cup butter or margarine, softened

1/2 teaspoon ground cinnamon

2/3 cup red raspberry preserves

Heat oven to 375°. Mix all ingredients except preserves with spoon until crumbly. Press two thirds of crumbly mixture in ungreased square pan, 9×9×2 inches. Spread with preserves. Sprinkle with remaining crumbly mixture; press gently into preserves.

Bake 20 to 25 minutes or until light golden brown. Cool completely. Cut into 8 rows by 6 rows bars.

1 Bar: Calories 60 (Calories from Fat 25); Fat 3g (Saturated 0g); Cholesterol 0mg; Sodium 25mg; Carbohydrate 8g (Dietary Fiber 0g); Protein 0g.

Lemon Squares

BAKE: 45 to 50 min per pan ● YIELD: 25 squares

1 cup all-purpose flour

1/2 cup butter or margarine, softened

1/4 cup powdered sugar

1 cup granulated sugar

2 teaspoons grated lemon peel, if desired

2 tablespoons lemon juice

1/2 teaspoon baking powder

1/4 teaspoon salt

2 eggs

Powdered sugar, if desired

Heat oven to 350°. Mix flour, butter and 1/4 cup powdered sugar with spoon. Press in ungreased square pan, 8×8×2 or 9×9×2 inches, building up 1/2-inch edge. Bake 20 minutes.

Beat remaining ingredients except powdered sugar with electric mixer on high speed about 3 minutes or until light and fluffy. Pour over baked layer. Bake 25 to 30 minutes or just until almost no indentation remains when touched lightly in center. Cool completely. Sprinkle with powdered sugar. Cut into 5 rows by 5 rows.

1 Square: Calories 90 (Calories from Fat 35); Fat 4g (Saturated 1g); Cholesterol 15mg; Sodium 80mg; Carbohydrate 13g (Dietary Fiber 0g); Protein 1g.

Cookie Tips

One fresh lemon will give you about 2 to 3 tablespoons of juice. To get the most juice out of a lemon or lime, it should be at room temperature. Some people zap whole lemons in the microwave on High for about 20 seconds or so to warm them.

"I Don't Have That"

For a tart-sweet treat, substitute lime juice and grated lime peel for the lemon juice and grated peel. For a brighter green color, add 4 drops green food color to the filling ingredients.

Cherry-Almond Bars

BAKE: 30 to 35 min per pan ● YIELD: 24 bars

Maraschino Cherries

Is that pronounced "mar-uh-SKEE-noh" or "mar-uh-SHEE-noh?" Either way is fine. Although any cherry will do, these sweet beauties are generally made from Royal Ann cherries. They are soaked in a sugar syrup and dyed red or green. The red cherries are flavored with almond and the green with mint.

Make It Your Way

Green Cherry-Almond Bars are just as attractive as pink ones. Replace the red maraschino cherries in the bars with green ones and replace red maraschino cherry juice in the glaze with green. This makes a great treat to serve for Saint Patrick's Day.

1 jar (10 ounces) maraschino cherries
1 cup all-purpose flour
1/2 cup butter or margarine, softened
1/4 cup powdered sugar
2 eggs
1 cup sliced almonds
1/2 cup granulated sugar
1/4 cup all-purpose flour
1/2 teaspoon baking powder
Pink Glaze (below)

Heat oven to 350°. Drain cherries, reserving juice for Pink Glaze. Chop cherries; set aside. Mix 1 cup flour, the butter and powdered sugar with spoon. Press in ungreased square pan, 9×9×2 inches. Bake about 10 minutes or until set.

Beat eggs in medium bowl with fork. Stir in cherries and remaining ingredients except Pink Glaze. Spread over baked layer. Bake 20 to 25 minutes or until golden brown. Cool completely. Drizzle with Pink Glaze. Cut into 6 rows by 4 rows.

Pink Glaze

1/2 cup powdered sugar
1/4 teaspoon almond extract
2 to 3 teaspoons reserved maraschino cherry juice

Mix all ingredients until smooth and thin enough to drizzle.

1 Bar: Calories 140 (Calories from Fat 65); Fat 7g (Saturated 1g); Cholesterol 20mg; Sodium 65mg; Carbohydrate 17g (Dietary Fiber 0g); Protein 2g.

Zucchini Bars

BAKE: 25 to 30 min per pan • YIELD: 24 bars

2/3 cup packed brown sugar

1/4 cup butter or margarine, softened

1/2 teaspoon vanilla

1 egg

1 cup all-purpose flour

1 teaspoon baking soda

1/2 teaspoon ground cinnamon

1/2 teaspoon ground cloves

1 small zucchini, shredded and drained (1 cup)

1/2 cup chopped nuts

Clove-Spiced Frosting (below)

Heat oven to 350°. Grease square pan, 8×8×2 or 9×9×2 inches. Mix brown sugar, butter, vanilla and egg in large bowl. Stir in flour, baking soda, cinnamon and cloves. Stir in zucchini and nuts.

Spread batter in pan. Bake 25 to 30 minutes or until toothpick inserted in center comes out clean. Cool completely. Frost with Clove-Spiced Frosting. Cut 6 rows by 4 rows.

Clove-Spiced Frosting

3/4 cup powdered sugar

1 tablespoon butter or margarine, softened

1/8 teaspoon ground cloves

3 to 4 teaspoons milk

Mix all ingredients until smooth and spreadable.

1 Bar: Calories 100 (Calories from Fat 35); Fat 4g (Saturated 1g); Cholesterol 10mg; Sodium 85mg; Carbohydrate 15g (Dietary Fiber 0g); Protein 1g.

Make It Your Way

Christmas Bars feature pretty green and red speckles. Add 1/2 cup chopped dried cranberries to the recipe.

"I Don't Have That"

No cloves in the spice rack? Replace with ground nutmeg in both the bars and the frosting.

Banana-Nut Bars

BAKE: 25 to 30 min per pan ● YIELD: 24 bars

Cookie Tips

When baking bar cookies, be sure to use the correct size pan to prevent under- or overbaking them. The three most common pan sizes are 8×8×2 inches, 9×9×2 inches or 13×9×2 inches.

Make It Your Way

For those who really love the flavor of bananas, create **Double Banana–Nut Dessert.** Don't frost the bars. Instead, cut the bars into 12 to 16 pieces and top with banana-nut ice cream. Drizzle with chocolate syrup.

1 cup sugar

1 cup mashed very ripe bananas (2 medium)

1/3 cup vegetable oil

2 eggs

1 cup all-purpose flour

1 teaspoon baking powder

1/2 teaspoon baking soda

1/2 teaspoon ground cinnamon

1/4 teaspoon salt

1/2 cup chopped nuts

Cream Cheese Frosting (below)

Heat oven to 350°. Grease rectangular pan, 13×9×2 inches. Mix sugar, bananas, oil and eggs in large bowl with spoon. Stir in flour, baking powder, baking soda, cinnamon and salt. Stir in nuts.

Spread batter in pan. Bake 25 to 30 minutes or until toothpick inserted in center comes out clean. Cool completely. Frost with Cream Cheese Frosting. Cut into 6 row by 4 rows. Store covered in refrigerator.

Cream Cheese Frosting

1 package (3 ounces) cream cheese, softened

1/3 cup butter or margarine, softened

1 teaspoon vanilla

2 cups powdered sugar

Mix cream cheese, butter and vanilla in medium bowl. Gradually beat in powdered sugar with spoon until smooth and spreadable.

1 Bar: Calories 190 (Calories from Fat 80); Fat 9g (Saturated 2g); Cholesterol 20mg; Sodium 115mg; Carbohydrate 25g (Dietary Fiber 0g); Protein 2g.

Pumpkin Spice Bars (top) (page 81), Zucchini Bars (middle) (page 77),
Banana-Nut Bars (bottom)

Double Apple Bars

BAKE: 25 to 30 min per pan ● YIELD: 24 bars

3/4 cup packed brown sugar

3/4 cup applesauce

1/4 cup vegetable oil

1 egg

1 1/4 cups all-purpose flour

1/2 teaspoon baking soda

1/2 teaspoon ground cinnamon

1/4 teaspoon salt

1/2 cup chopped unpeeled all-purpose apple

Powdered sugar, if desired

Heat oven to 350°. Mix brown sugar, applesauce, oil and egg in large bowl. Stir in flour, baking soda, cinnamon and salt. Stir in apple.

Spread batter in ungreased square pan, 9×9×2 inches. Bake 25 to 30 minutes or until toothpick inserted in center comes out clean; cool. Sprinkle with powdered sugar. Cut into 6 rows by 4 rows.

1 Bar: Calories 85 (Calories from Fat 25); Fat 3g (Saturated 0g); Cholesterol 10mg; Sodium 55mg; Carbohydrate 13g (Dietary Fiber 0g); Protein 1g.

Pumpkin-Spice Bars

BAKE: 25 to 30 min per pan ● YIELD: 48 bars

4 eggs

2 cups sugar

1 cup vegetable oil

1 can (15 ounces) pumpkin

2 cups all-purpose flour

2 teaspoons baking powder

2 teaspoons ground cinnamon

1 teaspoon baking soda

1/2 teaspoon salt

1/2 teaspoon ground ginger

1/4 teaspoon ground cloves

1 cup raisins

Cream Cheese Frosting (page 78)

1/2 cup chopped nuts

Heat oven to 350°. Grease jelly roll pan, 15 1/2 × 10 1/2 × 1 inch. Mix eggs, sugar, oil and pumpkin in large bowl with spoon. Stir in flour, baking powder, cinnamon, baking soda, salt, ginger and cloves. Stir in raisins.

Spread batter in pan. Bake 25 to 30 minutes or until toothpick inserted in center comes out clean. Cool completely. Frost with Cream Cheese Frosting. Sprinkle with nuts. Cut into 8 rows by 6 rows. Store covered in refrigerator.

1 Bar: Calories 160 (Calories from Fat 70); Fat 8g (Saturated 2g); Cholesterol 20mg; Sodium 95mg; Carbohydrate 21g (Dietary Fiber 0g); Protein 2g.

Cookie Tips

All the spices of pumpkin pie in a wonderfully moist bar. Keep the bars moist by storing in a tightly covered container.

"I Don't Have That"

Use 2 1/2 teaspoons pumpkin pie spice instead of cinnamon, ginger and cloves.

Cinnamon-Coffee Bars

BAKE: 20 to 22 min per pan ● YIELD: 32 bars

Cookie Tips

To double your pleasure, serve these bars with freshly brewed cinnamon-flavored coffee.

"I Don't Have That"

Cold coffee can be substituted for the milk in the glaze. It will add subtle coffee flavor and light tan color.

1 cup packed brown sugar
1/3 cup butter or margarine, softened
1 egg
1 1/2 cups all-purpose flour
1/2 cup water
1 tablespoon instant coffee (dry)
1 teaspoon baking powder
1/2 teaspoon ground cinnamon
1/4 teaspoon salt
1/4 teaspoon baking soda
1/2 cup raisins
1/4 cup chopped nuts
White Glaze (below)

Heat oven to 350°. Grease and flour rectangular pan, 13×9×2 inches. Beat brown sugar, butter and egg in large bowl with electric mixer on medium speed, or mix with spoon. Stir in remaining ingredients except raisins, nuts and White Glaze. Stir in raisins and nuts.

Spread batter in pan. Bake 20 to 22 minutes or until top springs back when touched in center. Drizzle with White Glaze while warm. Let cool. Cut into 8 rows by 4 rows bars.

White Glaze

1 cup powdered sugar
1/4 teaspoon vanilla
4 to 5 teaspoons milk

Mix all ingredients until smooth and thin enough to drizzle.

1 Bar: Calories 100 (Calories from Fat 25); Fat 3g (Saturated 1g); Cholesterol 5mg; Sodium 70mg; Carbohydrate 17g (Dietary Fiber 0g); Protein 1g.

Fudgy Layer Squares

PREP: 10 min ● COOL: 15 min ● CHILL: 2 hr ● YIELD: 36 squares

1/2 cup butter or margarine

1 1/2 ounces unsweetened baking chocolate

1 3/4 cups graham cracker crumbs

1 cup flaked coconut

1/2 cup chopped nuts

1/4 cup granulated sugar

2 tablespoons water

1 teaspoon vanilla

2 cups powdered sugar

1/4 cup butter or margarine, softened

2 tablespoons milk

1 teaspoon vanilla

1 1/2 ounces unsweetened baking chocolate

Cookie Tips

For an easy way to drizzle, pour the melted chocolate into a small resealable bag. Cut a tiny hole at one end and squeeze chocolate over the bars.

Did you know that nuts frozen in their shells are easier to crack and the meat is easier to remove?

Line square pan, 9×9×2 inches, with aluminum foil. Melt 1/2 cup butter and 1 1/2 ounces chocolate in 3-quart saucepan over low heat, stirring frequently, until smooth; remove from heat. Stir in graham cracker crumbs, coconut, nuts, granulated sugar, water and 1 teaspoon vanilla. Press in pan. Refrigerate while continuing with recipe.

Mix remaining ingredients except chocolate. Spread over refrigerated crumb mixture. Refrigerate 15 minutes.

Melt 1 1/2 ounces chocolate in 1-quart saucepan over low heat, stirring frequently, until smooth. Drizzle over frosting. Refrigerate about 2 hours or until chocolate is almost firm. Remove from pan, using foil to lift; fold back foil. Cut into 6 rows by 6 rows. Store covered in refrigerator.

1 Square: Calories 120 (Calories from Fat 65); Fat 7g (Saturated 2g); Cholesterol 0mg; Sodium 75mg; Carbohydrate 13g (Dietary Fiber 0g); Protein 1g.

Toffee Bars

BAKE: 25 to 30 min per pan ● YIELD: 32 bars

Cookie Tips

To make smoother cuts, spray knife with cooking spray before cutting bars.

Toffee, a brittle confection, is a flavor created by the blending together of butter and brown sugar.

1 cup packed brown sugar

1 cup butter or margarine, softened

1 teaspoon vanilla

1 egg yolk

2 cups all-purpose flour

1/4 teaspoon salt

4 ounces milk chocolate, broken into pieces

1/2 cup chopped nuts

Heat oven to 350°. Beat brown sugar, butter, vanilla and egg yolk in large bowl with electric mixer on medium speed, or mix with spoon. Stir in flour and salt. Press in ungreased rectangular pan, $13 \times 9 \times 2$ inches. Bake 25 to 30 minutes or until very light brown (crust will be soft).

Immediately place milk chocolate pieces on baked crust. Let stand about 5 minutes or until softened; spread evenly. Sprinkle with nuts. Cool 30 minutes. Cut into 8 rows by 4 rows while warm.

1 Bar: Calories 135 (Calories from Fat 70); Fat 8g (Saturated 2g); Cholesterol 5mg; Sodium 90mg; Carbohydrate 15g (Dietary Fiber 0g); Protein 1g.

Mousse Bars

BAKE: 35 to 45 min per pan ● COOL: 15 min ● CHILL: 2 hr ● YIELD: 16 bars

1 1/2 cups vanilla wafer crumbs (about 40 wafers)

1/4 cup butter or margarine, melted

3/4 cup whipping (heavy) cream

1 package (6 ounces) semisweet chocolate chips (1 cup)

3 eggs

1/3 cup sugar

1/8 teaspoon salt

Chocolate Topping (below)

Heat oven to 350°. Mix wafer crumbs and butter with spoon. Press in ungreased square pan, 8×8×2 or 9×9×2 inches. Bake 10 minutes.

Heat whipping cream and chocolate chips over low heat, stirring frequently, until chocolate is melted; remove from heat. Cool 5 minutes. Beat eggs, sugar and salt in large bowl with wire whisk until foamy. Pour chocolate mixture into egg mixture, stirring constantly. Pour over baked layer. Bake 25 to 35 minutes or until center springs back when touched lightly. Cool 15 minutes.

Spread with Chocolate Topping. Refrigerate uncovered about 2 hours or until chilled. Cut into 4 rows by 4 rows. Store covered in refrigerator.

Chocolate Topping

1/2 cup semisweet chocolate chips

1 tablespoon shortening

Melt chocolate chips and shortening over low heat, stirring frequently, until smooth.

1 Bar: Calories 220 (Calories from Fat 125); Fat 14g (Saturated 6g); Cholesterol 60mg; Sodium 100mg; Carbohydrate 22g (Dietary Fiber 1g); Protein 3g.

Super Bars and Brownies **85**

Tiramisu Cheesecake Bars

BAKE: 20 to 25 min per pan ● COOL: 30 min ● CHILL: 1 hr ● YIELD: 18 squares

1/4 teaspoon rum extract mixed with 1/4 cup water can be substituted for the rum.

How easy would it be to turn these cheesecake squares into a sophisticated, elegant little dessert? Line small dessert plates with doilies, and place squares on the doilies. Squeeze a dollop of canned whipped cream onto bars. Gently place a chocolate-covered espresso bean on the dollop of whipped cream. Sprinkle the whipped cream with a very light dusting of baking cocoa.

1 1/2 cups vanilla wafer cookie crumbs (about 40 wafers)

2 teaspoons instant espresso coffee (dry)

3 tablespoons butter or margarine, melted

2 packages (8 ounces each) cream cheese, softened

1/2 cup sugar

2 eggs

1/2 cup whipping (heavy) cream

1/4 cup rum

1 teaspoon vanilla

1/2 cup semisweet chocolate chips

2 tablespoons shortening

Heat oven to 350°. Grease square pan, 9×9×2 inches. Mix cookie crumbs, 1 teaspoon coffee and the butter thoroughly with fork. Press evenly in bottom of pan. Refrigerate while preparing cream cheese mixture.

Beat cream cheese in small bowl with electric mixer on medium speed until smooth and fluffy. Beat in sugar, eggs, whipping cream, rum and vanilla. Spread cream cheese mixture over crust. Bake 20 to 25 minutes or just until center is set.

Melt chocolate chips, shortening and remaining 1 teaspoon coffee in 1-quart saucepan over low heat, stirring constantly, until smooth. Pour over hot cheesecake, and spread evenly. Cool 30 minutes at room temperature. Cover loosely and refrigerate about 1 hour or until firm. Cut into 6 rows by 3 rows.

1 Serving: Calories 180 (Calories from Fat 115); Fat 13g (Saturated 8g); Cholesterol 50mg; Sodium 90 mg; Carbohydrate 14g (Dietary Fiber 0g); Protein 2g.

Dream Bars

BAKE: 30 to 35 min per pan ● COOL: 30 min ● YIELD: 32 bars

1/3 cup butter or margarine, softened
1/3 cup packed brown sugar
1 cup all-purpose flour
Almond-Coconut Topping (below)

Heat oven to 350°. Mix butter and brown sugar in small bowl with spoon. Stir in flour. Press in ungreased rectangular pan, 13×9×2 inches. Bake 10 minutes.

Spread Almond-Coconut Topping over baked layer. Bake 20 to 25 minutes or until topping is golden brown. Cool 30 minutes. Cut 8 rows by 4 rows while warm.

Almond-Coconut Topping

2 eggs, beaten
1 cup shredded coconut
1 cup chopped almonds
3/4 cup packed brown sugar
2 tablespoons all-purpose flour
1 teaspoon baking powder
1 teaspoon vanilla
1/4 teaspoon salt

Mix all ingredients.

1 Bar: Calories 95 (Calories from Fat 35); Fat 4g (Saturated 1g); Cholesterol 15mg; Sodium 50mg; Carbohydrate 13g (Dietary Fiber 0g); Protein 2g.

Cookie Tips

This bar cookie makes a dazzling taste treat with a homemade flavor beyond compare! Serve with a mug of hot chocolate for a winning combination.

"I Don't Have That"

Make an all-nut topping by leaving out the coconut and using 2 cups almonds.

Lemon Cream Oat Bars

BAKE: 30 min per pan ● YIELD: 24 bars

Cookie Tips

Always use quick-cooking or old-fashioned oatmeal in recipes. Avoid instant oatmeal, which will become mushy when baked in dough.

"I Don't Have That"

1 tablespoon of grated orange peel can replace the lemon peel in these bars.

1 can (14 ounces) sweetened condensed milk
2 teaspoons grated lemon peel
1/4 cup lemon juice
1 1/4 cups all-purpose flour
1 cup quick-cooking or old-fashioned oats
1/2 cup packed brown sugar
1/2 cup butter or margarine, softened
1/4 teaspoon baking soda
1/4 teaspoon salt

Heat oven to 375°. Grease square pan, 9×9×2 inches. Mix milk, lemon peel and lemon juice in medium bowl until thickened; set aside. Mix remaining ingredients in medium bowl with spoon until crumbly. Press half of the crumbly mixture in pan. Bake about 10 minutes or until set.

Spread milk mixture over baked layer. Sprinkle remaining crumbly mixture over milk mixture; press gently into milk mixture. Bake about 20 minutes or until edges are golden brown and center is set but soft. Cool completely. Cut into 6 rows by 4 rows.

1 Bar: Calories 130 (Calories from Fat 55); Fat 6g (Saturated 2g); Cholesterol 5mg; Sodium 105mg; Carbohydrate 21g (Dietary Fiber 0g); Protein 3g.

Lemon Cream Oat Bars, Caramel Candy Bars (page 90)

Caramel Candy Bars

BAKE: 30 to 35 min per pan ● COOL: 30 min ● YIELD: 48 bars

Cookie Tips

For a holiday or housewarming gift, wrap individual bars in colored plastic wrap and pack in a basket with a bow.

Make It Your Way

If you love the chocolate and peanut butter flavor combination, make **Chocolate Peanut Bars** by substituting chocolate caramels for the vanilla caramels and peanut butter chips for the chocolate chips. Use peanuts rather than walnuts. Delicious!

1 package (14 ounces) vanilla caramels

1/3 cup milk

2 cups all-purpose flour

2 cups quick-cooking or old-fashioned oats

1 1/2 cups packed brown sugar

1 teaspoon baking soda

1/2 teaspoon salt

1 egg

1 cup butter or margarine, softened

1 package (6 ounces) semisweet chocolate chips (1 cup)

1 cup chopped walnuts or dry-roasted peanuts

Heat oven to 350°. Heat caramels and milk in 2-quart saucepan over low heat, stirring frequently, until smooth; remove from heat.

Mix flour, oats, brown sugar, baking soda and salt in large bowl with spoon. Stir in egg and butter until mixture is crumbly. Press half of the crumbly mixture in ungreased rectangular pan, 13×9×2 inches. Bake 10 minutes.

Sprinkle chocolate chips and walnuts over baked layer. Drizzle with caramel mixture. Sprinkle with remaining crumbly mixture; press gently into caramel mixture. Bake 20 to 25 minutes or until golden brown. Cool 30 minutes. Loosen edges from sides of pan. Cool completely. Cut into 8 rows by 4 rows.

1 Bar: Calories 155 (Calories from Fat 65); Fat 7g (Saturated 2g); Cholesterol 5mg; Sodium 120mg; Carbohydrate 22g (Dietary Fiber 1g); Protein 2g.

Mixed Nut Bars

BAKE: 25 min per pan ● YIELD: 32 bars

1 cup packed brown sugar

1 cup butter or margarine, softened

1 teaspoon vanilla

1 egg yolk

2 cups all-purpose flour

1/4 teaspoon salt

8 ounces vanilla-flavored candy coating, chopped, or 1 1/4 cups vanilla milk (white) chips

1 can (12 ounces) salted mixed nuts

Heat oven to 350°. Beat brown sugar, butter, vanilla and egg yolk in large bowl with electric mixer on medium speed, or mix with spoon. Stir in flour and salt. Press in ungreased rectangular pan, 13×9×2 inches. Bake about 25 minutes or until light brown.

Immediately sprinkle candy coating evenly over baked layer. Let stand about 5 minutes or until softened; spread evenly. Sprinkle with nuts; press gently into topping. Cool completely. Cut into 8 rows by 4 rows bars.

1 Bar: Calories 210 (Calories from Fat 125); Fat 14g (Saturated 3g); Cholesterol 10mg; Sodium 160mg; Carbohydrate 19g (Dietary Fiber 1g); Protein 3g.

Cookie Tips

Don't throw away that left-over egg white! Cover and refrigerate for up to 24 hours. It can be used in baked products or added to scrambled eggs.

"I Don't Have That"

Substitute salted cashews, pecans or peanuts for the mixed nuts.

Pecan Pie Squares

BAKE: 45 min per pan ● YIELD: 60 squares

Cookie Tips

A real Southern-style taste treat—the flavor of pecan pie without having to roll out the dough!

Make It Your Way

Walnut Pie Squares are just as delicious and are made by substituting walnuts for the pecans.

3 cups all-purpose flour

3/4 cup butter or margarine, softened

1/3 cup sugar

1/2 teaspoon salt

Pecan Filling (below)

Heat oven to 350°. Grease jelly roll pan, 15 1/2 × 10 1/2 × 1 inch. Beat flour, butter, sugar and salt in large bowl with electric mixer on low speed until crumbly (mixture will be dry). Press firmly in pan. Bake about 20 minutes or until light golden brown.

Pour Filling over baked layer; spread evenly. Bake about 25 minutes or until filling is set. Cool completely. Cut into 10 rows by 6 rows.

Pecan Filling

4 eggs, slightly beaten

1 1/2 cups sugar

1 1/2 cups corn syrup

3 tablespoons butter or margarine, melted

1 1/2 teaspoons vanilla

2 1/2 cups chopped pecans

Mix all ingredients except pecans in large bowl until well blended. Stir in pecans.

1 Square: Calories 140 (Calories from Fat 65); Fat 7g (Saturated 1g); Cholesterol 15mg; Sodium 65mg; Carbohydrate 18g (Dietary Fiber 0g); Protein 1g.

Pecan Pie Squares

No-Bake Peanut Butter Squares

PREP: 10 min ● CHILL: 3 hr ● YIELD: 36 squares

Cookie Tips

A great refrigerated bar to make on a hot day when you want a sweet treat but you'd rather not turn on your oven.

Make It Your Way

For an interesting variation, make **No-Bake Chocolate Peanut Butter Squares** by replacing the graham cracker crumbs with chocolate graham cracker crumbs.

2 cups powdered sugar

1 cup butter or margarine, softened

1 cup peanut butter

1 teaspoon vanilla

2 3/4 cups graham cracker crumbs

1 cup chopped peanuts

1 package (12 ounces) semisweet chocolate chips (2 cups)

1/4 cup peanut butter

Line square pan, 9×9×2 inches, with aluminum foil. Beat powdered sugar, butter, 1 cup peanut butter and the vanilla in large bowl with electric mixer on medium speed, or mix with spoon. Stir in graham cracker crumbs and peanuts (mixture will be stiff). Press in pan.

Melt chocolate chips and 1/4 cup peanut butter over low heat, stirring frequently, until smooth. Spread over bars. Refrigerate about 1 hour or until chocolate is firm. Remove from pan, using foil to lift; fold back foil. Cut into 6 rows by 6 rows. Refrigerate about 2 hours or until firm. Store covered in refrigerator.

1 Square: Calories 225 (Calories from Fat 135); Fat 15g (Saturated 4g); Cholesterol 0mg; Sodium 140mg; Carbohydrate 20g (Dietary Fiber 1g); Protein 4g.

No-Bake Peanut Butter Squares, No-Bake Honey-Oat Bars (page 96)

No-Bake Honey-Oat Bars

PREP: 10 min ● YIELD: 24 bars

Cookie Tips

These are like homemade chewy granola bars. Pack a couple in your briefcase for an afternoon energy boost.

"I Don't Have That"

Use dried cherries or cranberries in place of the dried fruit bits.

1/4 cup sugar

1/4 cup butter or margarine

1/3 cup honey

1/2 teaspoon ground cinnamon

1 cup diced dried fruit and raisin mixture

1 1/2 cups Wheaties® cereal

1 cup quick-cooking oats

1/2 cup sliced almonds

Butter square pan, 9×9×2 inches. Heat sugar, butter, honey and cinnamon to boiling in 3-quart saucepan over medium heat, stirring constantly. Boil 1 minute, stirring constantly; remove from heat. Stir in dried fruit. Stir in remaining ingredients.

Press mixture in pan with back of wooden spoon. Cool completely. Cut into 6 rows by 4 rows.

1 Bar: Calories 85 (Calories from Fat 25); Fat 3g (Saturated 1g); Cholesterol 0mg; Sodium 35mg; Carbohydrate 14g (Dietary Fiber 1g); Protein 1g.

Coconut Macaroon Bars

BAKE: 37 to 45 min per pan ● CHILL: 2 hr ● YIELD: 24 bars

3/4 cup all-purpose flour

1/4 cup powdered sugar

1/4 cup butter or margarine, softened

1/2 teaspoon almond extract

1 egg yolk

1 cup chopped walnuts

1 can (14 ounces) sweetened condensed milk

1 package (7 ounces) flaked coconut (about 2 2/3 cups)

1/2 cup semisweet chocolate chips

Heat oven to 350°. Grease square pan, 9×9×2 inches. Mix flour, powdered sugar, butter, almond extract and egg yolk with spoon (mixture will be crumbly). Press in pan. Bake 12 to 15 minutes or until edges are light brown and center is set.

Mix walnuts, milk and coconut. Spread over baked layer. Bake 25 to 30 minutes or until golden brown. Immediately sprinkle with chocolate chips. Let stand about 5 minutes or until softened; spread carefully. Refrigerate uncovered 1 to 2 hours or until chocolate is firm. Cut into 6 rows by 4 rows. Store covered in refrigerator.

1 Bar: Calories 180 (Calories from Fat 100); Fat 11g (Saturated 5g); Cholesterol 15mg; Sodium 65mg; Carbohydrate 17g (Dietary Fiber 0g); Protein 3g.

Cookie Tips

Attention coconut lovers! Here is a cookie that tastes just like a chocolate-covered coconut candy bar.

Macaroons

A macaroon has several definitions. It can be a chewy coconut cookie, a crunchy almond cookie or a diverse combination of nuts and chocolate in a meringue.

CHAPTER 3

Giant Colorful Candy
  Cookies *100*
Malted Milk Cookies *101*
Mini Cookie Pizzas *102*
Spicy Iced Applesauce
  Cookies *104*
Mini Elephant Ears *105*
Halloween Cutout Cookies *106*
Ginger Cookie Clock *108*
Magic Window Cookies *109*
Candy Corn Shortbread *110*
Witches' Brooms *112*
Witches' Hats *113*
Cobweb Cookies *113*
Ghost Cookies *114*
Multigrain Cutouts *115*

Black-Eyed Susans *116*
Bumblebees *118*
Cookie Pizza *119*
Caramel Apple Cookies *120*
Caramel-Pecan Cookies *122*
Gingerpop Cookies *124*
Rocky Road Cookies *125*
Peanut Butter and Jam Bars *126*
Chocolate-Peanut Butter
  No-Bakes *128*
Chocolate-Peanut
  Windmills *129*
Goldfish Drops *131*
Ice-Cream Sandwiches *131*
Animal Cookies *133*
Cinnamon Footballs *135*

Kid Kookies

*Witches' Brooms (page 112),
Witches' Hats (page 113)*

Kids know what they like, and they love these cookies! The colorful little candy-coated chocolate pieces make these cookies fun to look at and to eat!

Giant Colorful Candy Cookies

BAKE: 11 to 14 min per sheet ● YIELD: About 18 cookies

Cookie Tips

Once you've used cookie/ice-cream scoops to make cookies, you'll never go back to doing it with two spoons. Look for the scoops in grocery stores, specialty cookware shops and cake decorating shops.

"I Don't Have That"

Candy-coated peanut butter covered candies can be used instead of the chocolate candies.

1 cup packed brown sugar

3/4 cup granulated sugar

1 cup butter or margarine, softened

1 teaspoon vanilla

2 eggs

2 1/2 cups all-purpose flour

3/4 teaspoon salt

3/4 teaspoon baking soda

2 cups candy-coated chocolate candies

Heat oven to 375°. Beat sugars, butter, vanilla and eggs in large bowl with electric mixer on medium speed, or mix with spoon. Stir in flour, salt and baking soda. Stir in candies.

Drop dough by level 1/4 cupfuls or #16 cookie/ice-cream scoop about 2 inches apart onto ungreased cookie sheet. Flatten dough slightly with fork. Bake 11 to 14 minutes or until edges are light brown. Cool 3 to 4 minutes; carefully remove from cookie sheet to wire rack.

1 Cookie: Calories 350 (Calories from Fat 145); Fat 16g (Saturated 5g); Cholesterol 25mg; Sodium 300mg; Carbohydrate 49g (Dietary Fiber 1g); Protein 4g.

Malted Milk Cookies

BAKE: 10 to 11 min per sheet ● YIELD: About 5 dozen cookies

2 cups packed brown sugar

1 cup butter or margarine, softened

1/3 cup sour cream

2 teaspoons vanilla

2 eggs

4 3/4 cups all-purpose flour

3/4 cup natural-flavor malted milk powder

2 teaspoons baking powder

1/2 teaspoon baking soda

1/2 teaspoon salt

Malted Milk Frosting (below)

Heat oven to 375°. Beat brown sugar, butter, sour cream, vanilla and eggs in large bowl with electric mixer on medium speed, or mix with spoon. Stir in remaining ingredients except Malted Milk Frosting.

Roll one third of dough at a time 1/4 inch thick on lightly floured surface. Cut into 2 1/2-inch rounds. Place about 2 inches apart on ungreased cookie sheet. Bake 10 to 11 minutes or until almost no indentation remains when touched in center. Immediately remove from cookie sheet to wire rack. Cool completely. Frost with Malted Milk Frosting.

Malted Milk Frosting

3 cups powdered sugar

1/2 cup natural-flavor malted milk powder

1/3 cup butter or margarine, softened

3 to 4 tablespoons milk

1 1/2 teaspoons vanilla

Mix all ingredients until smooth and spreadable.

1 Cookie: Calories 150 (Calories from Fat 35); Fat 4g (Saturated 1g); Cholesterol 10mg; Sodium 105mg; Carbohydrate 26g (Dietary Fiber 0g); Protein 2g.

Cookie Tips

Malted milk powder isn't something you use daily, so to keep it tasting fresh, store the opened jar in the refrigerator or freezer up to 12 months. You'll find malted milk powder in your supermarkets with other ice-cream toppings.

Make It Your Way

To make **Chocolate Malted Milk Cookies**, substitute chocolate-flavored malted milk powder for the natural malted milk powder in both the cookie dough and frosting. To double the malt flavor, sprinkle frosting with coarsely crushed malted milk balls and press them in slightly to help them stick.

Mini Cookie Pizzas

PREP: 10 min ● YIELD: 14 cookies

Cookie Tips

To make the drizzle look like cheese, color the melted candy coating mixture orange by mixing 1 part red and 2 parts yellow food color. For another fun idea, shred vanilla-flavored candy coating to look like shredded cheese.

Trail Mix

Usually, trail mix is a combination of seeds, nuts and dried fruits.

14 purchased sugar cookies (4 inches in diameter)

1 tub Betty Crocker Rich & Creamy chocolate ready-to-spread frosting

Colored sugar, if desired

2 cups assorted candies or trail mix

2 ounces vanilla-flavored candy coating

2 teaspoons shortening

Frost each cookie with about 2 tablespoons of the frosting; sprinkle with colored sugar. Top with 1 heaping tablespoon of the assorted candies.

Melt candy coating and shortening in 1-quart saucepan over low heat, stirring constantly, until smooth. Drizzle over cookies.

1 Cookie: Calories 400 (Calories from Fat 205); Fat 23g (Saturated 11g); Cholesterol 15mg; Sodium 100mg; Carbohydrate 45g (Dietary Fiber 2g); Protein 5g.

Mini Cookie Pizzas

Spicy Iced Applesauce Cookies

CHILL: 1 hr ● BAKE: 7 to 9 min per sheet ● YIELD: About 3 dozen cookies

Cookie Tips

Cut shapes as close together as possible; that way, you'll get more cookies out of your dough.

The icing comes out snowy white and stays white even when it hardens; it would make a great icing to use for decorating gingerbread houses.

1 1/4 cups packed brown sugar

1/4 cup butter or margarine, softened

1/4 cup applesauce

1 egg

2 1/4 cups all-purpose flour

2 teaspoons baking powder

1/2 teaspoon salt

1/2 teaspoon ground cinnamon

1/2 teaspoon ground nutmeg

1/2 teaspoon ground cloves

Icing (below)

Colored sugar, if desired

Beat brown sugar, butter, applesauce and egg in large bowl with electric mixer on medium speed, or mix with spoon. Stir in remaining ingredients except Icing and colored sugar. Cover and refrigerate at least 1 hour until chilled.

Heat oven to 375°. Grease cookie sheet. Roll dough 1/8 inch thick on floured cloth-covered surface. Cut with 2 1/2-inch cookie cutters. Place cookies about 1 inch apart on cookie sheet. Bake 7 to 9 minutes or until edges are light brown. Immediately remove from cookie sheet to wire rack. Cool completely. Frost with Icing. Sprinkle with colored sugar. Let icing dry about 2 hours before stacking cookies.

Icing

1 envelope unflavored gelatin

1/2 cup cold water

1/2 cup granulated sugar

1 cup powdered sugar

1/2 teaspoon baking powder

1 teaspoon vanilla

Dash of salt

Sprinkle gelatin on cold water in 1 1/2-quart saucepan to soften. Stir in granulated sugar. Heat to rolling boil; reduce heat. Simmer uncovered 10 minutes, stirring frequently. Pour hot mixture over powdered sugar in small bowl; beat with electric mixer on medium speed until smooth. Beat in remaining ingredients on high speed, scraping bowl frequently, until soft peaks form and icing is glossy.

1 Cookie: Calories 100 (Calories from Fat 20); Fat 2g (Saturated 0g); Cholesterol 5mg; Sodium 90mg; Carbohydrate 20g (Dietary Fiber 0g); Protein 1g.

Mini Elephant Ears

BAKE: 8 to 10 min per sheet ● YIELD: About 2 1/2 dozen cookies

Sugar

1/2 package (17 1/4-ounce size) frozen puff pastry (1 sheet), thawed

1/2 cup sugar

1 teaspoon ground cinnamon

Heat oven to 375°. Lightly grease cookie sheet. Sprinkle sugar over kitchen counter or breadboard. Roll pastry into 1/8-inch-thick rectangle, 12×9 1/2 inches, on sugared surface. Mark a line lengthwise down center of rectangle. Fold long sides of rectangle toward center line, leaving 1/4 inch uncovered at center. Fold rectangle lengthwise in half to form strip, 12×2 1/2 inches, pressing pastry together.

Cut strip crosswise into 1/4-inch slices. Mix 1/2 cup sugar and the cinnamon. Coat slices with sugar mixture. Place about 2 inches apart on cookie sheet. Bake 8 to 10 minutes, turning after 5 minutes, until cookies begin to turn golden brown. Immediately remove from cookie sheet to wire rack. Cool completely.

1 Cookie: Calories 25 (Calories from Fat 10); Fat 1g (Saturated 0g); Cholesterol 0mg; Sodium 25mg; Carbohydrate 4g (Dietary Fiber 0g); Protein 0g.

Make It Your Way

Here's another idea, Chocolate and Peanut Butter–Dipped Elephant Ears! Melt 1 ounce semi-sweet baking chocolate in 1-quart saucepan over low heat, stirring occasionally. Melt 3 tablespoons peanut butter-flavored chips in another 1-quart saucepan over low heat, stirring occasionally. Dip one end of cookie into chocolate and the other into peanut butter for two taste treats in one cookie. Place on waxed paper until chocolate and peanut butter are firm.

Halloween Cutout Cookies

CHILL: 1 to 2 hr ● BAKE: 5 to 7 min per sheet ● YIELD: 6 to 7 dozen cookies

Cookie Tips

When rolling out dough, always start at the center and roll toward the outside edges.

To prevent sticking, dip cookie cutters into baking mix, flour or powdered sugar and shake off the excess before cutting dough.

The egg yolk paint is perfectly safe to use because the cookies are baked after it's been painted on.

1 1/2 cups powdered sugar

1/2 cup butter or margarine, softened

1/2 teaspoon vanilla

2 eggs

4 cups Bisquick® Original baking mix

11 drops yellow food color

7 drops red food color

2 tablespoons baking cocoa

Egg Yolk Paint (below)

Beat powdered sugar, butter, vanilla and eggs in large bowl with electric mixer on medium speed, or mix with spoon. Stir in baking mix until soft dough forms. Divide dough in half. Mix yellow and red food colors into 1 half to make orange dough; mix cocoa into other half to make chocolate dough. Cover and refrigerate doughs separately 1 to 2 hours or until chilled.

Heat oven to 400°. Roll one-fourth of the dough at a time 1/8 inch thick on floured cloth-covered surface. (Keep remaining dough refrigerated until ready to roll.) Cut orange dough with 2- to 3-inch pumpkin-shaped cookie cutter and chocolate dough with medium-size cat-shaped cookie cutter. Place 1 inch apart on ungreased cookie sheet.

Prepare Egg Yolk Paint. Paint faces on pumpkins and cats. Bake 5 to 7 minutes or until edges are light brown. Remove from cookie sheet to wire rack.

Egg Yolk Paint

1 egg yolk

1/4 teaspoon water

Food colors

Mix egg yolk and water. Divide mixture among a few small custard cups. Tint each with a different food color. If paint thickens while standing, stir in a few drops water.

1 Cookie: Calories 50 (Calories from Fat 20); Fat 2g (Saturated 1g); Cholesterol 10mg; Sodium 110mg; Carbohydrate 7g (Dietary Fiber 0g); Protein 1g.

Halloween Cutout Cookies

Ginger Cookie Clock

BAKE: 10 min per pan ● YIELD: About 3 1/2 dozen 1 1/2-inch pieces

Cookie Tips

You don't have to decorate your giant cookie only as a clock. For variety, try decorating it as a jack-o'-lantern, ladybug, face or anything else you like. Squeezing dough through a garlic press or potato ricer is very handy for making dough into "hair."

Make It Your Way

Create **Giant Pizza Cookie Slices** by pressing all the dough into the pizza pan or onto the cookie sheet. Use a pizza cutter to cut the dough into 16 wedges. After baking and cooling the pizza cookie, decorate with frosting and candy. Recut along the lines to serve the slices.

1 cup sugar

1/2 cup butter or margarine, softened

1/4 cup molasses

1 egg

2 cups all-purpose flour

1 1/2 teaspoons baking soda

1/2 teaspoon salt

1/2 teaspoon ground cinnamon

1/2 teaspoon ground ginger

1/4 teaspoon ground cloves

Sugar

Heat oven to 375°. Grease 12-inch pizza pan or large cookie sheet. Mix 1 cup sugar, the butter, molasses and egg in large bowl with electric mixer on medium speed, or mix with spoon. Stir in remaining ingredients except sugar.

Reserve 1/3 cup dough. Press remaining dough in pan or into 12-inch circle on cookie sheet. Shape reserved dough into numbers and arrows; place on dough in pan to resemble the face of a clock. Sprinkle with sugar. Bake about 10 minutes or until golden brown. Cool completely. Cut or break into pieces.

1 Piece: Calories 65 (Calories from Fat 20); Fat 2g (Saturated 1g); Cholesterol 5mg; Sodium 100mg; Carbohydrate 11g (Dietary Fiber 0g); Protein 1g.

Shape reserved dough into desired design and place on dough in pan.

Magic Window Cookies

CHILL: 1 hr ● BAKE: 7 to 9 min per sheet ● YIELD: About 6 dozen 3-inch cookies

1 cup sugar

3/4 cup butter or margarine, softened

1 teaspoon vanilla or 1/2 teaspoon lemon extract

2 eggs

2 1/2 cups all-purpose flour

1 teaspoon baking powder

1/4 teaspoon salt

4 rolls (about 0.9 ounces each) ring-shaped hard candy

Beat sugar, butter, vanilla and eggs in large bowl with electric mixer on medium speed, or mix with spoon. Stir in flour, baking powder and salt. Cover and refrigerate about 1 hour or until firm.

Heat oven to 375°. Cover cookie sheet with aluminum foil. Roll one third of dough at a time 1/8 inch thick on lightly floured cloth-covered surface. Cut into desired shapes. Place 1 inch on foil. Cut out designs from cookies, using smaller cutters or your own patterns. Place whole or partially crushed pieces of candy in cutouts, depending on size and shape of design, mixing colors as desired. (To crush candy, place in heavy plastic bag and tap lightly with rolling pin; because candy melts easily, leave pieces as large as possible.)

Bake 7 to 9 minutes or until cookies are very light brown and candy is melted. If candy has not completely spread within cutout design, immediately spread with knife. Cool completely on foil. Remove cookies gently.

1 **Cookie:** Calories 55 (Calories from Fat 20); Fat 2g (Saturated 0g); Cholesterol 5mg; Sodium 40mg; Carbohydrate 8g (Dietary Fiber 0g); Protein 1g.

Cookie Tips

Use Halloween cookie cutters and cut out sections to be filled with hard candy. When making the "magic windows," try different colors of candy. Place candy pieces to form stripes, polka dots and swirls.

Make It Your Way

Make **Christmas Magic Window Cookies** by cutting dough with Christmas cutters and filling the holes with red and green candies. Create the hole for a hanger by pressing a drinking straw through the dough before baking.

Candy Corn Shortbread

CHILL: 2 hr ● BAKE: 10 to 12 min per sheet ● YIELD: About 3 dozen cookies

3/4 cup butter or margarine, softened

1/4 cup sugar

2 cups all-purpose flour

Yellow food color

Red food color

Beat butter and sugar in large bowl with electric mixer on medium speed, or mix with spoon. Stir in flour. Divide dough into 6 equal parts. Combine 3 parts dough; mix with 10 drops yellow food color and 4 drops red food color to make orange dough. Combine 2 parts dough; mix with 7 drops yellow food color to make yellow dough. Leave remaining part dough plain.

Pat orange dough into 3/4-inch-thick rectangle, 9 × 2 inches, on plastic wrap. Pat yellow dough into 1/2-inch-thick rectangle, 9 × 1 3/4 inches. Place yellow rectangle centered on orange rectangle. Shape plain dough into 9-inch roll, 3/4 inch in diameter. Place roll on center of yellow rectangle. Wrap plastic wrap around dough, pressing dough into triangle so that dough will resemble a kernel of corn when sliced. Refrigerate about 2 hours or until firm.

Heat oven to 350°. Cut dough into 1/4-inch slices. Place about 1 inch apart on ungreased cookie sheet. Bake 10 to 12 minutes or until set. Remove from cookie sheet to wire rack.

1 Cookie: Calories 70 (Calories from Fat 35); Fat 4g (Saturated 1g); Cholesterol 0mg; Sodium 45mg; Carbohydrate 7g (Dietary Fiber 0g); Protein 1g.

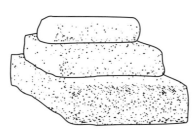

Stack dough so that the orange rectangle is on the bottom and the uncolored roll of dough is on top.

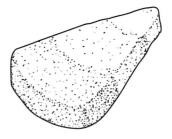

Press dough into triangle so that sliced wedges resemble a kernel of corn.

Candy Corn Shortbread, Magic Window Cookies (page 109)

Witches' Brooms

BAKE: 12 min per sheet ● YIELD: 20 cookies

Cookie Tips

Sweep up lots of Halloween fun when you serve these bewitchen' treats. They're great to serve for birthday and school parties.

Don't try to rush when melting chocolate. Chocolate burns easily when exposed to high heat. That's why we recommended melting it over low heat.

1/2 cup packed brown sugar

1/2 cup butter or margarine, softened

2 tablespoons water

1 teaspoon vanilla

1 1/2 cups all-purpose flour

1/8 teaspoon salt

10 pretzel rods (about 8 1/2 inches long), cut crosswise in half

2 teaspoons shortening

2/3 cup semisweet chocolate chips

1/3 cup butterscotch-flavored chips

Heat oven to 350°. Beat brown sugar, butter, water and vanilla in medium bowl with electric mixer on medium speed, or mix with spoon. Stir in flour and salt. Shape dough into twenty 1 1/4-inch balls.

Place pretzel rod halves on ungreased cookie sheet. Press ball of dough onto cut end of each pretzel rod. Press dough with fork to resemble bristles of broom. Bake about 12 minutes or until set but not brown. Remove from cookie sheet to wire rack. Cool completely.

Cover cookie sheet with waxed paper. Place brooms on waxed paper. Melt shortening and chocolate chips in 1-quart saucepan over low heat, stirring occasionally, until smooth; remove from heat. Spoon melted chocolate over brooms, leaving about 1 inch at top of pretzel handle and bottom halves of cookie bristles uncovered.

Place butterscotch chips in microwavable bowl. Microwave uncovered on Medium-High (70%) 30 to 50 seconds, stirring after 30 seconds, until chips can be stirred smooth. Drizzle over chocolate. Let stand until chocolate is firm.

1 Cookie: Calories 170 (Calories from Fat 70); Fat 8g (Saturated 3g); Cholesterol 0mg; Sodium 190mg; Carbohydrate 23g (Dietary Fiber 0g); Protein 2g.

Witches' Hats

PREP: 20 min ● CHILL: 15 min ● YIELD: 32 cookies

32 foil-wrapped milk chocolate kisses, unwrapped

1 package (11 1/2 ounces) fudge-striped shortbread cookies (32 cookies)

1 tube (4.25 ounces) orange or red decorating icing

Attach chocolate kiss to chocolate bottom of each cookie with decorating icing. Pipe decorating icing around base of each chocolate kiss to form a ribbon and bow.

1 Cookie: Calories 100 (Calories from Fat 45); Fat 5g (Saturated 3g); Cholesterol 5mg; Sodium 20mg; Carbohydrate 13g (Dietary Fiber 0g); Protein 1g.

"I Don't Have That"

Any 1 1/2 to 2 1/2-inch solid chocolate or chocolate-covered cookies can be used instead of the shortbread cookies.

Cobweb Cookies

COOK: 30 to 60 seconds per cookie ● YIELD: About 2 1/2 dozen cookies

3/4 cup all-purpose flour

1/2 cup granulated sugar

1/4 cup vegetable oil

1/4 cup milk

1/2 teaspoon vanilla

2 eggs

Powdered sugar

Beat all ingredients except powdered sugar with electric mixer on medium speed until smooth, or mix with spoon. Pour batter into plastic squeeze bottle with narrow opening.

Heat 10-inch skillet over medium heat until hot; grease lightly with vegetable oil or shortening. Working quickly, squeeze batter to form 4 straight, thin lines that intersect at a common center point to form a star shape. To form cobweb, squeeze thin streams of batter to connect lines. Cook 30 to 60 seconds or until bottom is golden brown; carefully turn. Cook until golden brown. Remove from skillet to wire rack; cool. Sprinkle with powdered sugar.

1 Cookie: Calories 45 (Calories from Fat 20); Fat 2g (Saturated 0g); Cholesterol 15mg; Sodium 5mg; Carbohydrate 6g (Dietary Fiber 0g); Protein 1g.

Cookie Tips

Recycle empty plastic squeeze-type honey bottles. They would work very well in this recipe to hold the batter.

Ghost Cookies

CHILL: 3 hr ● BAKE: 6 to 8 min per sheet ● YIELD: About 4 1/2 dozen cookies

Cookie Tips

When using cookie cutters with one wide end and one narrow end, alternate the direction of the cookie cutter as you are cutting out the cookies. In other words, cut out the first cookie with the wide end toward you, then cut out the next cookie with the narrow end toward you. That way, you can cut more cookies out of the dough.

To save space on your wire cooling racks, do the same thing, alternate the direction of each cookie. The first cookie you put down has the wide end toward you; then put the next cookie down with the narrow end toward you.

1/2 cup granulated sugar

1/2 cup packed brown sugar

1/2 cup peanut butter

1/4 cup butter or margarine, softened

1/4 cup shortening

1 egg

1 1/4 cups all-purpose flour

3/4 teaspoon baking soda

1/2 teaspoon baking powder

1/4 teaspoon salt

Creamy White Frosting (below)

Chocolate chips or small black gumdrops

Beat sugars, peanut butter, butter, shortening and egg in large bowl with electric mixer on medium speed, or mix with spoon. Stir in flour, baking soda, baking powder and salt. Cover and refrigerate about 3 hours or until firm.

Heat oven to 375°. Divide dough in half. Roll each half 1/8 inch thick on lightly floured surface. Cut into 3×2-inch ghost shapes. Place 1 inch apart on ungreased cookie sheet. Bake 6 to 8 minutes or until light brown. Cool 2 minutes; remove from cookie sheet to wire rack. Cool completely. Generously frost with Creamy White Frosting. Use chocolate chips or slices of gumdrops for eyes.

Creamy White Frosting

6 cups powdered sugar

2/3 cup butter or margarine, softened

1/3 cup milk

Beat powdered sugar and butter in large bowl with electric mixer on medium speed, or mix with spoon. Stir in milk until smooth and spreadable.

1 Cookie: Calories 140 (Calories from Fat 55); Fat 6g (Saturated 1g); Cholesterol 5mg; Sodium 85mg; Carbohydrate 20g (Dietary Fiber 0g); Protein 1g.

Multigrain Cutouts

BAKE: 12 to 14 min per sheet ● YIELD: About 6 dozen 2- to 3-inch cookies

1 cup sugar

2/3 cup shortening

3 1/4 cups whole wheat flour

1/4 cup cornmeal

1/4 cup wheat germ

3/4 cup milk

1 teaspoon baking powder

1/2 teaspoon salt

1/2 teaspoon vanilla

Baked-On Frosting (below)

Heat oven to 350°. Beat sugar and shortening in large bowl with electric mixer on medium speed, or mix with spoon. Stir in remaining ingredients except Baked-On Frosting.

Roll about one third of dough at a time 1/8 inch thick on lightly floured surface. Cut with sports-shape cookie cutters. Place 1 inch on ungreased cookie sheet.

Place Baked-On Frosting in decorating bag with #5 writing tip. Pipe frosting on unbaked cookies to outline or decorate. Bake 12 to 14 minutes or until edges are light brown. Cool 1 to 2 minutes; remove from cookie sheet to wire rack.

Baked-On Frosting

2/3 cup all-purpose flour

2/3 cup butter or margarine, softened

1 tablespoon hot water

Mix flour and butter until smooth. Stir in hot water.

1 Cookie: Calories 70 (Calories from Fat 35); Fat 4g (Saturated 1g); Cholesterol 0mg; Sodium 45mg; Carbohydrate 8g (Dietary Fiber 0g); Protein 1g.

Cookie Tips

This recipe makes a not-too-sweet cookie that can be cut into any shape to carry out a party theme.

Wheat Germ

Wheat germ is the embryo of the wheat kernel and is a very concentrated source of vitamins. It also is a good source of fiber, which contributes great texture to these cookies.

Black-Eyed Susans

CHILL: 2 hr ● BAKE: 10 to 12 min per sheet ● YIELD: About 3 dozen cookies

Cookie Tips

The interesting shape and color of these cookies makes them a real plus on a mixed cookie tray.

Make It Your Way

Change Black-Eyed Susans into **Spring Blossoms** in a snap of the fingers! Leave the dough plain or tint dough with food coloring as desired. Additionally, try rolling the balls in colored sugar. Use chocolate-covered candies, mints or décor sprinkles for the centers.

3/4 cup butter or margarine, softened

1/2 cup sugar

1 teaspoon vanilla

12 drops yellow food color

1 egg

1 package (3 ounces) cream cheese, softened

2 cups all-purpose flour

About 3 dozen large semisweet chocolate chips

Beat butter, sugar, vanilla, food color, egg and cream cheese in large bowl with electric mixer on medium speed, or mix with spoon. Stir in flour. Cover and refrigerate about 2 hours or until firm.

Heat oven to 375°. Shape dough into 1 1/4-inch balls. Place about 2 inches apart on ungreased cookie sheet. Make 3 cuts with scissors in top of each ball about three fourths of the way through to make 6 wedges. Spread wedges apart slightly to form flower petals (cookies will flatten as they bake).

Bake 10 to 12 minutes or until set and edges begin to brown. Immediately press 1 chocolate chip in center of each cookie. Remove from cookie sheet to wire rack.

1 Cookie: Calories 85 (Calories from Fat 45); Fat 5g (Saturated 2g); Cholesterol 10mg; Sodium 55mg; Carbohydrate 9g (Dietary Fiber 0g); Protein 1g.

Cut balls from top into 6 wedges about 3/4 way through dough.

Spring Blossoms (variation)

Bumblebees

CHILL: 2 hr ● BAKE: 11 to 13 min per sheet ● YIELD: About 4 dozen cookies

Cookie Tips

These "cute-as-a-bug" cookies are perfect for a child's birthday party.

Cookies baked on dark sheets may brown too quickly. You can prevent this by either lowering the temperature of the oven by 25° or lining the sheets with aluminum foil or baking parchment paper.

1/2 cup peanut butter

1/2 cup shortening

1/3 cup packed brown sugar

1/3 cup honey

1 egg

1 3/4 cups all-purpose flour

3/4 teaspoon baking soda

1/2 teaspoon baking powder

8 dozen pretzel twists

8 dozen pretzel sticks

Beat peanut butter, shortening, brown sugar, honey and egg in large bowl with electric mixer on medium speed, or mix with spoon. Stir in flour, baking soda and baking powder. Cover dough with plastic wrap and refrigerate about 2 hours or until firm.

Heat oven to 350°. Shape dough into 1-inch balls (dough will be slightly sticky). For each cookie, place 2 pretzel twists side by side with the bottoms (the bottom comes to a rounded point, similar to the bottom of a heart shape) touching on ungreased cookie sheet. Place 1 ball of dough on center, and flatten slightly. Break 2 pretzel sticks in half. Gently press 3 pretzel stick halves into dough for stripes on bee. Break fourth pretzel piece in half. Poke pieces into 1 end of dough for antennae.

Bake 11 to 13 minutes or until light golden brown. Immediately remove from cookie sheet to wire rack.

1 Cookie: Calories 115 (Calories from Fat 35); Fat 4g (Saturated 1g); Cholesterol 5mg; Sodium 260mg; Carbohydrate 18g (Dietary Fiber 0g); Protein 2g.

Cookie Pizza

BAKE: 15 min per pan • YIELD: About 16 servings

1/2 cup packed brown sugar

1/4 cup granulated sugar

1/2 cup butter or margarine, softened

1 teaspoon vanilla

1 egg

1 1/4 cups all-purpose flour

1/2 teaspoon baking soda

1/2 package (12-ounce size) miniature semisweet chocolate chips (1 cup)

1 cup frozen (thawed) whipped topping or whipped topping from a pressurized can

1/4 cup chopped walnuts

1/4 cup flaked or shredded coconut, toasted (see right)

1/2 cup candy-coated chocolate candies

Heat oven to 350°. Beat sugars, butter, vanilla and egg in large bowl with electric mixer on medium speed, or mix with spoon. Stir in flour and baking soda (dough will be stiff). Stir in chocolate chips. Press dough in ungreased 12-inch pizza pan or into 12-inch circle on cookie sheet. Bake about 15 minutes or until golden brown. Cool completely in pan.

Just before serving, spread whipped topping over cookie. Top with walnuts, coconut and candies. Cut into wedges. Store leftovers covered in the refrigerator.

1 Serving: Calories 245 (Calories from Fat 115); Fat 13g (Saturated 5g); Cholesterol 15mg; Sodium 125mg; Carbohydrate 30g (Dietary Fiber 1g); Protein 3g.

Cookie Tips

Here's a couple of tricks to press out the dough without having it stick to your hands: Dampen hands with cold water (don't dry them!), lightly dust hands with flour, spray hands with cooking spray or place hands in plastic bags.

To toast coconut, bake uncovered in ungreased shallow pan in 350° oven 5 to 7 minutes, stirring occasionally, until golden brown. Or cook in ungreased heavy skillet over medium-low heat 6 to 14 minutes, stirring frequently until browning begins, then stirring constantly until golden brown.

"I Don't Have That"

Any type of candies, nuts or peanuts can be used instead of the topping ideas we've listed in the recipe.

Caramel Apple Cookies

BAKE: 8 to 9 min per sheet ● YIELD: About 2 dozen cookies

Make It Your Way

Here's another fall idea, try making **Leaf Cookies**. Make the dough as directed above—except omit red food color paste and Caramel Glaze. Divide dough into 3 equal parts. Stir 8 drops yellow food color into 1 part dough to make yellow dough. Stir 8 drops yellow and 3 drops red food color into another part dough to make orange dough. Stir 10 drops red, 8 drops green and 3 drops yellow food color into remaining dough to make brown dough.

Drop small portions of each of the 3 colors of dough close together in random pattern onto lightly floured cloth-covered surface. Roll doughs together into marbled pattern to 1/8-inch thickness. Cut with 2 1/2- to 3-inch leaf-shaped cookie cutter. Place on ungreased cookie sheet. Bake 6 to 7 minutes or until no indentation remains when touched in center. Remove from cookie sheet; cool on wire rack. About 4 dozen cookies.

1 cup sugar

1/2 cup butter or margarine, softened

1/2 cup shortening

1 1/2 teaspoons vanilla

2 eggs

3 cups all-purpose flour

1/2 teaspoon baking soda

1/2 teaspoon salt

Red paste food color, if desired

About 24 wooden sticks with rounded ends

Caramel Glaze (below)

Heat oven to 400°. Beat sugar, butter and shortening in large bowl with electric mixer on medium speed, or mix with spoon. Stir in vanilla and eggs. Stir in flour, baking soda and salt. Stir in food color to tint dough red.

Roll dough 1/4 inch thick on lightly floured cloth-covered surface. Cut with 3-inch round or apple-shaped cookie cutter. Place 2 inches apart on ungreased cookie sheet. Insert wooden stick into side of each cookie. Bake 8 to 9 minutes or until edges are light brown. Cool 2 minutes; remove from cookie sheet to wire rack. Cool completely. Spread top third of each cookie (opposite wooden stick) with Caramel Glaze. Hold cookie upright to allow glaze to drizzle down cookie.

Caramel Glaze

1 package (14 ounces) vanilla caramels

1/4 cup water

Heat caramels and water in 2-quart saucepan over low heat, stirring frequently, until melted and smooth. If glaze becomes too stiff, heat over low heat, stirring constantly, until softened.

1 Cookie: Calories 235 (Calories from Fat 90); Fat 10g (Saturated 3g); Cholesterol 20mg; Sodium 170mg; Carbohydrate 33g (Dietary Fiber 0g); Protein 3g.

Leaf Cookie (variation), Caramel Apple Cookies

Caramel-Pecan Cookies

BAKE: 12 to 15 min per sheet ● YIELD: About 32 cookies

1/2 cup packed brown sugar

1/2 cup butter or margarine, softened

2 tablespoons water

1 teaspoon vanilla

1 1/2 cups all-purpose flour

1/8 teaspoon salt

8 vanilla caramels

160 pecan halves (about 2 1/4 cups)

Chocolate Glaze (below)

Heat oven to 350°. Beat brown sugar, butter, water and vanilla in large bowl with electric mixer on medium speed, or mix with spoon. Stir in flour and salt.

Cut each caramel into 4 pieces with sharp knife. For each cookie, group 5 pecan halves on ungreased cookie sheet. Shape 1 teaspoon dough around each caramel piece to form a ball. Press ball firmly onto center of each group of pecans.

Bake 12 to 15 minutes or until set but not brown. Immediately remove from cookie sheet to wire rack. Cool completely. Spread tops of cookies with Chocolate Glaze.

Chocolate Glaze

1 ounce unsweetened baking chocolate

1 cup powdered sugar

1 teaspoon vanilla

2 to 4 teaspoons water

Melt chocolate in 1-quart saucepan over low heat, stirring occasionally. Stir in powdered sugar, vanilla and water until smooth and spreadable.

1 Cookie: Calories 140 (Calories from Fat 80); Fat 9g (Saturated 1g); Cholesterol 0mg; Sodium 50mg; Carbohydrate 15g (Dietary Fiber 1g); Protein 1g.

Caramel-Pecan Cookies

Gingerpop Cookies

CHILL: 15 min ● BAKE: 8 to 10 min per sheet ● YIELD: About 18 cookies

Cookie Tips

When you work with liquid food color, go slowly to get the exact shade of color you want. Add one drop at a time and mix it in the dough or frosting completely before adding more color.

Food Coloring

There are two types of food coloring widely available: liquid and paste. Liquid food coloring is easy to find at your supermarket. Paste coloring can be found in cake decorating or specialty food stores. Paste colors are preferred by many people because the colors are much more vivid than liquid colors.

1 package (14 1/2 ounces) Betty Crocker gingerbread cake and cookie mix

1/3 cup lukewarm water

About 18 wooden sticks with rounded ends

Sugar

Easy Pink Frosting (below)

Candy-coated chocolate candies, candy corn, licorice or gumdrops, if desired

Mix gingerbread mix (dry) and water in large bowl with spoon. Cover dough with plastic wrap and refrigerate about 15 minutes or until slightly firm.

Heat oven to 375°. Shape dough into 1 1/4-inch balls. Insert wooden stick into side of each ball until tip of stick is in center of ball. Place balls about 2 inches apart on ungreased cookie sheet.

Press bottom of glass into dough to grease, then dip into sugar; press on balls to flatten slightly. Bake 8 to 10 minutes or until edges are firm. Cool 1 minute; remove from cookie sheet with spatula to wire rack. Cool completely. Spread Easy Pink Frosting over each cookie with knife, then immediately top with candies to make a face design or decorate as desired.

Easy Pink Frosting

1 cup vanilla ready-to-spread frosting

2 drops red food color

Mix ingredients until pink and smooth.

1 Cookie: Calories 175 (Calories from Fat 45); Fat 5g (Saturated 3g); Cholesterol 1mg; Sodium 160mg; Carbohydrate 31g (Dietary Fiber 0g); Protein 1g.

Rocky Road Cookies

BAKE: 8 to 12 min per sheet ● YIELD: About 4 dozen cookies

1 cup semisweet chocolate chips

1/2 cup butter or margarine

1 1/2 cups all-purpose flour

1 cup sugar

1/2 teaspoon baking powder

1/2 teaspoon vanilla

1/4 teaspoon salt

2 eggs

1 cup chopped nuts

About 48 miniature marshmallows

Melt 1/2 cup of the chocolate chips and the butter in 1-quart saucepan over low heat, stirring occasionally, until smooth; remove from heat. Cool slightly.

Heat oven to 400°. Mix melted chocolate mixture, flour, sugar, baking powder, vanilla, salt and eggs in large bowl with spoon. Stir in nuts and remaining 1/2 cup chocolate chips.

Drop dough by rounded teaspoonfuls about 2 inches apart onto ungreased cookie sheet. Press 1 marshmallow into center of each cookie. Bake 8 to 12 minutes or until almost no indentation remains when touched in center. Immediately remove from cookie sheet to wire rack.

1 Cookie: Calories 90 (Calories from Fat 45); Fat 5g (Saturated 1g); Cholesterol 10mg; Sodium 45mg; Carbohydrate 10g (Dietary Fiber 0g); Protein 1g

Cookie Tips

Beginner cookie makers can help with this recipe by pressing the marshmallows into the cookie dough.

Make It Your Way

Try using colored or the fun seasonal-shaped miniature marshmallows in place of the little white ones.

Peanut Butter and Jam Bars

BAKE: 20 to 25 min per pan ● YIELD: 32 bars

Cookie Tips

Everyone will like these cookies when served with a glass of milk for the kids and a cup of coffee for the adults.

"I Don't Have That"

Feel free to use whichever preserve you have on hand. Kids would love these bars with grape jelly. In fact, any jam, jelly or preserve will work.

1/2 cup granulated sugar

1/2 cup packed brown sugar

1/2 cup shortening

1/2 cup peanut butter

1 egg

1 1/4 cups all-purpose flour

3/4 teaspoon baking soda

1/2 teaspoon baking powder

1/2 cup red raspberry jam

Vanilla Drizzle (below)

Heat oven to 350°. Beat sugars, shortening, peanut butter and egg in large bowl with electric mixer on medium speed, or mix with spoon. Stir in flour, baking soda and baking powder.

Reserve 1 cup dough. Press remaining dough in ungreased rectangular pan, 13×9×2 inches. Spread with jam. Crumble reserved dough and sprinkle over jam; gently press into jam. Bake 20 to 25 minutes or until golden brown. Cool completely. Drizzle with Vanilla Drizzle. Cut into 8 rows by 4 rows.

Vanilla Drizzle

2 tablespoons butter or margarine

1 cup powdered sugar

1 teaspoon vanilla

3 to 4 teaspoons hot water

Melt butter in 1-quart saucepan over low heat; remove from heat. Stir in powdered sugar and vanilla. Stir in hot water, 1 teaspoon at a time, until smooth and thin enough to drizzle.

1 Bar: Calories 135 (Calories from Fat 55); Fat 6g (Saturated 1g); Cholesterol 5mg; Sodium 70mg; Carbohydrate 18g (Dietary Fiber 0g); Protein 2g.

Peanut Butter and Jam Bars

Chocolate–Peanut Butter No-Bakes

PREP: 12 min ● CHILL: 1 hr ● YIELD: About 2 dozen cookies

Cookie Tips

If you don't want to take the time to drop the mixture onto waxed paper do this— pat the mixture on a cookie sheet and refrigerate as directed. Cut into squares.

Make It Your Way

To make **Double–Peanut Butter No-Bakes** substitute peanut butter–flavored chips for the chocolate chips.

1 package (6 ounces) semisweet chocolate chips (1 cup)

1/4 cup light corn syrup

1/4 cup peanut butter

2 tablespoons milk

1 teaspoon vanilla

2 cups quick-cooking oats

1 cup peanuts

Cover cookie sheet with waxed paper. Heat chocolate chips, corn syrup, peanut butter, milk and vanilla in 3-quart saucepan over medium heat, stirring constantly, until chocolate is melted and mixture is smooth; remove from heat. Stir in oats and peanuts until well coated.

Drop mixture by rounded tablespoonfuls onto waxed paper. Refrigerate uncovered about 1 hour or until firm. Store covered in refrigerator.

1 Cookie: Calories 125 (Calories from Fat 65); Fat 7g (Saturated 2g); Cholesterol 0mg; Sodium 20mg; Carbohydrate 13g (Dietary Fiber 1g); Protein 4g.

Chocolate-Peanut Windmills

CHILL: 2 hr ● BAKE: 6 min per sheet ● YIELD: About 2 dozen cookies

1 cup sugar

1/4 cup butter or margarine, softened

1/4 cup shortening

1/2 teaspoon vanilla

1 egg

2 ounces unsweetened baking chocolate, melted and cooled

1 3/4 cups all-purpose flour

1 teaspoon baking powder

1/8 teaspoon salt

1/2 cup finely chopped peanuts

Cookie Tips

A great way to evenly cut cookie dough is to use a pizza cutter and a plastic ruler.

"I Don't Have That"

Instead of using chopped peanuts, cover the cookie dough with candy sprinkles.

Beat sugar, butter, shortening, vanilla and egg in large bowl with electric mixer on medium speed, or mix with spoon. Stir in chocolate. Stir in flour, baking powder and salt. Cover and refrigerate about 2 hours or until firm.

Heat oven to 400°. Divide dough in half. Roll each half into rectangle, 12×9 inches, on lightly floured cloth-covered surface. Sprinkle each rectangle with half of the peanuts; gently press into dough. Cut dough into 3-inch squares. Place about 2 inches apart on ungreased cookie sheet.

Cut squares diagonally from each corner almost to center. Fold every other point to center to resemble pinwheel. Bake about 6 minutes or until set. Remove from cookie sheet to wire rack.

1 Cookie: Calories 140 (Calories from Fat 65); Fat 7g (Saturated 2g); Cholesterol 10mg; Sodium 60mg; Carbohydrate 17g (Dietary Fiber 0g); Protein 2g.

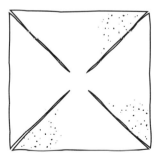

Cut squares diagonally from each corner almost to center.

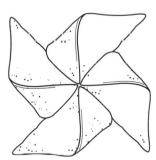

Fold every other point to center to resemble pinwheel.

Goldfish Drops

PREP: 12 min ● STAND: 1 hr ● YIELD: About 3 dozen cookies

1 cup butterscotch-flavored chips

1 tablespoon shortening

1 package (6 ounces) original flavor tiny fish-shaped crackers (about 3 1/2 cups)

1 cup broken pretzel sticks

Grease cookie sheet. Melt butterscotch chips and shortening in 3-quart saucepan over low heat, stirring constantly, until smooth; remove from heat. Stir in crackers and pretzels until well coated.

Drop mixture by rounded tablespoonfuls onto cookie sheet. Let stand about 1 hour or until firm. Carefully remove from cookie sheet.

1 Cookie: Calories 60 (Calories from Fat 25); Fat 3g (Saturated 1g); Cholesterol 0mg; Sodium 65mg; Carbohydrate 7g (Dietary Fiber 0g); Protein 1g.

Cookie Tips

If the combination of sweet and salty is one of your favorites, this is the cookie for you!

Make It Your Way

Goldfish Peanut Drops are easy to make by substituting vanilla milk (white) chips for the butterscotch chips and salted peanuts for the pretzel sticks.

Ice-Cream Sandwiches

BAKE: 9 to 10 min per sheet ● FREEZE: 1 hr ● YIELD: About 15 sandwich cookies

Peanut Butter Cookies (page 170)

2 cups ice cream (any flavor), slightly softened

Assorted candies or chopped dry-roasted peanuts, if desired

Prepare and bake Peanut Butter Cookies; cool completely. For each sandwich, press 1 rounded tablespoon ice cream between the bottoms of 2 cookies. Roll edge of sandwich cookie in candies. Place in rectangular pan.

Freeze uncovered about 1 hour or until firm. Wrap each sandwich cookie in plastic wrap. Store in freezer in plastic freezer bag.

1 Sandwich Cookie: Calories 210 (Calories from Fat 100); Fat 11g (Saturated 3g); Cholesterol 20mg; Sodium 180mg; Carbohydrate 24g (Dietary Fiber 0g); Protein 4g.

Make It Your Way

You can use any cookie you like in this book. Or, purchase store-bought cookies to make preparing these treats a snap!

Goldfish Drops

Animal Cookies

CHILL: 2 hr ● BAKE: 10 to 12 min per sheet ● YIELD: About 1 1/2 dozen cookies

1/2 cup granulated sugar

1/2 cup packed brown sugar

1/2 cup butter or margarine, softened

1 teaspoon vanilla

1 egg

2 cups all-purpose flour

1 teaspoon baking powder

1/2 teaspoon salt

1/2 teaspoon ground cinnamon

Heat oven to 350°. Beat sugars, butter, vanilla and egg in large bowl with electric mixer on medium speed, or mix with spoon. Stir in remaining ingredients. (If dough is too soft to shape, cover and refrigerate about 2 hours or until firm.)

Shape dough by 2 tablespoonfuls into slightly flattened balls and ropes. Arrange on ungreased cookie sheet to form animals as desired. Use small pieces of dough for facial features if desired. Bake about 10 to 12 minutes or until edges are golden brown. Remove from cookie sheet to wire rack.

1 Cookie: Calories 75 (Calories from Fat 25); Fat 3g (Saturated 1g); Cholesterol 5mg; Sodium 80mg; Carbohydrate 11g (Dietary Fiber 0g); Protein 1g.

Cookie Tips

Some animal forms you make may have very thin parts (like legs, arms or tails) and thick parts. To prevent the thinner parts from over-browning, bake on two cookie sheets that have been stacked together to form one sheet. Or use insulated sheets.

Make It Your Way

Have fun spelling your children's names with **Letter and Number Cookies.** Prepare dough as directed. Shape level tablespoonfuls dough into ropes, about 8 inches long and about 1/4 inch thick. Shape into letters and numbers as desired on ungreased cookie sheet and bake 8 to 10 minutes. Cool 3 minutes and remove from cookie sheet. About 3 dozen cookies.

Arrange balls or ropes of dough on cookie sheet to form animal as desired.

Cinnamon Footballs

BAKE: 12 to 14 min per sheet ● YIELD: About 2 dozen cookies

1/2 cup packed brown sugar

1/2 cup butter or margarine, softened

1 teaspoon vanilla

1 1/2 cups all-purpose flour

1/2 teaspoon ground cinnamon

1/8 teaspoon salt

About 24 blanched whole almonds

Decorating Glaze (below)

Heat oven to 350°. Beat brown sugar, butter and vanilla in large bowl with electric mixer on medium speed, or mix with spoon. Stir in flour, cinnamon and salt until dough holds together. (If dough is dry, mix in 1 to 2 tablespoons milk.)

Shape dough by scant tablespoonfuls around almonds to form football shapes. Place about 1 inch apart on ungreased cookie sheet. Bake 12 to 14 minutes or until set but not brown. Remove from cookie sheet to wire rack. Cool completely. Place Decorating Glaze in decorating bag with #3 writing tip. Pipe glaze on cookies to resemble football laces.

Decorating Glaze

1/2 cup powdered sugar

1 1/2 to 3 teaspoons water

Mix powdered sugar and water just enough to make a paste that can be piped from decorating bag.

1 Cookie: Calories 100 (Calories from Fat 45); Fat 5g (Saturated 1g); Cholesterol 0mg; Sodium 60mg; Carbohydrate 13g (Dietary Fiber 0g); Protein 1g.

Blanched Almonds

Blanched almonds are almonds that have the skin removed, and they are widely available in grocery stores.

Make It Your Way

When it's no longer football season, make **Cinnamon Baseballs.** Substitute pitted dates, cut in half crosswise, for the almonds. Mold dough around date half into baseball shape. Pipe on laces.

Cinnamon Footballs, Multigrain Cutouts (page 115)

CHAPTER 4

Chocolate Cookies *138*

Chocolate Chip Cookies *140*

Peanut Butter–Chocolate Chip Cookies *141*

Oatmeal Cookies *142*

Lemon Cookies *142*

Granola Cookies *143*

Brownie Drop Cookies *143*

Rolled Sugar Cookies *144*

Carrot-Molasses Cookies *146*

Easy Decorated Gingerbread Cookies *148*

Rocky Road Bars *149*

German Chocolate Bars *150*

Chocolate Chip–Pecan Bars *152*

Caramel Fudge Bars *153*

Almond Bars *154*

Peanut Butter–Toffee Bars *156*

Apricot-Cherry Bars *157*

Carrot-Raisin Bars *158*

Triple Chocolate-Cherry Bars *158*

Peanut Butter and Jelly Bars *159*

Easy-Yet-Elegant Raspberry Bars *160*

Lemon Bars *161*

Luscious Lemon-Raspberry Bars *162*

Chocolate-Raspberry Cheesecake Bars *164*

Lemon Cheesecake Bars *166*

Tuxedo Cheesecake Bars *167*

Fix 'em with a Mix

Rocky Road Bars (page 149),
Caramel Fudge Bars (page 153)

The convenience of a cake mix makes baking so easy! How to make cookies from a box of cake mix is requested over and over again. We're sure you'll agree that these are quick, easy and delicious.

Chocolate Cookies

BAKE: 8 to 10 min per sheet ● YIELD: About 4 dozen cookies

Cookie Tips

The tops of these cookies look crinkled, and they have a soft, chewy texture.

Make It Your Way

To make **Chocolate Chip Chocolate Cookies**, stir in 2/3-cup miniature semisweet chocolate chips into the dough.

1 package Betty Crocker SuperMoist devil's food cake mix

1/2 cup vegetable oil

2 eggs

Sugar

Heat oven to 350°. Mix cake mix (dry), oil and eggs in large bowl with spoon until dough forms.

Shape dough into 1-inch balls; roll in sugar. Place about 2 inches apart on ungreased cookie sheet. Bake 8 to 10 minutes or until set. Remove from cookie sheet to wire rack.

1 Cookie: Calories 75 (Calories from Fat 20); Fat 2g (Saturated 1g); Cholesterol 10mg; Sodium 85mg; Carbohydrate 13g (Dietary Fiber 0g); Protein 1g.

Chocolate Cookies, Lemon Cookies (page 142)

Chocolate Chip Cookies

BAKE: 9 to 11 min per sheet ● YIELD: About 5 dozen cookies

Cookie Tips

Did you know that frozen nuts are easier to chop than room temperature nuts?

The cap on the vanilla extract bottles are a handy little measure, most caps hold between 1/2 and 1 teaspoon.

1 package Betty Crocker SuperMoist butter pecan, chocolate chip*, chocolate fudge, devil's food, German chocolate or yellow cake mix

1/2 cup butter or margarine, softened

1 teaspoon vanilla

2 eggs

1/2 cup chopped nuts

1 package (6 ounces) semisweet chocolate chips (1 cup)

Heat oven to 350°. Beat half of the cake mix (dry), the butter, vanilla and eggs in large bowl with electric mixer on medium speed until smooth, or mix with spoon. Stir in remaining cake mix, the nuts and chocolate chips.

Drop dough by rounded teaspoonfuls about 2 inches apart onto ungreased cookie sheet. Bake 9 to 11 minutes or until edges are set (centers will be soft). Cool 1 minute; remove from cookie sheet to wire rack.

1 Cookie: Calories 75 (Calories from Fat 35); Fat 4g (Saturated 1g); Cholesterol 5mg; Sodium 80mg; Carbohydrate 9g (Dietary Fiber 0g); Protein 1g.

*If using chocolate chip cake mix, bake 12 to 15 minutes.

Peanut Butter–Chocolate Chip Cookies

BAKE: 8 to 10 min per sheet • YIELD: About 4 1/2 dozen cookies

1 package Betty Crocker SuperMoist devil's food or white cake mix

1/3 cup water

1/4 cup butter or margarine, softened

3/4 cup peanut butter

2 eggs

1 package (12 ounces) semisweet chocolate chips (2 cups)

Heat oven to 375°. Beat half of the cake mix (dry), the water, butter, peanut butter and eggs in large bowl with electric mixer on medium speed until smooth, or mix with spoon. Stir in remaining cake mix and the chocolate chips.

Drop dough by rounded teaspoonfuls about 2 inches apart onto ungreased cookie sheet. Bake 8 to 10 minutes (centers will be soft). Cool 1 minute; remove from cookie sheet to wire rack.

1 Cookie: Calories 105 (Calories from Fat 55); Fat 6g (Saturated 2g); Cholesterol 10mg; Sodium 115mg, Carbohydrate 12g (Dietary Fiber 1g); Protein 2g.

Cookie Tips

Cake mix cookies tend to be sweeter than cookies made from scratch.

Make It Your Way

Making these cookies into a pan of **Peanut Butter–Chocolate Chip Bars** is easy: Grease and flour a jelly roll pan, 15 1/2 × 10 1/2 × 1 inch and spread dough in the pan. Bake devil's food bars about 23 minutes and white bars about 20 minutes. Cool completely. Cut into 6 rows by 5 rows.

Oatmeal Cookies

BAKE: 14 min per sheet ● YIELD: About 5 dozen cookies

Cookie Tips

Measure vegetable oil in a liquid measuring cup instead of a "nested" or dry type of measuring cup for an accurate amount.

Make It Your Way

To make **Oatmeal Raisin Cake Mix Cookies** substitute raisins for the pecans.

1 package Betty Crocker SuperMoist yellow cake mix

2 cups quick-cooking oats

1 cup sugar

1 cup vegetable oil

2 eggs

1 cup chopped pecans

1 1/2 teaspoons vanilla

Heat oven to 350°. Mix cake mix (dry), oats and sugar in large bowl with spoon. Mix oil and eggs; stir into oat mixture thoroughly. Stir in pecans and vanilla.

Drop dough by rounded tablespoonfuls about 2 inches apart onto ungreased cookie sheet. Bake 12 to 14 minutes or until light brown. Remove from cookie sheet to wire rack.

1 Cookie: Calories 110 (Calories from Fat 55); Fat 6g (Saturated 1g); Cholesterol 5mg; Sodium 60mg; Carbohydrate 13g (Dietary Fiber 0g); Protein 1g.

Lemon Cookies

BAKE: 8 min per sheet ● YIELD: About 4 dozen cookies

Make It Your Way

If you like tart lemon flavor, try **Double Lemon Cookies**. Measure 2 tablespoons lemon juice plus enough oil to equal 1/2 cup, instead of just the 1/2 cup oil. Continue as directed.

1 package Betty Crocker SuperMoist lemon cake mix

1/2 cup vegetable oil

2 eggs

1 tub Betty Crocker Whipped or Rich & Creamy lemon ready-to-spread frosting

Heat oven to 350°. Grease cookie sheet. Mix cake mix (dry), oil and eggs in large bowl with spoon until dough forms.

Drop dough by teaspoonfuls onto cookie sheet. Bake about 8 minutes or until set. Remove from cookie sheet to wire rack. Cool completely. Frost.

1 Cookie: Calories 110 (Calories from Fat 45); Fat 5g (Saturated 2g); Cholesterol 10mg; Sodium 70mg; Carbohydrate 16g (Dietary Fiber 0g); Protein 0g.

Granola Cookies

BAKE: 10 to 12 min per sheet ● YIELD: About 5 dozen cookies

1 package Betty Crocker SuperMoist yellow cake mix

3/4 cup shortening

1/2 cup packed brown sugar

2 eggs

1 1/2 cups Nature Valley® low-fat fruit granola

1/2 cup chopped nuts, if desired

Heat oven to 375°. Beat half of the cake mix (dry), the shortening, brown sugar and eggs in large bowl with electric mixer on medium speed until smooth, or mix with spoon. Stir in remaining cake mix, the granola and nuts.

Drop dough by teaspoonfuls about 2 inches apart onto ungreased cookie sheet. Bake 10 to 12 minutes or until light brown. Cool 1 minute; remove from cookie sheet to wire rack.

1 Cookie: Calories 80 (Calories from Fat 35); Fat 4g (Saturated 1g); Cholesterol 5mg; Sodium 65mg; Carbohydrate 10g (Dietary Fiber 0g); Protein 1g.

Cookie Tips

The granola will add a lot of chewy texture and just a little crunch to these cookies.

In our testing in the Betty Crocker Kitchens, we use only large-size eggs. Using jumbo, extra-large or small eggs may cause a cookie dough to be too soft or dry.

Brownie Drop Cookies

BAKE: 6 to 8 min per sheet ● YIELD: About 4 dozen cookies

1 package (15 ounces) Betty Crocker fudge brownie mix

1/4 cup water

1 egg

1/2 cup chopped nuts

Heat oven to 375°. Lightly grease cookie sheet. Mix brownie mix, water and egg in large bowl with spoon. Stir in nuts (dough will be stiff).

Drop dough by rounded teaspoonfuls onto cookie sheet. Bake 6 to 8 minutes or until set. Cool slightly; remove from cookie sheet to wire rack.

1 Cookie: Calories 40 (Calories from Fat 10); Fat 1g (Saturated 0g); Cholesterol 4mg; Sodium 35mg; Carbohydrate 8g (Dietary Fiber 0g); Protein 0g.

Make It Your Way

For extra fudgy cookies, try **Double Chocolate Drops**. Just stir in 1/2 cup semisweet chocolate chips.

Indulge in **Coffee Liqueur Brownie Drops** by substituting coffee liqueur for the water.

Rolled Sugar Cookies

BAKE: 5 to 7 min per sheet ● YIELD: About 5 dozen 2 1/2-inch cookies

1 package Betty Crocker SuperMoist yellow cake mix

1/2 cup shortening

1/3 cup butter or margarine, softened

1 teaspoon vanilla, almond extract or lemon extract

1 egg

White or colored granulated sugar

Heat oven to 375°. Beat half of the cake mix (dry), the shortening, butter, vanilla and egg in large bowl with electric mixer on medium speed until smooth, or mix with spoon. Stir in remaining cake mix.

Divide dough into 4 equal parts. Roll each part 1/8 inch thick on lightly floured cloth-covered surface with cloth-covered rolling pin. Cut into desired shapes; sprinkle with sugar. Place 2 inches apart on ungreased cookie sheet.

Bake 5 to 7 minutes or until light brown. Cool slightly; remove from cookie sheet to wire rack.

1 Cookie: Calories 70 (Calories from Fat 35); Fat 4g (Saturated 1g); Cholesterol 5mg; Sodium 75mg; Carbohydrate 8g (Dietary Fiber 0g); Protein 0g.

Rolled Sugar Cookies

Carrot-Molasses Cookies

CHILL: 2 hr ● BAKE: 8 to 10 min per sheet ● YIELD: About 3 1/2 dozen cookies

1 package Betty Crocker SuperMoist carrot cake mix

1/4 cup butter or margarine, softened

2 tablespoons light molasses

2 eggs

1/2 cup chopped nuts, if desired

1 tub Betty Crocker Rich & Creamy cream cheese ready-to-spread frosting, if desired

Beat half of the cake mix (dry), the butter, molasses and eggs in large bowl with electric mixer on medium speed until smooth, or mix with spoon. Stir in remaining cake mix and the nuts. Refrigerate about 2 hours or until chilled.

Heat oven to 375°. Lightly grease cookie sheet. Drop dough by rounded teaspoonfuls about 2 inches apart onto cookie sheet. Bake 8 to 10 minutes or until edges are set (centers will be soft). Remove from cookie sheet to wire rack. Cool completely. Frost with frosting. (Cover and refrigerate any remaining frosting.)

1 Cookie: Calories 75 (Calories from Fat 25); Fat 3g (Saturated 1g); Cholesterol 10mg; Sodium 100mg; Carbohydrate 11g (Dietary Fiber 0g); Protein 1g.

Carrot-Molasses Cookies

Easy Decorated Gingerbread Cookies

BAKE: 8 to 10 min per sheet ● YIELD: About 2 dozen cookies

Cookie Tips

Yes, this is a no-roll ginger-bread cookie recipe. Isn't that a nice change? Kids will love making these cookies and coming up with fun decorating ideas.

Make It Your Way

Here's how to make easy **Rolled Gingerbread People and Snowmen**. Prepare cookie dough as directed above and divide in half. Place one half on floured cloth-covered surface. Roll 1/8 inch thick. Cut with floured cutter. Bake on ungreased cookie sheet and cool as directed above. Repeat with the remaining dough. Frost and decorate as desired.

1 package Betty Crocker gingerbread cake and cookie mix

1/4 cup hot water

2 tablespoons all-purpose flour

2 tablespoons butter or margarine, melted

Sugar

1 tub Betty Crocker Rich & Creamy vanilla ready-to-spread frosting

Miniature chocolate chips, raisins, cut-up gumdrops, colored sugar, miniature marshmallows, red cinnamon candies, shredded coconut, chocolate shot or shoestring licorice, if desired

Heat oven to 375°. Mix gingerbread mix, hot water, flour and butter in medium bowl with spoon until dough forms.

Shape dough into 1-inch balls. Place about 2 inches apart on ungreased cookie sheet. Press bottom of glass into dough to grease, then dip into sugar; press on shaped dough to flatten to 2 1/2 inches in diameter.

Bake 8 to 10 minutes or until edges are firm (do not overbake). Cool 1 minute; remove from cookie sheet to wire rack. Cool completely. Frost with frosting. (Cover and refrigerate any remaining frosting.) Decorate as desired with chocolate chips and candies.

1 Cookie: Calories 165 (Calories from Fat 55); Fat 6g (Saturated 3g); Cholesterol 0mg; Sodium 130mg; Carbohydrate 27g (Dietary Fiber 0g); Protein 1g.

Rocky Road Bars

BAKE: 30 to 35 min per pan • YIELD: 24 bars

1 package Betty Crocker SuperMoist milk chocolate cake mix

1/2 cup butter or margarine, melted

1/4 cup packed brown sugar

1/3 cup water

2 eggs

1 cup chopped nuts

3 cups miniature marshmallows

1/3 cup Betty Crocker Rich & Creamy chocolate ready-to-spread frosting

Heat oven to 350°. Grease and flour rectangular pan, 13×9×2 inches. Mix half of the cake mix (dry), the butter, brown sugar, water and eggs in large bowl with spoon until smooth. Stir in remaining cake mix and the nuts. Spread in pan.

Bake 22 minutes; sprinkle with marshmallows. Bake 10 to 13 minutes or until marshmallows are puffed and golden.

Microwave frosting in microwavable bowl uncovered on High 15 seconds. Drizzle over bars. Cool completely. For easier cutting, use plastic knife dipped in hot water. Cut into 6 rows by 4 rows.

1 Bar: Calories 205 (Calories from Fat 90); Fat 10g (Saturated 3g); Cholesterol 20mg; Sodium 250mg; Carbohydrate 28g (Dietary Fiber 1g); Protein 2g.

Make It Your Way

Expect rave reviews when you make **Chocolate-Chip Rocky Road Bars.** Sprinkle 1 cup semisweet chocolate chips on the bars before sprinkling with the marshmallows. Continue as directed.

"I Don't Have That"

Devil's food, German chocolate or chocolate fudge flavors can be substituted for the milk chocolate flavored mix.

German Chocolate Bars

BAKE: 35 to 40 min per pan ● YIELD: 48 bars

Cookie Tips

This take-off of German Chocolate Cake is one of our most frequently requested recipes. We hope you like it too.

Make It Your Way

For deliciously easy dessert, place 2 bars on individual serving plates. Top with canned whipped cream and then grated milk chocolate from a candy bar.

2/3 cup butter or margarine, softened
1 package Betty Crocker SuperMoist German chocolate cake mix
1 package (6 ounces) semisweet chocolate chips (1 cup)
1 tub Betty Crocker Rich & Creamy coconut pecan ready-to-spread frosting
1/4 cup milk

Heat oven to 350°. Lightly grease rectangular pan, 13×9×2 inches. Cut butter into cake mix (dry) in medium bowl, using pastry blender or crisscrossing 2 knives, until crumbly. Press half of the mixture (2 1/2 cups) in bottom of pan. Bake 10 minutes.

Sprinkle chocolate chips over baked layer; drop frosting by tablespoonfuls over chocolate chips. Stir milk into remaining cake mixture. Drop by teaspoonfuls onto frosting layer.

Bake 25 to 30 minutes or until cake portion is slightly dry to touch. Cool completely. Cover and refrigerate until firm. Cut into 8 rows by 6 rows. Store covered in refrigerator.

1 Bar: Calories 135 (Calories from Fat 70); Fat 8g (Saturated 5g); Cholesterol 15mg; Sodium 120mg; Carbohydrate 15g (Dietary Fiber 0g); Protein 1g.

German Chocolate Bars

Chocolate Chip–Pecan Bars

BAKE: 26 to 29 min per pan • YIELD: 32 bars

Cookie Tips

A pastry blender is a very efficient, easy-to-use tool to have on hand. It blends butter or shortening into dry ingredients without much effort. Pastry blenders are inexpensive and can be found in the cooking and baking utensil section of most discount stores.

"I Don't Have That"

Golden Vanilla- or yellow-flavored mix can be substituted for the French vanilla.

1 package Betty Crocker SuperMoist French vanilla cake mix
1/2 cup butter or margarine, softened
2 cups pecan halves
2/3 cup butter or margarine
2/3 cup packed brown sugar
1 package (6 ounces) semisweet chocolate chips (1 cup)

Heat oven to 350°. Mix cake mix (dry) and 1/2 cup butter in medium bowl, using pastry blender or crisscrossing 2 knives, until crumbly. Press firmly in bottom of ungreased rectangular pan, 13×9×2 inches. Bake 13 to 14 minutes or until light brown.

Sprinkle pecan halves evenly over baked layer. Heat 2/3 cup butter and the brown sugar to boiling in 2-quart saucepan over medium heat, stirring occasionally; boil and stir 1 minute. Spoon mixture evenly over pecans.

Bake about 13 to 15 minutes or until bubbly and light brown. Sprinkle chocolate chips over warm bars; cool. Cut into 8 rows by 4 rows.

1 Bar: Calories 220 (Calories from Fat 125); Fat 14g (Saturated 6g); Cholesterol 20mg; Sodium 160mg; Carbohydrate 22g (Dietary Fiber 1g); Protein 2g.

Caramel Fudge Bars

BAKE: 35 to 40 min per pan ● YIELD: 24 bars

1 package Betty Crocker Original Supreme brownie mix (with Chocolate Syrup Pouch)

1/4 cup milk

1 teaspoon vanilla

1 egg

1/2 package (14-ounce size) vanilla caramels (25 caramels)

1 can (14 ounces) sweetened condensed milk

Heat oven to 350°. Grease bottom only of rectangular pan, $13 \times 9 \times 2$ inches. Mix brownie mix (dry); do not add chocolate syrup from pouch, milk, vanilla and egg with spoon; reserve 1 cup. Press remaining brownie mixture in bottom of pan. Bake 10 minutes.

Heat caramels and chocolate syrup from pouch in 2-quart saucepan over medium-low heat, stirring occasionally, until caramels are melted. Stir in milk. Pour over baked layer. Break up reserved brownie mixture; sprinkle over caramel.

Bake 25 to 30 minutes or until bubbly around edges. Cool completely; refrigerate for easier cutting. Cut into 4 rows by 6 rows. Store tightly covered and, if desired, in refrigerator.

1 Bar: Calories 185 (Calories from Fat 25); Fat 3g (Saturated 2g); Cholesterol 15mg; Sodium 120mg; Carbohydrate 36g (Dietary Fiber 0g); Protein 3g.

Cookie Tips

These bars are more like a candy, and if you like "ooey-gooey" sweets, you'll love these. Make sure to keep them stored in the refrigerator so they don't get too soft.

Make It Your Way

Make **Chocolate–Caramel Fudge Bars** by substituting chocolate-flavored sweetened condensed milk for regular.

Almond Bars

BAKE: 22 to 28 min per pan • YIELD: 32 bars

1 package Betty Crocker SuperMoist white cake mix
1/2 cup butter or margarine, softened
2 eggs
Almond Topping (below)

Heat oven to 350°. Beat cake mix (dry), butter and eggs with electric mixer on low speed until dough forms or mix with a spoon. Press in bottom of ungreased jelly roll pan, 15 1/2 × 10 1/2 × 1 inch. Bake 20 to 25 minutes or until golden brown and crust begins to pull away from sides of pan or until toothpick inserted in center comes out clean.

Immediately spread Almond Topping over crust. Set oven control to broil. Place pan on middle rack in oven. Broil 2 to 3 minutes or until Almond Topping is golden brown and bubbly (watch carefully—Almond Topping burns easily). Cool completely. Cut into 8 rows by 4 rows.

Almond Topping

2/3 cup sliced almonds
2/3 cup butter or margarine
1/2 cup sugar
1 tablespoon plus 1 teaspoon all-purpose flour
1 tablespoon milk

Cook all ingredients in 2-quart saucepan over low heat, stirring constantly, until sugar is dissolved and mixture thickens slightly.

1 Bar: Calories 150 (Calories from Fat 80); Fat 9g (Saturated 2g); Cholesterol 10mg; Sodium 180mg; Carbohydrate 16g (Dietary Fiber 0g); Protein 1g.

Almond Bars, Apricot Cherry Bars (page 157)

Peanut Butter–Toffee Bars

BAKE: 20 to 25 min per pan ● YIELD: 60 bars

Cookie Tips

Almond toffee bits can become rancid, so be sure to do a "taste-test" before adding them to your recipe. Store toffee bits in the freezer to prevent them from becoming rancid.

There's a handy little tool called an offset spatula or spreader. The "spreader" part has a bend in it, making it very easy to frost bars in pans. This little gem is inexpensive and can be found in large department stores or specialty cookware stores.

1 package Betty Crocker SuperMoist yellow cake mix

1 cup crunchy peanut butter

1/2 cup water

2 eggs

1 package (10 ounces) almond toffee bits or milk chocolate toffee bits (1 3/4 cups)

1 package (12 ounces) semisweet chocolate chips (2 cups)

Heat oven to 350°. Grease and flour jelly roll pan, 15 1/2 × 10 1/2 × 1 inch. Mix cake mix (dry), peanut butter, water and eggs in large bowl with spoon. Stir in toffee bits. Spread evenly in pan.

Bake 20 to 25 minutes or until golden brown. Immediately sprinkle chocolate chips over hot bars. Let stand about 5 minutes or until chips are melted; spread evenly. Cool completely. Cut into 10 rows by 6 rows.

1 Bar: Calories 130 (Calories from Fat 65); Fat 7g (Saturated 3g); Cholesterol 10mg; Sodium 105mg; Carbohydrate 15g (Dietary Fiber 0g); Protein 2g.

Apricot-Cherry Bars

BAKE: 22 to 27 min per pan ● YIELD: 30 bars

1 package Betty Crocker SuperMoist yellow cake mix

1/4 cup water

1/4 cup butter or margarine, softened

1/4 cup packed brown sugar

2 eggs

1 cup cut-up dried apricots

1/2 cup drained chopped maraschino cherries

Powdered sugar

Heat oven to 375°. Grease and flour jelly roll pan, 15 1/2 × 10 1/2 × 1 inch. Beat half of the cake mix (dry), the water, butter, brown sugar and eggs in large bowl with electric mixer on medium speed until smooth, or mix with spoon. Stir in remaining cake mix, the apricots and cherries. Spread evenly in pan.

Bake 22 to 27 minutes or until toothpick inserted in center comes out clean. Cool completely. Sprinkle with powdered sugar. Cut into 6 rows by 5 rows.

1 Bar: Calories 120 (Calories from Fat 35); Fat 4g (Saturated 1g); Cholesterol 15mg; Sodium 140mg; Carbohydrate 20g (Dietary Fiber 0g); Protein 1g.

Cookie Tips

Use a kitchen scissors to quickly cut up dried apricots.

Make It Your Way

If you'd like, drizzle these bars with Cherry Glaze instead of sprinkling them with powdered sugar. To make the glaze, use this easy recipe: Mix together 1 cup powdered sugar and 6 tablespoons maraschino juice until smooth. Drizzle over cooled bars.

Carrot-Raisin Bars

BAKE: 15 to 20 min per pan ● YIELD: 48 bars

Make It Your Way

If you love coconut, you'll love our **Carrot-Raisin Coconut Bars**. Stir in 1 cup coconut with the raisins and nuts.

Using orange juice instead of the water gives these bars a nice flavor boost.

1 package Betty Crocker SuperMoist carrot cake mix

1/2 cup vegetable oil

1/4 cup water

2 eggs

3/4 cup raisins

1/2 cup chopped nuts

1 tub Betty Crocker Rich & Creamy cream cheese ready-to-spread frosting

Heat oven to 350°. Grease and flour jelly roll pan, 15 1/2 × 10 1/2 × 1 inch. Mix cake mix (dry), oil, water and eggs in large bowl with spoon. Stir in raisins and nuts. Spread evenly in pan.

Bake 15 to 20 minutes or until bars spring back when touched lightly in center. Cool completely. Frost with frosting. Cut into 8 rows by 6 rows.

1 Bar: Calories 120 (Calories from Fat 55); Fat 6g (Saturated 1g); Cholesterol 10mg; Sodium 90mg; Carbohydrate 16g (Dietary Fiber 0g); Protein 1g.

Triple Chocolate-Cherry Bars

BAKE: 28 to 38 min per pan ● YIELD: 48 bars

Make It Your Way

Make **Triple Chocolate-Strawberry Bars** by using strawberry pie filling instead of the cherry.

1 package Betty Crocker SuperMoist chocolate fudge cake mix

1 can (21 ounces) cherry pie filling

2 eggs, beaten

1 cup miniature semisweet chocolate chips

1 tub Betty Crocker Whipped chocolate ready-to-spread frosting

Heat oven to 350°. Spray jelly roll pan, 15 1/2 × 10 1/2 × 1 inch, with cooking spray. Mix cake mix (dry), pie filling, eggs and chocolate chips in large bowl with spoon. Pour into pan.

Bake 28 to 38 minutes or until toothpick inserted in center comes out clean. Cool completely. Frost with frosting. Cut into 8 rows by 6 rows.

1 Bar: Calories 125 (Calories from Fat 35); Fat 4g (Saturated 3g); Cholesterol 10mg; Sodium 100mg; Carbohydrate 22g (Dietary Fiber 1g); Protein 1g.

Peanut Butter and Jelly Bars

BAKE: 25 to 30 min per pan   •   YIELD: 32 bars

1 package Betty Crocker SuperMoist French vanilla cake mix

1/2 cup butter or margarine, softened

1 egg

1 jar (12 ounces) strawberry jelly (about 1 cup)

1 package (10 ounces) peanut butter chips

Heat oven to 375°. Grease rectangular pan, 13×9×2 inches. Mix cake mix (dry), butter and egg in large bowl with spoon (mixture will be stiff). Press evenly in pan, flouring fingers if necessary.

Microwave jelly in microwavable bowl uncovered on Medium (50%) 1 minute. Spread evenly over mixture in pan to within 1/2 inch of edges. Sprinkle peanut butter chips over jelly.

Bake 25 to 30 minutes or until golden brown around edges. Cool completely. Cut into 8 rows by 4 rows. For easier cutting, use sharp or wet knife.

1 Bar: Calories 170 (Calories from Fat 65); Fat 7g (Saturated 3g); Cholesterol 5mg; Sodium 150mg; Carbohydrate 26g (Dietary Fiber 0g); Protein 1g.

Cookie Tips

Shake out the brown bag blues! Your kids will smile at lunchtime when you include 1 or 2 of these yummy bars in their lunch bag.

"I Don't Have That"

Any flavor of jam, jelly or preserves can be used in this recipe.

Easy-Yet-Elegant Raspberry Bars

BAKE: 28 to 30 min per pan ● CHILL: 1 hr 15 min ● YIELD: 18 bars

1 package (1 pound 3.8 ounces) Betty Crocker fudge brownie mix

1 package (8 ounces) cream cheese, softened

1/2 cup powdered sugar

1/2 cup raspberry preserves

1 ounce unsweetened baking chocolate

1 tablespoon butter or margarine

Heat oven to 350°. Prepare and bake brownie mix as directed on package for fudgelike brownies in rectangular pan, 13×9×2 inches. Cool completely.

Beat cream cheese, powdered sugar and preserves in small bowl with electric mixer on medium speed until smooth. Spread over brownies. Refrigerate 15 minutes.

Microwave chocolate and butter in small microwavable bowl on Medium (50%) about 1 minute or until mixture can be stirred smooth. Drizzle over brownies. Refrigerate about 1 hour or until chocolate is firm. Cut into 6 rows by 3 rows. Store covered in refrigerator.

1 Bar: Calories 220 (Calories from Fat 70); Fat 8g (Saturated 4g); Cholesterol 15mg; Sodium 160mg; Carbohydrate 35g (Dietary Fiber 0g); Protein 2g.

Lemon Bars

BAKE: 34 to 36 min per pan ● YIELD: 30 bars

1 package Betty Crocker SuperMoist lemon cake mix

1/3 cup butter or margarine, softened

3 eggs

1 cup granulated sugar

1/2 teaspoon baking powder

1/4 teaspoon salt

2 teaspoons grated lemon peel

1/4 cup lemon juice

Powdered sugar, if desired

Heat oven to 350°. Mix cake mix (dry), butter and 1 of the eggs with spoon until crumbly; reserve 1 cup. Press remaining crumbly mixture lightly in bottom of ungreased rectangular pan, 13×9×2 inches. Bake about 17 minutes or until light brown.

Beat remaining 2 eggs, the granulated sugar, baking powder, salt, lemon peel and lemon juice with hand beater until light and foamy. Pour over hot baked layer. Sprinkle with reserved crumbly mixture.

Bake 17 to 19 minutes or until light brown and set. Sprinkle with powdered sugar; cool. Cut into 6 rows by 5 rows.

1 Bar: Calories 125 (Calories from Fat 35); Fat 4g (Saturated 1g); Cholesterol 20mg; Sodium 180mg; Carbohydrate 21g (Dietary Fiber 0g); Protein 1g.

Cookie Tips

Only grate the yellow portion of the lemon; the white portion, or pith, is very bitter.

Make It Your Way

For a bright lemon color, add 4 to 6 drops of yellow food coloring with the eggs and sugar mixture.

Luscious Lemon-Raspberry Bars

BAKE: 49 to 54 min per pan ● YIELD: 16 bars

Cookie Tips

Soften cream cheese quickly in the microwave. Remove the foil wrapper and place on waxed paper or microwave-safe plate, uncovered. Microwave on Medium (50%) 30 to 45 seconds for 3 ounces and 1 to 1 1/2 minutes for 8 ounces.

Jams, jellies and preserves are easier to spread if you stir them vigorously first.

1 package Betty Crocker Sunkist® lemon bar mix
1/2 package (8-ounce size) cream cheese, softened
1/4 cup raspberry preserves
Powdered sugar

Heat oven to 350°. Prepare filling and crust as directed in steps 1 and 2 of bar mix—except bake crust 12 minutes.

Drop cream cheese by spoonfuls onto hot crust and return pan to oven about 2 minutes to further soften cream cheese. Carefully spread cream cheese over crust. Stir filling mixture; pour over cream cheese.

Bake 35 to 40 minutes or until top begins to brown and center is set. Cool 10 minutes. Spread preserves over top. Cool completely. Sprinkle with powdered sugar. Cut into 4 rows by 4 rows. For easier cutting, use sharp or wet knife. Store covered in refrigerator.

1 Bar: Calories 170 (Calories from Fat 55); Fat 6g (Saturated 2g); Cholesterol 10mg; Sodium 105mg; Carbohydrate 28g (Dietary Fiber 0g); Protein 1g.

Luscious Lemon-Raspberry Bars

Chocolate-Raspberry Cheesecake Bars

BAKE: 48 min per pan ● CHILL: 2 hr ● YIELD: 24 bars

Cookie Tips

Cheesecakes are baked at low temperatures to prevent excess shrinkage. They are more easily cut when a wet knife is used, cleaning it after each cut.

Make It Your Way

Chocolate lover's will love this variation! To make **Chocolate-Chip Raspberry Cheesecake Dessert**, stir in 1 cup miniature semisweet chocolate chips into the filling mixture after the eggs have been added. Continue as directed.

1 package Betty Crocker SuperMoist chocolate fudge cake mix

1/2 cup butter or margarine, softened

2 packages (8 ounces each) cream cheese, softened

1 container (6 ounces) Yoplait® Original red raspberry yogurt (2/3 cup)

1 tub Betty Crocker Rich & Creamy chocolate ready-to-spread frosting

3 eggs

1 1/2 cups raspberry pie filling or topping

Heat oven to 325°. Lightly grease bottom only of rectangular pan, 13×9×2 inches. Beat cake mix (dry) and butter in large bowl with electric mixer on low speed until crumbly; reserve 1 cup. Press remaining crumbly mixture, using floured fingers, in bottom of pan.

Beat cream cheese, yogurt and frosting in same bowl on medium speed until smooth. Beat in eggs until blended. Pour into pan. Sprinkle with reserved crumbly mixture.

Bake about 48 minutes or until center is set. Refrigerate uncovered at least 2 hours before serving. Cut into 6 rows by 4 rows; serve with a dollop of pie filling. Store leftovers covered in refrigerator.

1 Serving: Calories 315 (Calories from Fat 160); Fat 18g (Saturated 9g); Cholesterol 50mg; Sodium 310mg; Carbohydrate 35g (Dietary Fiber 1g); Protein 4g.

Chocolate-Raspberry Cheesecake Bars, Lemon Cheesecake Bars (page 166)

Lemon Cheesecake Bars

BAKE: 25 min per pan ● YIELD: 48 bars

<table>
<tr><td>

Make It Your Way

To make **Lemon-Blueberry Cheesecake Bars,** stir in 1 cup dried blueberries after beating the 2 eggs into the cream cheese mixture. Continue as directed.

If you'd like a more tart lemon flavor, increase the lemon peel to 1 tablespoon.

</td><td>

1 package Betty Crocker SuperMoist lemon cake mix

1/3 cup butter or margarine, softened

3 eggs

1 package (8 ounces) cream cheese, softened

1 cup powdered sugar

2 teaspoons grated lemon peel

2 tablespoons lemon juice

Heat oven to 350°. Beat cake mix (dry), butter and 1 of the eggs in large bowl with electric mixer on low speed until crumbly. Press in bottom of ungreased rectangular pan, 13×9×2 inches.

Beat cream cheese in medium bowl with electric mixer on medium speed until smooth, or mix with spoon. Gradually beat in powdered sugar on low speed. Stir in lemon peel and lemon juice until smooth. Reserve 1/2 cup; refrigerate.

Beat remaining 2 eggs into remaining cream cheese mixture on medium speed until blended. Spread over cake mixture. Bake about 25 minutes or until set. Cool completely. Spread with reserved cream cheese mixture. Refrigerate until firm. Cut into 8 rows by 6 rows. Store covered in refrigerator.

1 Bar: Calories 85 (Calories from Fat 35); Fat 4g (Saturated 2g); Cholesterol 20mg; Sodium 110mg; Carbohydrate 11g (Dietary Fiber 0g); Protein 1g.

</td></tr>
</table>

Tuxedo Cheesecake Bars

BAKE: 55 to 65 min per pan ● CHILL: 2 hr ● YIELD: 36 bars

1 package Betty Crocker SuperMoist white cake mix

1/2 cup butter or margarine, softened

2 packages (8 ounces each) cream cheese, softened

**1 tub Betty Crocker Rich & Creamy vanilla
ready-to-spread frosting**

3 eggs

3 tablespoons baking cocoa

Heat oven to 325°. Beat cake mix (dry) and butter in large bowl with electric mixer on low speed until crumbly. Press in bottom of ungreased rectangular pan, 13×9×2 inches.

Beat cream cheese and frosting in same bowl on medium speed until smooth. Beat in eggs until blended; reserve 1 cup. Pour remaining mixture over crust. Beat cocoa into reserved mixture. Drop by tablespoonfuls randomly in 8 to 10 mounds onto mixture in pan. Cut through mixture with knife in S-shape curves in one continuous motion without cutting into crust. Turn pan 1/4 turn, and repeat cutting for swirled design.

Bake 55 to 65 minutes or until set. Cool completely. Refrigerate uncovered at least 2 hours. Cut into 6 rows by 6 rows. Store covered in refrigerator.

1 Bar: Calories 190 (Calories from Fat 100); Fat 11g (Saturated 7g); Cholesterol 40mg; Sodium 160mg; Carbohydrate 21g (Dietary Fiber 0g); Protein 2g.

Cookie Tips

To determine if a cheesecake is done, touch the center gently with your finger to see if it's still soft or if it has set (will leave a slight indentation). Don't be tempted to insert a knife in the center because the hole could cause cheesecake to crack.

Cheesecakes that are refrigerated while still hot or warm should not be covered. Why? If covered before they are completely cool, moisture will condense and drip onto the top of the cheesecake, making it quite wet. Cover only after cheesecakes are completely cooled.

CHAPTER 5

Peanut Butter Cookies *170*

The Ultimate Refrigerator Cookies *171*

Maple-Nut Refrigerator Cookies *172*

Chocolate-Peppermint Refrigerator Cookies *174*

Rum-Raisin Sandwich Cookies *176*

No-Roll Sugar Cookies *177*

Chocolate-Orange–Chocolate Chip Cookies *178*

Russian Tea Cakes *179*

Cinnamon Espresso Cookies *180*

Chocolate-Almond Tea Cakes *181*

Butterscotch-Oatmeal Crinkles *182*

Snickerdoodles *183*

Three-Leaf Clovers *184*

Thumbprint Cookies *185*

Almond Bonbons *186*

Peanut Butter Hidden Middles *188*

Honey-Oat Sandwich Cookies *189*

Lemon Decorator Cookies *190*

Meringue-Topped Almond Cookies *192*

Banana-Cornmeal Cookies *193*

Cinnamon Twists *194*

Coconut-Fudge Cups *195*

Ginger Shortbread Wedges *196*

Kringla *196*

No-Bake Apricot Balls *197*

Chocolate-Bourbon Balls *198*

Fig-Filled Whole Wheat Cookies *199*

Pistachio-Chocolate Checkers *200*

Cappuccino-Pistachio Shortbread *202*

Sunflower Cookies *203*

Anise Biscotti *204*

Orange-Almond Biscotti *205*

Hand-Shaped and Pressed Cookies

Cinnamon Espresso Cookie (page 180),
Cappuccino-Pistachio Shortbread (page 202)

Good, ol'-fashioned peanut butter cookies are an enduring favorite. For even more peanut butter flavor, check out our Rich Peanut Butter Chip Cookies variation below or Peanut Butter Hidden Middles (page 188).

Peanut Butter Cookies

BAKE: 9 to 10 min per sheet ● YIELD: About 2 1/2 dozen cookies

Cookie Tips

Either smooth or chunky peanut butter can be used for these cookies. The difference between the two is the amount of processing. Smooth peanut butter is processed until no peanut pieces remain.

Make It Your Way

To make **Rich Peanut Butter Chip Cookies,** omit granulated sugar and use all brown sugar (1 cup) and omit shortening and use all butter (1/2 cup total). After you stir in the flour, baking soda, baking powder and salt, stir in 1 cup peanut butter chips. Shape dough into balls as directed. Dip tops of balls into sugar but do not flatten. Bake as directed.

1/2 cup granulated sugar

1/2 cup packed brown sugar

1/2 cup peanut butter

1/4 cup butter or margarine, softened

1/4 cup shortening

1 egg

1 1/4 cups all-purpose flour

3/4 teaspoon baking soda

1/2 teaspoon baking powder

1/4 teaspoon salt

Granulated sugar

Heat oven to 375°. Beat 1/2 cup granulated sugar, the brown sugar, peanut butter, butter, shortening and egg in large bowl with electric mixer on medium speed, or mix with spoon. Stir in flour, baking soda, baking powder and salt.

Shape dough into 1 1/4-inch balls. Place about 3 inches apart on ungreased cookie sheet. Flatten slightly in crisscross pattern with fork or potato masher dipped into granulated sugar. Bake 9 to 10 minutes or until light brown. Cool 5 minutes; remove from cookie sheet to wire rack.

1 Cookie: Calories 110 (Calories from Fat 55); Fat 6g (Saturated 1g); Cholesterol 5mg; Sodium 100mg; Carbohydrate 12g (Dietary Fiber 0g); Protein 2g.

The Ultimate Refrigerator Cookies

CHILL: 2 hr ● BAKE: 6 to 8 min per sheet ● YIELD: About 6 dozen cookies

1 cup packed brown sugar

1 cup butter or margarine, softened

1 teaspoon vanilla

1 egg

3 cups all-purpose flour

1 1/2 teaspoons ground cinnamon

1/2 teaspoon baking soda

1/2 teaspoon salt

1/3 cup chopped nuts

Beat brown sugar, butter, vanilla and egg in large bowl with electric mixer on medium speed, or mix with spoon. Stir in flour, cinnamon, baking soda and salt. Stir in nuts. Shape dough into rectangle, 10 × 3 inches. Wrap and refrigerate about 2 hours or until firm.

Heat oven to 375°. Cut rectangle into 1/8-inch slices. Place 2 inches apart on ungreased cookie sheet. Bake 6 to 8 minutes or until light brown. Cool slightly; remove from cookie sheet to wire rack.

1 Cookie: Calories 60 (Calories from Fat 25); Fat 3g (Saturated 1g); Cholesterol 5mg; Sodium 55mg; Carbohydrate 7g (Dietary Fiber 0g), Protein 1g

Cookie Tips

If you like thin, crisp cookies, the refrigerator technique is for you. The thinner you slice the dough, the crisper the cookies will be. Watch the cookies carefully while they are in the oven to prevent overbaking.

To intensify the nut flavor in these cookies, toast the nuts before adding to the dough. To toast nuts, bake uncovered in ungreased shallow pan in 350° oven about 10 minutes, stirring occasionally, until golden brown.

Maple-Nut Refrigerator Cookies

CHILL: 2 hr ● BAKE: 8 to 10 min per sheet ● YIELD: About 4 dozen cookies

Cookie Tips

When you don't have time to bake all the cookies, wrap the dough tightly and refrigerate up to 3 days or freeze up to 1 month.

Make It Your Way

Prepare Creamy Filling (page 218) but replace vanilla with 1/4 teaspoon maple extract. Make **Maple-Nut Sandwich Cookies** by putting cookies together in pairs with about 1 teaspoon filling each.

3/4 cup packed brown sugar

3/4 cup butter or margarine, softened

1/4 teaspoon maple extract

1 1/2 cups all-purpose flour

1 teaspoon baking powder

1/4 teaspoon salt

1 cup chopped pecans

Beat brown sugar, butter and maple extract in large bowl with electric mixer on medium speed, or mix with spoon. Stir in flour, baking powder and salt. Stir in pecans. Shape into roll, 12 inches long. Wrap and refrigerate about 2 hours or until firm.

Heat oven to 375°. Cut roll into 1/4-inch slices. Place 2 inches apart on ungreased cookie sheet. Bake 8 to 10 minutes or until edges are golden brown. Remove from cookie sheet to wire rack.

1 Cookie: Calories 75 (Calories from Fat 45); Fat 5g (Saturated 1g); Cholesterol 0mg; Sodium 55mg; Carbohydrate 7g (Dietary Fiber 0g); Protein 1g.

Maple-Nut Refrigerator Cookie

Chocolate-Peppermint Refrigerator Cookies

CHILL: 2 hr ● BAKE: 8 to 10 min per sheet ● YIELD: About 4 dozen cookies

Cookie Tips

Each time you slice a cookie, roll the roll a quarter turn to prevent flattening on one side.

Make It Your Way

To make **Chocolate-Wintergreen Refrigerator Cookies**, omit peppermint candies. Stir 1/4 cup chocolate shot, 1/4 teaspoon wintergreen extract and 4 drops green food color into plain dough. Continue as directed.

1 1/2 cups powdered sugar

1 cup butter or margarine, softened

1 egg

2 2/3 cups all-purpose flour

1/4 teaspoon salt

1/4 cup baking cocoa

1 tablespoon milk

1/4 cup finely crushed hard peppermint candy

Beat powdered sugar, butter and egg in large bowl with electric mixer on medium speed, or mix with spoon. Stir in flour and salt. Divide dough in half. Stir cocoa and milk into one half and peppermint candy into other half.

Roll or pat chocolate dough into rectangle, 12 × 6 1/2 inches, on waxed paper. Shape peppermint dough into roll, 12 inches long; place on chocolate dough. Wrap chocolate dough around peppermint dough, using waxed paper to help lift. Press edges together. Wrap and refrigerate about 2 hours or until firm.

Heat oven to 375°. Cut roll into 1/4-inch slices. Place about 1 inch apart on ungreased cookie sheet. Bake 8 to 10 minutes or until set. Remove from cookie sheet to wire rack.

1 Cookie: Calories 80 (Calories from Fat 35); Fat 4g (Saturated 1g); Cholesterol 5mg; Sodium 60mg; Carbohydrate 10g (Dietary Fiber 0g); Protein 1g.

Chocolate-Peppermint Refrigerator Cookies,
The Ultimate Refrigerator Cookie (page 171)

Rum-Raisin Sandwich Cookies

CHILL: 2 hr ● BAKE: 7 to 9 min per sheet ● YIELD: About 3 dozen cookies

1 cup powdered sugar

1 cup butter or margarine, softened

1 egg

2 1/4 cups all-purpose flour

1/4 teaspoon cream of tartar

1 cup raisins, finely chopped

Rum Frosting (below)

Beat powdered sugar, butter and egg in large bowl with electric mixer on medium speed, or mix with spoon. Stir in flour and cream of tartar. Stir in raisins. Divide dough in half. Shape each half into roll, 10 inches long. Wrap and refrigerate about 2 hours or until firm.

Heat oven to 375°. Cut rolls into 1/4-inch slices. Place about 1 inch apart on ungreased cookie sheet. Bake 7 to 9 minutes or until set. Remove from cookie sheet to wire rack. Cool completely. Spread about 1 teaspoon Rum Frosting between bottoms of pairs of cookies.

Rum Frosting

2 cups powdered sugar

1/4 cup butter or margarine, softened

1/4 teaspoon rum extract

2 tablespoons milk

Mix all ingredients until smooth and spreadable.

1 Cookie: Calories 145 (Calories from Fat 65); Fat 7g (Saturated 1g); Cholesterol 5mg; Sodium 75mg; Carbohydrate 19g (Dietary Fiber 0g); Protein 1g.

No-Roll Sugar Cookies

CHILL: 2 hr ● BAKE: 6 to 8 min per sheet ● YIELD: About 9 1/2 dozen cookies

1 cup granulated sugar

1 cup powdered sugar

1 cup butter or margarine, softened

1 cup vegetable oil

2 teaspoons vanilla

3 1/2 cups all-purpose flour

3/4 cup cornstarch

1 teaspoon baking soda

1 teaspoon cream of tartar

1/2 teaspoon salt

Granulated sugar

Beat sugars, butter, oil and vanilla in large bowl with electric mixer on medium speed, or mix with spoon. Stir in remaining ingredients except granulated sugar. Cover and refrigerate about 2 hours or until firm.

Heat oven to 375°. Shape dough into 1-inch balls. Place about 2 inches apart on ungreased cookie sheet. Press bottom of glass into dough to grease, then dip into granulated sugar; press on shaped dough until about 1/4 inch thick. Bake 6 to 8 minutes or until set but not brown. Immediately remove from cookie sheet to wire rack.

1 Cookie: Calories 70 (Calories from Fat 35); Fat 4g (Saturated 2g); Cholesterol 5mg; Sodium 30mg; Carbohydrate 9g (Dietary Fiber 0g); Protein 0g.

Cookie Tips

The powdered sugar and cornstarch in these cookies produce a very delicate, tender, melt-in-your mouth cookie.

Make It Your Way

To make **Brown Sugar Maple No-Roll Sugar Cookies,** substitute 1 cup packed brown sugar for the 1 cup granulated sugar and substitute 2 teaspoons maple extract for the 2 teaspoons vanilla.

Chocolate-Orange–Chocolate Chip Cookies

BAKE: 9 to 11 minutes per sheet • YIELD: About 2 1/2 dozen cookies

Cookie Tips

One medium orange will give you the 1 to 2 tablespoons of grated peel you'll need for this recipe.

1 cup sugar

2/3 cup butter or margarine, softened

1 tablespoon grated orange peel

1 egg

1 1/2 cups all-purpose flour

1/3 cup baking cocoa

1/4 teaspoon salt

1/4 teaspoon baking powder

1/4 teaspoon baking soda

1 cup chopped pecans

1 package (6 ounces) semisweet chocolate morsels (1 cup)

1/3 cup sugar

1 teaspoon grated orange peel

Heat oven to 350°. Beat 1 cup sugar, butter, 1 tablespoon grated orange peel and the egg in large bowl with electric mixer on medium speed, or mix with spoon. Stir in flour, cocoa, salt, baking powder and baking soda. Stir in pecans and chocolate morsels.

Shape dough into 1 1/2-inch balls. Mix 1/3 cup sugar and 1 teaspoon grated orange peel. Roll balls in sugar mixture. Place about 3 inches apart on ungreased cookie sheet. Flatten to about 1/2-inch thickness with bottom of glass. Bake 9 to 11 minutes or until set. Cool slightly; remove from cookie sheet. Cool on wire rack.

1 Cookie: Calories 160 (Calories from Fat 80); Fat 9g (Saturated 2g); Cholesterol 10mg; Sodium 80mg; Carbohydrate 19g (Dietary Fiber 1g); Protein 1g.

Russian Tea Cakes

BAKE: 8 to 9 min per sheet ● YIELD: About 4 dozen cookies

1 cup butter or margarine, softened

1/2 cup powdered sugar

1 teaspoon vanilla

2 1/4 cups all-purpose flour

1/4 teaspoon salt

3/4 cup finely chopped nuts

Powdered sugar

Heat oven to 400°. Beat butter, 1/2 cup powdered sugar and the vanilla in large bowl with electric mixer on medium speed, or mix with spoon. Stir in flour and salt. Stir in nuts.

Shape dough into 1-inch balls. Place about 2 inches apart on ungreased cookie sheet. Bake 8 to 9 minutes or until set but not brown. Immediately remove from cookie sheet; roll in powdered sugar. Cool completely on wire rack. Roll in powdered sugar again.

1 Cookie: Calories 75 (Calories from Fat 45); Fat 5g (Saturated 1g); Cholesterol 0mg; Sodium 55mg; Carbohydrate 7g (Dietary Fiber 0g); Protein 1g.

Cookie Tips

These rich little cookies are extra special when made with macadamia nuts.

Make It Your Way

Toasted Coconut Tea Cakes are a special treat for coconut lovers. Omit nuts and place 3/4 cup coconut in an ungreased shallow pan. Bake uncovered at 350° for 5 to 7 minutes, stirring occasionally, until golden brown. Allow coconut to cool before adding to dough.

Cinnamon Espresso Cookies

CHILL: 1 hr ● BAKE: 8 to 10 min per sheet ● YIELD: About 4 1/2 dozen cookies

Cookie Tips

While the dough chills, take advantage of the extra time. You can run a few errands, get some laundry done, balance your checkbook, write a few letters or just hang out.

"I Don't Have That"

Any instant coffee (crystals or granules) will work in place of instant espresso, giving you a milder coffee flavor.

1 1/2 tablespoons instant espresso coffee (dry)

1 tablespoon hot water

1/2 cup butter or margarine, softened

1/4 cup shortening

1 cup granulated sugar

1/2 cup packed brown sugar

1 egg

2 cups all-purpose flour

1 teaspoon baking powder

1 teaspoon instant espresso coffee (dry)

1 teaspoon ground cinnamon

1/4 teaspoon salt

Espresso Coating (below)

Dissolve 1 1/2 tablespoons espresso in hot water in large bowl. Add butter, shortening, sugars and egg. Beat with electric mixer on medium speed until fluffy. Beat in flour, baking powder, 1 teaspoon espresso, cinnamon and salt on low speed.

Divide dough in half. Shape each half into roll, 10 inches long. Wrap each roll with plastic wrap and refrigerate 30 minutes. Prepare Espresso Coating. Roll each roll of dough in coating (reserve any remaining coating). Rewrap in plastic wrap and refrigerate at least 30 minutes longer.

Heat oven to 375°. Cut each roll into 3/8-inch slices. Place about 2 inches apart on ungreased cookie sheet. Sprinkle with remaining coating. Bake 8 to 10 minutes or until edges are light brown. Cool slightly; remove from cookie sheet to wire rack.

Espresso Coating

1/2 cup granulated sugar

2 teaspoons instant espresso coffee (dry)

Mix ingredients on a large plate or piece of waxed paper.

1 Cookie: Calories 75 (Calories from Fat 25); Fat 3g (Saturated 1g); Cholesterol 5mg; Sodium 40mg; Carbohydrate 11g (Dietary Fiber 0g); Protein 1g.

Chocolate-Almond Tea Cakes

BAKE: 12 to 15 min per sheet ● YIELD: About 3 1/2 dozen cookies

3/4 cup butter or margarine, softened

1/3 cup powdered sugar

1 1/4 cups all-purpose flour

1/2 cup hot cocoa mix (dry)

1/2 cup chopped slivered almonds, toasted (page 64)

Powdered sugar

Heat oven to 325°. Beat butter and 1/3 cup powdered sugar in medium bowl with electric mixer on medium speed, or mix with spoon. Stir in flour, cocoa mix and almonds. (If dough is soft, cover and refrigerate until firm enough to shape.)

Shape dough into 1-inch balls. Place about 2 inches apart on ungreased cookie sheet. Bake 12 to 15 minutes or until set. Dip tops into powdered sugar while warm. Cool completely on wire rack. Dip tops into powdered sugar again.

1 Cookie: Calories 60 (Calories from Fat 35); Fat 4g (Saturated 1g); Cholesterol 0mg; Sodium 45mg; Carbohydrate 7g (Dietary Fiber 0g); Protein 1g.

Cookie Tips

Any of the flavored hot cocoa mixes will do the trick in these tasty little morsels.

These cookies are dipped twice into the powdered sugar because the sugar from the first dip gets absorbed into the cookie.

Butterscotch-Oatmeal Crinkles

BAKE: 10 to 12 min per sheet ● YIELD: About 5 dozen cookies

Cookie Tips

You can use either light brown or dark brown sugar in your recipes. The larger amount of molasses gives dark brown sugar its darker color and stronger flavor.

If your want to add a crunchy texture to these oatmeal cookies, lightly toast the oatmeal before adding it to the other ingredients (see page viii for directions).

2 cups packed brown sugar

1/2 cup butter or margarine, softened

1/2 cup shortening

1 teaspoon vanilla

2 eggs

2 1/4 cups all-purpose flour

2 cups old-fashioned or quick-cooking oats

1 1/2 teaspoons baking powder

1/2 teaspoon salt

1/2 cup granulated or powdered sugar

Heat oven to 350°. Grease cookie sheet. Beat brown sugar, butter, shortening, vanilla and eggs in large bowl with electric mixer on medium speed, or mix with spoon. Stir in flour, oats, baking powder and salt.

Shape dough into 1-inch balls; roll in granulated sugar. Place about 2 inches apart on cookie sheet. Bake 10 to 12 minutes or until almost no indentation remains when touched lightly in center. Immediately remove from cookie sheet to wire rack.

1 Cookie: Calories 95 (Calories from Fat 35); Fat 4g (Saturated 1g); Cholesterol 5mg; Sodium 55mg; Carbohydrate 14g (Dietary Fiber 0g); Protein 1g.

Snickerdoodles

BAKE: 10 min per sheet ● YIELD: About 4 dozen cookies

1/4 cup sugar

1 tablespoon ground cinnamon

1 1/2 cups sugar

1/2 cup shortening

1/2 cup butter or margarine, softened

2 eggs

2 3/4 cups all-purpose flour

2 teaspoons cream of tartar

1 teaspoon baking soda

1/4 teaspoon salt

Heat oven to 400°. Mix 1/4 cup sugar and the cinnamon; set aside. Beat 1 1/2 cups sugar, the shortening, butter and eggs in large bowl with electric mixer on medium speed, or mix with spoon. Stir in flour, cream of tartar, baking soda and salt.

Shape dough into 1 1/4-inch balls. Roll in sugar-cinnamon mixture. Place about 2 inches apart on ungreased cookie sheet. Bake about 10 minutes or until centers are almost set. Remove from cookie sheet to wire rack.

1 Cookie: Calories 90 (Calories from Fat 35); Fat 4g (Saturated 1g); Cholesterol 10mg; Sodium 65mg; Carbohydrate 13g (Dietary Fiber 0g); Protein 1g.

Cookie Tips

Long ago, little cookies that could be made quickly were given the nonsense name, *Snickerdoodles.*

"I Don't Have That"

If your cinnamon container is empty, substitute 1 tablespoon apple pie spice.

Three-Leaf Clovers

BAKE: 10 to 12 min per sheet ● YIELD: About 2 dozen cookies

Cookie Tips

Just mixing these cookies is a pleasure! The delicious aroma of cloves is perfect on an autumn afternoon. Serve cookies with a cup of tea.

Cloves

Cloves are the aromatic dried unopened buds of the clove tree. The flavor is powerful and spicy.

1 cup butter or margarine, softened

1/3 cup sugar

2 tablespoons honey

1 egg

2 1/3 cups all-purpose flour

1/2 teaspoon ground cloves

2 tablespoons sugar

1/4 teaspoon ground cloves

Heat oven to 350°. Mix butter, 1/3 cup sugar, the honey and egg in large bowl with spoon. Stir in flour and 1/2 teaspoon cloves.

Shape dough into 3/4-inch balls. For each cookie, arrange 3 balls of dough together to form a triangle about 2 inches apart on ungreased cookie sheet. Mix 2 tablespoons sugar and 1/4 teaspoon cloves. Press bottom of glass into dough to grease, then dip into sugar-clove mixture; press on triangles until 1/4 inch thick. Bake 10 to 12 minutes or until edges are light brown. Remove from cookie sheet to wire rack.

1 Cookie: Calories 140 (Calories from Fat 70); Fat 8g (Saturated 2g); Cholesterol 10mg; Sodium 90mg; Carbohydrate 15g (Dietary Fiber 0g); Protein 2g.

Thumbprint Cookies

BAKE: 10 min per sheet ● YIELD: About 2 1/2 dozen cookies

1/4 cup packed brown sugar

1/4 cup butter or margarine, softened

1/4 cup shortening

1/2 teaspoon vanilla

1 egg yolk

1 cup all-purpose flour

1/4 teaspoon salt

1 egg white

1 cup finely chopped nuts

About 5 tablespoons jam or jelly (any flavor)

Heat oven to 350°. Beat brown sugar, butter, shortening, vanilla and egg yolk in large bowl with electric mixer on medium speed, or mix with spoon . Stir in flour and salt.

Shape dough into 1-inch balls. Beat egg white slightly with fork. Dip each ball into egg white; roll in nuts. Place about 1 inch apart on ungreased cookie sheet. Press thumb into center of each cookie to make indentation. Bake about 10 minutes or until light brown. Quickly remake indentations with end of wooden spoon if necessary. Remove cookies from cookie sheet to wire rack. Fill thumbprints with about 1/2 measuring teaspoon jam.

1 Cookie: Calories 95 (Calories from Fat 55); Fat 6g (Saturated 1g); Cholesterol 5mg; Sodium 45mg; Carbohydrate 9g (Dietary Fiber 0g); Protein 1g.

Cookie Tips

These cookies were often called "Thimble Cookies" in older cookbooks because a thimble was used to make the indentation. Besides jam, other ideas for fillings are gumdrops, frosting, caramel fudge ice-cream topping or baking chips.

You'll be done in a flash if you use a food processor to finely chop nuts.

Almond Bonbons

BAKE: 10 to 12 min per sheet • YIELD: About 3 dozen cookies

Try wrapping the dough around candied cherries, dried apricots or malted milk balls instead of the almond paste. Tint the glaze for a more festive look and decorate as desired.

To make a really attractive serving tray or for gifts, pack small cookies in mini paper cupcake liners or fluted bonbon cups.

1 1/2 cups all-purpose flour

1/2 cup butter or margarine, softened

1/3 cup powdered sugar

2 tablespoons milk

1/2 teaspoon vanilla

1/2 package (7- or 8-ounce size) almond paste

Almond Glaze (below)

Sliced almonds, toasted, if desired (page 64)

Heat oven to 375°. Beat flour, butter, powdered sugar, milk and vanilla in large bowl with electric mixer on medium speed, or mix with spoon. Cut almond paste into 1/2-inch slices; cut each slice into fourths.

Shape 1-inch ball of dough around each piece of almond paste. Gently roll to form ball. Place about 1 inch apart on ungreased cookie sheet. Bake 10 to 12 minutes or until set and bottom is golden brown. Remove from cookie sheet to wire rack. Cool completely. Dip tops of cookies into Almond Glaze. Garnish with sliced almonds.

Almond Glaze

1 cup powdered sugar

1/2 teaspoon almond extract

4 to 5 teaspoons milk

Mix all ingredients until smooth and spreadable.

1 Cookie: Calories 70 (Calories from Fat 25); Fat 3g (Saturated 1g); Cholesterol 0mg; Sodium 30mg; Carbohydrate 10g (Dietary Fiber 0g); Protein 1g.

Almond Bonbons

Peanut Butter Hidden Middles

BAKE: 7 to 9 min per sheet • YIELD: About 3 dozen cookies

1 pouch (1 pound 1.5 ounces) Betty Crocker peanut butter cookie mix

1/3 cup vegetable oil

1 egg

36 miniature marshmallows

12 one-inch chocolate-covered peanut butter cup candies

12 chocolate-covered peanut-buttery candy balls (about 1/2 inch in diameter)

Sugar

Heat oven to 375°. Empty cookie mix into large bowl. Break up lumps in mix with spoon. Stir in oil and egg until soft dough forms.

Divide dough into thirds. Shape one-third dough by tablespoonfuls around 3 miniature marshmallows. Shape one-third dough by tablespoonfuls around 1 peanut butter cup. Shape one-third dough by tablespoonfuls around 1 candy ball. Roll each ball in sugar. Place about 2 inches apart on ungreased cookie sheet. Bake 7 to 9 minutes or until light golden brown. Cool 1 to 2 minutes; remove from cookie sheet to wire rack.

1 Cookie: Calories 115 (Calories from Fat 45); Fat 5g (Saturated 2g); Cholesterol 5mg; Sodium 75mg; Carbohydrate 17g (Dietary Fiber 0g); Protein 1g.

Honey-Oat Sandwich Cookies

BAKE: 8 to 10 min per sheet ● YIELD: About 3 dozen cookies

1 cup packed brown sugar

1/2 cup butter or margarine, softened

1/2 cup shortening

1/3 cup honey

2 eggs

1 teaspoon vanilla

1 1/2 cups all-purpose flour

1 1/2 cups quick-cooking or old-fashioned oats

2 teaspoons baking soda

Granulated sugar

About 1 cup thick fruit preserves (any flavor)

Heat oven to 350°. Beat brown sugar, butter, shortening, honey, eggs and vanilla in large bowl with electric mixer on medium speed, or mix with spoon. Stir in flour, oats and baking soda.

Shape dough into 1 1/4-inch balls. Place about 2 inches apart on ungreased cookie sheet. Press bottom of glass into dough to grease, then dip into granulated sugar; press on shaped dough to flatten slightly. Bake 8 to 10 minutes or until almost no indentation remains when touched in center. Remove from cookie sheet to wire rack. Cool completely. Spread about 1 1/2 teaspoons jam between bottoms of pairs of cookies.

1 Cookie: Calories 145 (Calories from Fat 55); Fat 6g (Saturated 1g); Cholesterol 10mg; Sodium 110mg; Carbohydrate 21g (Dietary Fiber 0g); Protein 2g.

Cookie Tips

For soft cookies, let the filled cookies stand overnight; for crisp cookies, fill just before serving.

Honey

Honey is the sweet, thick fluid produced by bees from the nectar collected from flowers. Did you know that the flavor of honey varies according to the location and type of flowers the bees feed on?

Lemon Decorator Cookies

CHILL: 2 hr ● BAKE: 7 to 9 min per sheet ● YIELD: About 5 dozen cookies

Cookie Tips

Regular cookie presses will work well with this recipe, but if you want to customize the look of your cookies, create your own designs using a carrot.

Here's a tip to remember when making dough into balls: Using a level measuring tablespoon of dough will create a perfect 1-inch ball.

1 cup butter or margarine, softened

1 package (3 ounces) cream cheese, softened

1/2 cup sugar

1 tablespoon grated lemon peel

2 cups all-purpose flour

Carrot Press (below)

Sugar

Beat butter and cream cheese in large bowl with electric mixer on medium speed, or mix with spoon. Stir in 1/2 cup sugar and the lemon peel. Gradually stir in flour. Cover and refrigerate about 2 hours or until firm. Prepare Carrot Press.

Heat oven to 375°. Shape dough into 1-inch balls. Place about 2 inches apart on ungreased cookie sheet. Flatten to about 1/4-inch thickness with Carrot Press dipped into sugar. Bake 7 to 9 minutes or until set but not brown. Remove from cookie sheet to wire rack.

Carrot Press

Cut carrot, about 1 1/2 inches in diameter, into 2-inch lengths. Cut decorative design about 1/8 inch deep in cut end of carrot, using small, sharp knife, tip of vegetable peeler or other small, sharp kitchen tool.

1 Cookie: Calories 65 (Calories from Fat 35); Fat 4g (Saturated 1g); Cholesterol 0mg; Sodium 40mg; Carbohydrate 6g (Dietary Fiber 0g); Protein 1g.

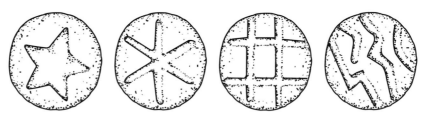

Cut decorative designs about 1/8 inch deep in ends of carrot pieces.

Lemon Decorator Cookies

Meringue-Topped Almond Cookies

BAKE: 13 to 15 min per sheet • YIELD: About 3 dozen cookies

Cookie Tips

Separating eggs is much easier to do while the eggs are cold. Bring the whites and yolks to room temperature before using in the recipe.

Almond Paste

Almond paste is a commercially prepared mixture of almonds, sugar and water that is packed in 6- to 8-ounce packages and cans. It is used in cookies. Do not substitute marzipan for almond paste.

2 egg whites

1/4 teaspoon cream of tartar

1/2 cup granulated sugar

1 package (7 or 8 ounces) almond paste

1/2 cup butter or margarine, softened

1 cup packed brown sugar

1 teaspoon vanilla

2 egg yolks

1 1/2 cups all-purpose flour

Granulated sugar

About 3 dozen blanched whole almonds

Heat oven to 350°. Beat egg whites and cream of tartar in medium bowl with electric mixer on high speed until foamy. Beat in 1/2 cup granulated sugar, 1 tablespoon at a time; continue beating until stiff and glossy. Set aside.

Break almond paste into small pieces in large bowl. Beat in butter on medium speed until smooth. Stir in brown sugar, vanilla and egg yolks. Stir in flour.

Shape dough into 1 1/4-inch balls. Place about 2 inches apart on ungreased cookie sheet. Press bottom of glass into dough to grease, then dip into granulated sugar; press on shaped dough to flatten slightly. Spread about 1 rounded teaspoonful meringue on each cookie, and top with almond. Bake 13 to 15 minutes or until meringue is golden brown. Remove from cookie sheet to wire rack.

1 Cookie: Calories 120 (Calories from Fat 45); Fat 5g (Saturated 1g); Cholesterol 10mg; Sodium 35mg; Carbohydrate 17g (Dietary Fiber 0g); Protein 2g.

Banana-Cornmeal Cookies

BAKE: 10 to 12 min per sheet ● YIELD: About 4 dozen cookies

1 cup packed brown sugar

1/2 cup granulated sugar

1/2 cup butter or margarine, softened

1/2 cup mashed very ripe banana (1 medium)

1 egg

2 1/2 cups all-purpose flour

1 cup yellow cornmeal

1 teaspoon baking powder

1/2 teaspoon salt

1 teaspoon ground cinnamon

1/4 cup granulated sugar

1/2 teaspoon ground cinnamon

Heat oven to 375°. Grease cookie sheet. Beat brown sugar, 1/2 cup granulated sugar, the butter, banana and egg in large bowl with electric mixer on medium speed, or mix with spoon. Stir in flour, cornmeal, baking powder, salt and 1 teaspoon cinnamon. (If dough is too soft to shape, cover and refrigerate about 2 hours or until firm.)

Mix 1/4 cup granulated sugar and 1/2 teaspoon cinnamon. Shape dough into 1 1/4-inch balls. Place about 3 inches apart on cookie sheet. Flatten slightly in crisscross pattern with fork dipped into cinnamon sugar mixture. Bake 10 to 12 minutes or until light brown. Immediately remove from cookie sheet to wire rack.

1 Cookie: Calories 80 (Calories from Fat 20); Fat 2g (Saturated 0g); Cholesterol 5mg; Sodium 60mg; Carbohydrate 15g (Dietary Fiber 0g); Protein 1g.

Cinnamon Twists

BAKE: 8 to 10 min per sheet ● YIELD: About 4 dozen cookies

1 cup sugar

1/2 cup butter or margarine, softened

2 teaspoons vanilla

1 egg

1 3/4 cups all-purpose flour

2 teaspoons baking powder

1/2 teaspoon salt

1 teaspoon ground cinnamon

Heat oven to 375°. Beat sugar, butter, vanilla and egg in large bowl with electric mixer on medium speed, or mix with spoon. Stir in flour, baking powder and salt. Divide dough in half. Stir cinnamon into one half.

Shape 1 level teaspoonful each, plain and cinnamon dough, into 3-inch rope. Place ropes side by side; twist gently. Repeat with remaining dough. Place twists about 2 inches apart on ungreased cookie sheet. Bake 8 to 10 minutes or until very light brown. Remove from cookie sheet to wire rack.

1 Cookie: Calories 55 (Calories from Fat 20); Fat 2g (Saturated 0g); Cholesterol 5mg; Sodium 70mg; Carbohydrate 8g (Dietary Fiber 0g); Protein 1g.

Coconut-Fudge Cups

BAKE: 18 to 20 min per pan ● YIELD: About 2 dozen cookies

1/4 cup butter or margarine, softened

1 package (3 ounces) cream cheese, softened

3/4 cup all-purpose flour

1/4 cup powdered sugar

2 tablespoons baking cocoa

1/2 teaspoon vanilla

Coconut-Fudge Filling (below)

Heat oven to 350°. Beat butter and cream cheese in large bowl with electric mixer on medium speed, or mix with spoon. Stir in remaining ingredients except Coconut-Fudge Filling.

Shape dough into 1-inch balls. Press each ball in bottom and up side of each of 24 small ungreased muffin cups, 1 3/4×1 inch. Prepare Coconut-Fudge Filling. Spoon about 2 teaspoons filling into each cup. Bake 18 to 20 minutes or until almost no indentation remains when filling is touched lightly. Cool slightly; carefully remove from muffin cups to wire rack.

Coconut-Fudge Filling

2/3 cup sugar

2/3 cup flaked coconut

1/3 cup baking cocoa

2 tablespoons butter or margarine, softened

1 egg

Mix all ingredients until spreadable.

1 Cookie: Calories 95 (Calories from Fat 45); Fat 5g (Saturated 2g); Cholesterol 15mg, Sodium 50mg; Carbohydrate 12g (Dietary Fiber 0g); Protein 1g.

Cookie Tips

To quickly soften cream cheese, remove wrapper and place on a microwave-safe saucer. Microwave on Medium 30 seconds; then let stand 1 to 2 minutes.

Make It Your Way

Fudge Nut Cups are just as delicious as the originals. Simply replace the coconut in the filling with 2/3 cup chopped nuts to make Fudge Nut Filling.

Ginger Shortbread Wedges

BAKE: 20 min per pan • YIELD: About 16 cookies

2/3 cup butter or margarine, softened

1/3 cup powdered sugar

3 tablespoons finely chopped crystallized ginger

1 1/3 cups all-purpose flour

2 teaspoons granulated sugar

Heat oven to 350°. Mix butter, powdered sugar and ginger in large bowl with electric mixer on medium speed, or mix with spoon. Stir in flour.

Pat dough into a 9-inch circle on an ungreased cookie sheet. Sprinkle with granulated sugar. Bake about 20 minutes or until golden brown. Cool 10 minutes. Cut into wedges.

1 Cookie: Calories 125 (Calories from Fat 70); Fat 8g (Saturated 2g); Cholesterol 0mg; Sodium 90mg; Carbohydrate 12g (Dietary Fiber 0g); Protein 1g.

Kringla

BAKE: 12 to 15 min per sheet • YIELD: About 6 dozen cookies

1 1/2 cups sugar

1 egg

2 1/2 cups sour cream

4 cups all-purpose flour

2 teaspoons baking soda

1/4 teaspoon salt

Heat oven to 350°. Mix sugar, egg and sour cream in large bowl with spoon. Stir in flour, baking soda and salt.

Spoon dough by rounded teaspoonfuls onto lightly floured surface; roll in flour to coat. Shape into rope, 7 to 8 inches long. Form each rope into figure 8, tucking ends under, on ungreased cookie sheet. Bake 12 to 15 minutes or until light golden brown. Immediately remove from cookie sheet to wire rack.

1 Cookie: Calories 60 (Calories from Fat 20); Fat 2g (Saturated 1g); Cholesterol 10mg; Sodium 45mg; Carbohydrate 10g (Dietary Fiber 0g); Protein 1g.

No-Bake Apricot Balls

YIELD: About 7 1/2 dozen cookies

1 package (6 ounces) dried apricots

1 cup hazelnuts

2 1/2 cups graham cracker crumbs

1 can (14 ounces) sweetened condensed milk

Place apricots and hazelnuts in food processor. Cover and process, using quick on-and-off motions, until finely chopped. Place mixture in large bowl. Stir in cracker crumbs and milk.

Shape mixture into 1-inch balls. Cover tightly and store in refrigerator up to 2 weeks or freeze up to 2 months.

1 Cookie: Calories 35 (Calories from Fat 10); Fat 1g (Saturated 0g); Cholesterol 0mg; Sodium 15mg; Carbohydrate 5g (Dietary Fiber 0g); Protein 1g.

Make It Your Way

Make **No-Bake Apple Balls** by replacing the apricots with dried apples and the hazelnuts with walnuts. Perk up the flavor with a dash of cinnamon.

Chocolate-Bourbon Balls

YIELD: About 5 dozen cookies ● CHILL: 5 days

"I Don't Have That"

1 tablespoon brandy extract plus enough water to equal 1/4 cup can be substituted for the bourbon.

Make It Your Way

Make **Vanilla Bourbon Balls** by substituting crushed vanilla wafers for the chocolate wafers and pecans for the almonds.

1 package (9 ounces) chocolate wafer cookies, finely crushed (2 1/3 cups)

2 cups finely chopped almonds

2 cups powdered sugar

1/4 cup bourbon

1/4 cup light corn syrup

Powdered sugar

Mix crushed cookies, almonds and 2 cups powdered sugar in large bowl. Stir in bourbon and corn syrup.

Shape mixture into 1-inch balls. Roll in powdered sugar. Cover tightly and refrigerate at least 5 days to blend flavors.

1 Cookie: Calories 65 (Calories from Fat 25); Fat 3g (Saturated 0g); Cholesterol 0mg; Sodium 25mg; Carbohydrate 9g (Dietary Fiber 0g); Protein 1g.

Fig-Filled Whole Wheat Cookies

BAKE: 12 to 14 min per sheet ● YIELD: About 3 dozen cookies

Fig Filling (below)

1 cup packed brown sugar

1/2 cup shortening

1 teaspoon vanilla

1 egg

1 2/3 cups whole wheat flour

1/4 teaspoon salt

Prepare Fig Filling. Heat oven to 375°. Beat brown sugar, shortening, vanilla and egg in large bowl with electric mixer on medium speed, or mix with spoon. Stir in flour and salt.

Divide dough into thirds. Pat each third into rectangle, 12×4 inches, on waxed paper. Spoon one third of the filling lengthwise down center of each rectangle in 1 1/2-inch-wide strip. Fold sides of dough over filling, using waxed paper to help lift and overlapping edges slightly. Press lightly to seal. Cut into 1-inch bars. Place seam sides down about 1 inch apart on ungreased cookie sheet. Bake 12 to 14 minutes or until light brown. Remove from cookie sheet to wire rack.

Fig Filling

1 1/3 cups finely chopped dried figs

1/4 cup sugar

1/3 cup finely chopped nuts

1/3 cup water

1 teaspoon grated orange peel

Heat all ingredients over medium heat about 5 minutes, stirring frequently, until thickened.

1 Cookie: Calories 100 (Calories from Fat 35); Fat 4g (Saturated 1g); Cholesterol 5mg; Sodium 20mg; Carbohydrate 16g (Dietary Fiber 1g); Protein 1g.

Pistachio-Chocolate Checkers

CHILL: 2 hr ● BAKE: 8 to 10 min per sheet ● YIELD: About 3 dozen cookies

1 1/2 cups powdered sugar

1 cup butter or margarine, softened

1 egg

2 2/3 cups all-purpose flour

1/4 teaspoon salt

1/4 cup baking cocoa

1 tablespoon milk

1/4 cup finely chopped pistachio nuts

2 or 3 drops green food color, if desired

Beat powdered sugar, butter and egg in large bowl with electric mixer on medium speed, or mix with spoon. Stir in flour and salt. Divide dough in half. Stir cocoa and milk into one half. Stir nuts and food color into other half.

Pat chocolate dough into rectangle, 6×5 inches. Cut crosswise into 8 strips, 3/4 inch wide. Repeat with pistachio dough. Place 2 strips of each color of dough side by side, alternating colors. Top with 2 strips of each dough, alternating colors to create checkerboard. Gently press strips together. Repeat with remaining strips to make second rectangle. Wrap and refrigerate about 2 hours or until firm.

Heat oven to 375°. Cut rectangles crosswise into 1/4-inch slices. Place about 1 inch apart on ungreased cookie sheet. Bake 8 to 10 minutes or until set. Remove from cookie sheet to wire rack.

1 Cookie: Calories 105 (Calories from Fat 55); Fat 6g (Saturated 1g); Cholesterol 5mg; Sodium 80mg; Carbohydrate 13g (Dietary Fiber 0g); Protein 2g.

Pistachio-Chocolate Checkers, Coconut-Fudge Cups (page 195)
Sunflower Cookies (page 203),

Cappuccino-Pistachio Shortbread

BAKE: 15 min per sheet ● YIELD: 32 cookies

Cookie Tips

Instant flavored coffees are very popular and come in individual envelopes, boxes of envelopes, cans, canisters and jars. Use your favorite flavor in this recipe.

For a Christmas theme, look for red or green pistachios! These colors would also work for Valentine's or Saint Patrick's Day. If you'd like, drizzle cookies with both semisweet and white chocolate.

2 tablespoons cappuccino-flavored instant coffee mix (dry)

1 tablespoon water

3/4 cup butter or margarine, softened

1/2 cup powdered sugar

2 cups all-purpose flour

1/2 cup chopped pistachio nuts

1 ounce semisweet baking chocolate or white baking bar

1 teaspoon shortening

Heat oven to 350°. Dissolve coffee mix in water in medium bowl. Add butter and powdered sugar. Beat with electric mixer on medium speed until creamy, or mix with spoon. Stir in flour and nuts, using hands if necessary, until stiff dough forms.

Divide dough in half. Shape each half into a ball. Pat each ball into 6-inch round, about 1/2 inch thick, on lightly floured surface. Cut each round into 16 wedges. Arrange wedges about 1/2 inch apart and with pointed ends toward center on ungreased cookie sheet. Bake about 15 minutes or until golden brown. Immediately remove from cookie sheet to wire rack. Cool completely.

Place chocolate and shortening in small microwavable bowl. Microwave uncovered on Medium (50%) 3 to 4 minutes, stirring after 2 minutes, until mixture can be stirred smooth and is thin enough to drizzle. Drizzle over cookies.

1 Cookie: Calories 95 (Calories from Fat 55); Fat 6g (Saturated 3g); Cholesterol 10mg; Sodium 30mg; Carbohydrate 9g (Dietary Fiber 0g); Protein 1g.

Sunflower Cookies

CHILL: 2 hr ● BAKE: 8 to 10 min per sheet ● YIELD: About 4 dozen cookies

1 cup sugar

1/2 cup butter or margarine, softened

1 teaspoon vanilla

1 egg

1 1/3 cups all-purpose flour

1 cup old-fashioned or quick-cooking oats

1/2 teaspoon baking powder

1/4 teaspoon salt

1/2 cup unsalted sunflower nuts

1/4 teaspoon yellow food color

Beat sugar, butter, vanilla and egg in large bowl with electric mixer on medium speed, or mix with spoon. Stir in flour, oats, baking powder and salt. Divide dough into one-third and two-thirds portions. Stir sunflower nuts into one-third dough. Stir food color into two-thirds dough.

Shape sunflower dough into two 3/4-inch rolls, 8 inches long. Divide yellow dough in half. Pat each half into rectangle, 8 × 4 inches, on lightly floured surface. Top each rectangle with roll of sunflower dough. Wrap yellow dough around roll of sunflower dough. Press edges together. Wrap and refrigerate about 2 hours or until firm.

Heat oven to 350°. Grease cookie sheet. Cut rolls into 1/4 inch slices. Place about 2 inches apart on cookie sheet. Cut slits in outer yellow edge about every 1/2 inch to shape tips of petals. Bake 8 to 10 minutes or until light brown. Remove from cookie sheet to wire rack.

1 Cookie: Calories 65 (Calories from Fat 25); Fat 3g (Saturated 1g); Cholesterol 5mg; Sodium 40mg; Carbohydrate 8g (Dietary Fiber 0g); Protein 1g.

Sunflower Nuts

Sunflower nuts are the dried seeds of the sunflower and are available plain or salted, dry-roasted or cooked in oil.

"I Don't Have That"

If you only have salted sunflower nuts in your cupboard, use them and eliminate the 1/4 teaspoon salt called for in the recipe.

Anise Biscotti

BAKE: 35 min per sheet ● COOL: 15 min ● YIELD: About 3 1/2 dozen cookies

1 cup sugar

1/2 cup butter or margarine, softened

2 teaspoons anise seed, ground

2 teaspoons grated lemon peel

2 eggs

3 1/2 cups all-purpose flour

1 teaspoon baking powder

1/2 teaspoon salt

Heat oven to 350°. Beat sugar, butter, anise seed, lemon peel and eggs in large bowl with electric mixer on medium speed, or mix with spoon. Stir in remaining ingredients. Divide dough in half. Shape each half into rectangle, 10×3 inches, on ungreased cookie sheet.

Bake about 20 minutes or until toothpick inserted in center comes out clean. Cool on cookie sheet 15 minutes. Cut crosswise into 1/2-inch slices. Turn slices cut sides down on cookie sheet.

Bake about 15 minutes or until crisp and light brown. Remove from cookie sheet to wire rack.

1 Cookie: Calories 85 (Calories from Fat 25); Fat 3g (Saturated 1g); Cholesterol 10mg; Sodium 70mg; Carbohydrate 13g (Dietary Fiber 0g); Protein 1g.

Orange-Almond Biscotti

BAKE: 35 min per sheet ● COOL: 15 min ● YIELD: About 3 1/2 dozen cookies

1 cup sugar

1/2 cup butter or margarine, softened

1 tablespoon grated orange peel

2 eggs

3 1/2 cups all-purpose flour

1 teaspoon baking powder

1/2 teaspoon salt

1/3 cup slivered almonds, toasted (page 64) and chopped

Heat oven to 350°. Beat sugar, butter, orange peel and eggs in large bowl with electric mixer on medium speed, or mix with spoon. Stir in flour, baking powder and salt. Stir in almonds. Divide dough in half. Shape each half into rectangle, 10×3 inches, on ungreased cookie sheet.

Bake about 20 minutes or until toothpick inserted in center comes out clean. Cool on cookie sheet 15 minutes. Cut crosswise into 1/2-inch slices. Turn slices cut sides down on cookie sheet.

Bake about 15 minutes or until crisp and light brown. Remove from cookie sheet to wire rack.

1 Cookie: Calories 85 (Calories from Fat 25); Fat 3g (Saturated 2); Cholesterol 15mg; Sodium 55mg; Carbohydrate 13g (Dietary Fiber 0g); Protein 2g.

Cookie Tips

When grating orange peel, be sure to grate only the orange part of the skin. The white part, or pith, is very bitter.

Make It Your Way

To make **Orange-Cashew Biscotti**; just substitute cashews for the almonds.

CHAPTER 6

Mary's Sugar Cookies *208*
Sour Cream–Sugar
  Cookies *209*
Easy Decorating Ideas *210*
Christmas Cookie Slices *214*
Yogurt Stack Cookies *215*
Sugar Cookie Tarts *216*
Cream Wafers *218*
Cream Squares *220*
Chocolate Shortbread *221*
Butterscotch Shortbread *222*
Chocolate-Glazed Graham
  Crackers *224*
Moravian Ginger Cookies *225*
Frosted Spice Cookies *226*

Gingerbread Cookies *227*
Joe Froggers *228*
Raspberry Logs *229*
Pecan Crisps *230*
Cinnamon-Nut Crisps *231*
Date-Nut Pinwheels *232*
Mint Ravioli Cookies *233*
Hungarian Poppy Seed
  Cookies *234*
Glazed Chocolate Pockets *236*
Sunshine Cookies *238*
Almond-Filled Crescents *239*
Peach Triangles *240*
Toffee Meringue Sticks *241*

Rolling in Dough

Mary's Sugar Cookies (page 208),
Bird's Nest Cookies (variation, page 216)

Sweet, crisp sugar cookies have made the grade throughout the years. Whether sprinkled with colored sugar, frosted or elaborately decorated, they're as popular as ever.

Mary's Sugar Cookies

CHILL: 2 hr ● BAKE: 7 to 8 min per sheet ● YIELD: About 5 dozen 2- to 2 1/2-inch cookies

Cookie Tips

One of the nice things about rolled cookies is that they will wait until you are ready to bake them. Because the dough can always be refrigerated (and can be frozen, too), they're very convenient. We love them because they present lots of opportunity for creativity. Simple cookies are ideal for teaching the beginning baker how to handle a rolling pin.

Make It Your Way

Fruit-Flavored Sugar Cookies are very easy to make. Just sprinkle the cut out cookies with fruit-flavored gelatin instead of granulated sugar. Or check out our Easy Decorating Ideas on pages 210–213, for more creative ways to decorate.

1 1/2 cups powdered sugar

1 cup butter or margarine, softened

1 teaspoon vanilla

1/2 teaspoon almond extract

1 egg

2 1/2 cups all-purpose flour

1 teaspoon baking soda

1 teaspoon cream of tartar

Granulated sugar

Beat powdered sugar and butter in large bowl with electric mixer on medium speed, or mix with spoon. Stir in vanilla, almond extract and egg. Stir in flour, baking soda and cream of tartar. Cover and refrigerate about 2 hours or until firm.

Heat oven to 375°. Roll half of dough at a time 1/8 inch thick on lightly floured cloth-covered surface. Cut into desired shapes. Place about 2 inches apart on ungreased cookie sheet. Sprinkle with granulated sugar. Bake 7 to 8 minutes or until light brown. Remove from cookie sheet to wire rack.

1 Cookie: Calories 60 (Calories from Fat 25); Fat 3g (Saturated 1g); Cholesterol 5mg; Sodium 60mg; Carbohydrate 7g (Dietary Fiber 0g); Protein 1g.

Sour Cream–Sugar Cookies

BAKE: 7 to 8 min per sheet ● YIELD: About 3 dozen 2 1/2-inch cookies

1 cup sugar

1/3 cup butter or margarine, softened

1/4 cup shortening

1/2 teaspoon lemon extract

1 egg

2 2/3 cups all-purpose flour

1 teaspoon baking powder

1/2 teaspoon baking soda

1/2 teaspoon salt

2/3 cup sour cream

Sugar

Heat oven to 375°. Beat 1 cup sugar, the butter, shortening, lemon extract and egg in large bowl with electric mixer on medium speed, or mix with spoon. Stir in flour, baking powder, baking soda, salt and sour cream.

Roll one third of dough at a time 1/4 inch thick on well-floured cloth-covered surface. Cut into desired shapes. Place about 2 inches apart on ungreased cookie sheet. Sprinkle with sugar. Bake 7 to 8 minutes or until almost no indentation remains when touched in center. Remove from cookie sheet to wire rack.

1 Cookie: Calories 95 (Calories from Fat 35); Fat 4g (Saturated 2g); Cholesterol 15mg; Sodium 80mg; Carbohydrate 14g (Dietary Fiber 0g); Protein 1g.

Cookie Tips

If some of your cut-out cookies are thicker than the others, don't reroll the dough. Instead, place the thinner ones in the center of the cookie sheet and the thicker ones around the edge to get more even browning.

A partly empty cookie sheet will produce unevenly baked cookies. If there isn't enough dough to fill a cookie sheet, use an upside-down cake pan.

Easy Decorating Ideas

Decorating cookies, at any age, is one of life's simple and memorable pleasures. What's great is you don't need to have any special skills to do it. Anyone can decorate cookies, elaborately or simply. Cookies with a touch of frosting or drizzle of chocolate are a special treat for your family, and they make heartwarming gifts. No matter how you've chosen to adorn your cookies, remember to have fun and let your creativity shine (and don't forget, you can eat your mistakes!).

EASY DECORATING

Before You Get Started

KEEP YOUR COOL Cookies or bars must be completely cooled before you begin to decorate, so frostings and glazes won't melt.

THE FUN STARTS HERE Most grocery stores carry many instant decorating items, such as colored sugar, nonpareils (tiny colored candy balls), frosting tubes with tips, tubes of colored gels, molded candy decorations and chocolate leaves. Candies, fruit snacks and dried fruits also make fun and easy decorations. *Note: The following decorating items are not edible: silver or gold dragées ("silver or gold shot") and gold or silver dust.*

OVER THE RAINBOW You can use either liquid or paste food color. Paste colors are concentrated, giving the most vivid, deep colors without thinning the frosting or glaze, and just a little bit goes a long way. Paste colors can be bought at cake decorating stores and some kitchen specialty shops. Liquid food color is readily available in grocery stores and is usually sold in or near the section of flavor extracts and spices in the baking aisle.

Frosting, Glaze and Paints

DECORATOR'S FROSTING OR GLAZE Stir together 2 cups powdered sugar, 1/2 teaspoon vanilla and 2 tablespoons milk or half-and-half until smooth and spreadable. This recipe makes enough to frost 3 to 5 dozen cookies. Add more milk for a thinner frosting or to create a glaze. Frosting can be tinted with food color. Stir in liquid food color, 1 drop at a time, until frosting is the desired color. If intense, vivid frosting color is desired, use paste food color. Why? Because you would have to use too much liquid color to get vivid color, and using too much liquid color will break down the frosting, causing it to separate and look curdled.

EGG YOLK PAINT Stir together 1 egg yolk and 1/4 teaspoon water. Divide mixture among several small custard cups. Tint with food color to desired brightness (Egg Yolk Paint creates very opaque, bright color). Paint on cookie dough before baking. If paint thickens while standing, add a few drops of water. **For food-safety reasons, use Egg Yolk Paint only on cookie dough that will be baked; do not paint on cookies that have already been baked.**

MILK PAINT Stir together small amounts of evaporated milk and food color. Paint on cookie dough before baking.

FOOD COLOR PAINT Stir together small amounts of water and food color. Paint on cookie dough before baking, or use to paint designs on frosted cookies.

Paint Your Cookie!

TO CREATE ANY TYPE OF DESIGN Cookies frosted with a glaze are best for cookie painting because the surface is smooth and flat. Before starting, make sure the glaze is completely dry and hardened. This prevents the colors from bleeding or creating a marbled effect. Either paint (using a small brush), drizzle or pipe (using a decorator's bag with a writing tip) a different color of Egg Yolk Paint, Milk Paint or Food Color Paint on glazed cookie. Allow paint to dry completely before storing cookies.

Basic Cookie Painting

TO CREATE A MARBLED LOOK Either paint (using a small brush), drizzle or pipe (using a decorator's bag with a writing tip) a different color of Egg Yolk Paint, Milk Paint or Food Color Paint on *freshly* glazed or frosted cookie (do not allow glaze or frosting to dry or harden before painting, or this technique won't work). Use a small brush or toothpick to swirl colors or create marbleized patterns. Allow paint to dry completely before storing cookies.

Marbled Look

TO CREATE COOKIE "FLOCKING" Pipe or drizzle a design on completely dried and hardened, glazed or frosted cookie. Sprinkle colored sugar over design while design is still fresh (do not allow design to dry or harden before flocking, or this technique won't work). Shake off any excess sugar. Or instead of adding a design, you can flock the entire surface of a freshly glazed or frosted cookie.

Cookie "Flocking"

Chocolate Creations

DRAMATIC DRIZZLES Melt desired chocolate, following the directions on pages xiii–xiv. Place cookies to be drizzled on a wire rack over a piece of waxed paper or aluminum foil; for bars, drizzle with chocolate while bars are in the pan and before cutting. Create drizzles using one of these two methods:

1. Dip a fork or small tableware-type spoon into melted chocolate, allowing the first large drop of chocolate to drip back into the bowl or saucepan. Then, using back-and-forth motions, drizzle chocolate over the cookies or bars.

2. Spoon melted chocolate into a decorator's bag with a writing tip, and squeeze out the chocolate. Or instead of using a decorator's bag, spoon melted chocolate into a small, resealable plastic bag, snip off a very tiny piece of one corner of the bag and gently squeeze out the melted chocolate.

Drizzle in straight lines, circles or squiggly lines—there are no rules! Allow the chocolate to harden before storing cookies or placing on serving platter.

Different ways to drizzle melted chocolate.

DUNK AND PLUNGE Melt desired chocolate, following the directions on pages xiii–xiv. Line work surface with waxed paper or aluminum foil, or use a cutting board. Holding cookie with tongs, dip sides, ends or the whole cookie into melted chocolate. Remove excess chocolate by pulling the cookie against the edge of the bowl or saucepan. Try melting more than one type of chocolate—let's say, milk chocolate and white chocolate—and dip each cookie into both kinds! Allow the chocolate to harden before storing cookies or placing on serving platter.

Dipping Cookies into Melted Chocolate

RUB IT THE RIGHT WAY Line work surface with waxed paper or aluminum foil, or use a cutting board. Rub room-temperature squares or bars of chocolate against the holes of a shredder or grater, using steady, even pressure. Large holes will make little curls; the small holes will make fine shreds. The grater will grate the chocolate.

Grating Chocolate

CURLS, CURLS, CURLS Line work surface with waxed paper or aluminum foil, or use a cutting board. Draw a vegetable peeler across room-temperature squares of semisweet or bars of milk chocolate, using steady, even pressure. The thin strips of chocolate you're shaving will curl automatically. Wider bars will give you larger curls.

Transfer curls onto cookies or bars by inserting a toothpick or thin skewer into the curl.

Making Chocolate Curls

Coconut Creations

TINTED COCONUT Place 1/2 cup flaked or shredded coconut in a resealable plastic bag or jar with tight-fitting lid. Add 1 or 2 drops of liquid food color. Seal bag or tighten lid. Shake to tint coconut with color.

Tinting Coconut

TOASTED COCONUT Sprinkle 1/2 cup flaked or shredded coconut in an ungreased heavy skillet. Cook over medium-low heat 6 to 14 minutes, stirring frequently until browning begins, then stirring constantly until golden brown.

Toasting Coconut

Colored Sugar

Place 1/2 cup granulated sugar in a resealable plastic bag. Add food color to tint as desired. Seal bag. Squeeze sugar in bag until it becomes colored. Sugar colored with liquid food color may clump; if it does, just break the sugar apart until clumps are gone. Check out our chart for how to create your own custom colors.

Color	Number of Drops of Liquid Food Color
Orange	2 drops yellow and 2 drops red
Peach	4 drops yellow and 1 drop red
Yellow	4 drops yellow
Pale Yellow	2 drops yellow
Green	8 drops green
Lime green	3 drops yellow and 1 drop green
Blue	5 drops blue
Turquoise blue	3 drops blue and 1 drop green
Baby blue	2 drops blue
Purple	3 drops red and 2 drops blue
Red	10 drops red
Rose	5 drops red and 1 drop blue
Pink	1 drop red

"Homemade" Colored Sugars

Paste food color gives vivid, deeper color; less paste color than liquid color is needed to achieve desired results. Before using paste color, be sure to stir it with a toothpick until smooth because paste colors can separate and thicken during storage. To measure paste color, dip toothpick into container and take out a tiny amount (the amount should look like a drop or two of liquid food color). Paste color will take longer to blend into the sugar than liquid color.

Nutty Ideas

Sprinkle chopped or ground nuts on bars or cookies right after they've been frosted, so the nuts stick to the fresh frosting. You may have to press the nuts in slightly

Sprinkling Chopped Nuts on Cookies

Melt desired chocolate, following the directions on pages xiii–xiv. Dip one half of pecan halves, walnut halves or whole almonds into melted chocolate, to use as a garnish. Place the nuts on waxed paper, and allow the chocolate to harden before using.

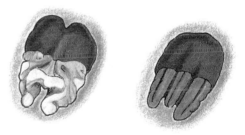

Dipping Nuts into Melted Chocolate

STAMPING OUT STAINS AND SPOTS

Food color can stain, just as deep-colored fruits and vegetables such as blueberries and beets can. For stains on your skin, wash with warm, soapy water. Bleach can be used on laminated countertops (check cleaning instructions for marble, granite, tile or other nonlaminated surfaces).

To treat fabric stains on fabric that cannot be bleached: With a clean cloth, blot the stain first to remove as much color as possible. Next, blot the stain with lukewarm water until no color is transferred onto your blotting cloth.

If the stain is still visible, use a commercial stain remover following the manufacturer's directions for the type of fabric and stain. If the stain is from a color that contains red dye #3 as an ingredient, soak the stain first in distilled white vinegar or lemon juice, then try blotting with lukewarm water and allow to dry before trying a commercial stain remover.

Christmas Cookie Slices

CHILL: 4 hrs ● BAKE: 8 to 10 min per sheet ● YIELD: About 7 dozen cookies

Make It Your Way

Pink and white **Peppermint Pinwheels** will attract attention! To make them, decrease vanilla to 1 teaspoon; add 1 teaspoon peppermint extract. Divide dough in half. Stir 1/2 teaspoon red or green food color into 1 half. Cover both halves and refrigerate 1 hour. Roll plain dough into rectangle, about 16 × 9 inches, on lightly floured surface. Repeat with colored dough; place on plain dough. Roll dough's together until about 1/4 inch thick. Roll up tightly, beginning at 16-inch side. Refrigerate as directed.

1 cup sugar

1 cup butter or margarine, softened

1 1/2 teaspoons vanilla

2 eggs

3 cups all-purpose flour

1 teaspoon salt

1/2 teaspoon baking soda

Beat sugar, butter, vanilla and eggs in large bowl with electric mixer on medium speed, or mix with spoon. Stir in flour, salt and baking soda. Divide into 3 equal parts. Shape each part into roll, about 1 1/2 inches in diameter. Wrap and refrigerate at least 4 hours.

Heat oven to 400°. Cut rolls into 1/8-inch slices. Place about 1 inch apart on ungreased cookie sheet. Bake 8 to 10 minutes or just until golden brown around edges. Immediately remove from cookie sheet. to wire rack.

1 Cookie: Calories 45 (Calories from Fat 20); Fat 2g (Saturated 1g); Cholesterol 10mg; Sodium 50mg; Carbohydrate 6g (Dietary Fiber 0g); Protein 1g.

Yogurt Stack Cookies

CHILL: 2 hr ● BAKE: 6 to 8 min per sheet ● YIELD: About 20 cookies

1 cup sugar

1/2 cup butter or margarine, softened

1/2 cup shortening

1/2 cup plain yogurt

1 egg

3 cups all-purpose flour

1 teaspoon baking powder

1/2 teaspoon baking soda

1/4 teaspoon salt

Yogurt Frosting (below)

1/3 cup fruit preserves (any flavor)

Beat sugar, butter and shortening in large bowl with electric mixer on medium speed, or mix with spoon. Stir in yogurt and egg. Stir in flour, baking powder, baking soda and salt. Cover and refrigerate about 2 hours or until firm.

Heat oven to 375°. Roll half of dough at a time 1/8 inch thick on lightly floured surface. Cut into 2-inch rounds. Place 2 inches apart on ungreased cookie sheet. Bake 6 to 8 minutes or until light brown. Remove from cookie sheet to wire rack. Cool completely.

Prepare Yogurt Frosting. Spread 1 cookie with 1/2 teaspoon frosting. Top with second cookie; spread with 1/2 teaspoon preserves. Top with third cookie. Repeat with remaining cookies, frosting and preserves. Store tightly covered in refrigerator.

Yogurt Frosting

1 cup powdered sugar

2 tablespoons plain yogurt

1 tablespoon butter or margarine, softened

1/4 teaspoon vanilla

Mix all ingredients until smooth and spreadable.

1 Cookie: Calories 245 (Calories from Fat 100); Fat 11g (Saturated 3g); Cholesterol 10mg; Sodium 150mg; Carbohydrate 34g (Dietary Fiber 0g); Protein 3g.

Cookie Tips

Remember not to place cut-out cookies on a warm cookie sheet; they'll spread too much and loose their shape before baking.

"I Don't Have That"

When there's no yogurt in the refrigerator, substitute sour cream in both the cookies and in the frosting.

Sugar Cookie Tarts

BAKE: 10 to 12 min per sheet ● YIELD: About 2 1/2 dozen cookies

Cookie Tips

In a hurry? A thin-rimmed glass or clean, empty food can makes a good substitute for a cookie cutter.

Make It Your Way

Bake these cookies, but leave out the fruit and replace Cream Cheese Spread with Creamy Frosting (page 221). Make **Bird's Nest Cookies** by spreading each cookie with frosting, sprinkling with plain, toasted or tinted coconut and centering 3 jelly beans in the middle of each. Directions for making tinted and toasted coconut are on page 212.

2 cups sugar

1 cup shortening

3/4 cup butter or margarine, softened

2 teaspoons vanilla

1 egg

3 1/2 cups all-purpose flour

1 teaspoon baking powder

1/4 teaspoon salt

Cream Cheese Spread (below)

Toppings (sliced fresh fruit, miniature chocolate chips, chopped pecans or jam with toasted sliced almonds)

Heat oven to 375°. Beat sugar, shortening, butter, vanilla and egg in large bowl with electric mixer on medium speed, or mix with spoon. Stir in flour, baking powder and salt.

Roll half of dough at a time 1/4 inch thick on lightly floured surface. Cut into 3-inch rounds. Place 2 inches apart on ungreased cookie sheet. Bake 10 to 12 minutes or until light brown. Cool 1 to 2 minutes; remove from cookie sheet to wire rack. Cool completely.

Prepare Cream Cheese Spread. Spread about 2 teaspoons spread over each cookie. Arrange Toppings on spread. Store covered in refrigerator.

Cream Cheese Spread

1 package (8 ounces) cream cheese, softened

1/2 cup powdered sugar

1 teaspoon vanilla

Mix all ingredients until smooth.

1 Cookie: Calories 245 (Calories from Fat 125); Fat 14g (Saturated 4g); Cholesterol 15mg; Sodium 115mg; Carbohydrate 28g (Dietary Fiber 0g); Protein 2g.

Sugar Cookie Tarts

Cream Wafers

CHILL: 1 hr ● BAKE: 7 to 9 min per sheet ● YIELD: About 5 dozen cookies

2 cups all-purpose flour
1 cup butter or margarine, softened
1/3 cup whipping (heavy) cream
Sugar
Creamy Filling (below)

Mix flour, butter and whipping cream with spoon. Cover and refrigerate about 1 hour or until firm.

Heat oven to 375°. Roll one-third of dough at a time 1/8 inch thick on lightly floured surface. (Keep remaining dough refrigerated until ready to roll.) Cut into 1 1/2-inch rounds. Generously cover large piece of waxed paper with sugar. Transfer rounds to waxed paper, using pancake turner. Turn each round to coat both sides. Place on ungreased cookie sheet. Prick each round with fork about 4 times.

Bake 7 to 9 minutes or just until set but not brown. Remove from cookie sheet to wire rack. Cool completely. Prepare Creamy Filling. Spread about 1/2 teaspoon filling between bottoms of pairs of cookies.

Creamy Filling

3/4 cup powdered sugar
1/4 cup butter or margarine, softened
1 teaspoon vanilla
Food color, if desired

Mix all ingredients until smooth. Add a few drops water if necessary.

1 Cookie: Calories 65 (Calories from Fat 35); Fat 4g (Saturated 1g); Cholesterol 0mg; Sodium 45mg; Carbohydrate 6g (Dietary Fiber 0g); Protein 1g.

Cream Wafers, Cream Squares (page 220)

Cream Squares

CHILL: 2 hr ● BAKE: 10 to 13 min per sheet ● YIELD: About 4 dozen cookies

Make It Your Way

Stir 1/2 cup mini chocolate chips into dough and make speckled **Chocolate Chip Cream Squares**.

Another variation, **Coffee Bean Mocha Squares** provide a delicious mocha (chocolate and coffee) flavor. Mix dough, except reduce flour to 3 3/4 cups and add 1/4 cup cocoa. Roll and cut dough into 2-inch squares, but don't make side cuts. After cookies are baked and cooled, frost with a double batch of Mocha Frosting (page 29) and press a chocolate-covered coffee bean in the center of each.

2 eggs

1 cup sugar

1 cup whipping (heavy) cream

4 cups all-purpose flour

3 teaspoons baking powder

1 teaspoon salt

Beat eggs in large bowl with electric mixer on medium speed until foamy. Gradually beat in sugar. Stir in whipping cream. Stir in flour, baking powder and salt. Cover and refrigerate about 2 hours or until firm.

Heat oven to 375°. Grease cookie sheet. Roll half of dough at a time into rectangle, 12×8 inches, on lightly floured surface. Cut into 2-inch squares. Place 2 inches apart on cookie sheet. Make two 1/2-inch cuts on all sides of each square. Bake 10 to 13 minutes or until edges are light brown. Remove from cookie sheet to wire rack.

1 Cookie: Calories 70 (Calories from Fat 20); Fat 2g (Saturated 1g); Cholesterol 15mg; Sodium 85mg; Carbohydrate 12g (Dietary Fiber 0g); Protein 1g.

Chocolate Shortbread

BAKE: 9 to 11 min per sheet ● YIELD: About 4 dozen cookies

2 cups powdered sugar

1 1/2 cups butter or margarine, softened

3 cups all-purpose flour

3/4 cup baking cocoa

2 teaspoons vanilla

4 ounces semisweet baking chocolate, melted and cooled

1/2 teaspoon shortening

Creamy Frosting (below)

Heat oven to 325°. Beat powdered sugar and butter in large bowl with electric mixer on medium speed until light and fluffy, or mix with spoon. Stir in flour, cocoa and vanilla.

Roll half of dough at a time 1/2 inch thick on lightly floured surface. Cut into 3-inch rounds. Place 2 inches apart on ungreased cookie sheet. Bake 9 to 11 minutes or until firm (cookies should not be dark brown). Remove from cookie sheet to wire rack. Cool completely.

Mix chocolate and shortening until smooth. Prepare Creamy Frosting. Spread each cookie with about 1 teaspoon frosting. Immediately make three concentric circles on frosting with melted chocolate. Starting at center, draw a toothpick through chocolate circles to make spider web design. Let stand until chocolate is firm.

Creamy Frosting

3 cups powdered sugar

1/3 cup butter or margarine, softened

1 1/2 teaspoons vanilla

About 2 tablespoons milk

Mix powdered sugar and butter in medium bowl. Stir in vanilla and milk. Beat with spoon until smooth and spreadable.

1 Cookie: Calories 160 (Calories from Fat 80); Fat 9g (Saturated 2g); Cholesterol 0mg; Sodium 85mg; Carbohydrate 20g (Dietary Fiber 1g); Protein 1g.

Butterscotch Shortbread

BAKE: 25 min per sheet ● YIELD: About 4 dozen cookies

Cookie Tips

This dough makes great cut-out cookies. After baking you can leave them plain, make sandwich cookies or frost them.

Shortbread

Shortbread comes from Scotland. Originally it was made in a large round cake with spokes notched like rays, radiating from the center, to symbolize the rays of the sun. In the eighteenth century, the triangular wedges were called "Petticoat Tails."

1/2 cup butter or margarine, softened
1/2 cup shortening
1/2 cup packed brown sugar
1/4 cup granulated sugar
2 1/4 cups all-purpose flour
1 teaspoon salt

Heat oven to 300°. Beat butter, shortening and sugars in large bowl with electric mixer on medium speed, or mix with spoon. Stir in flour and salt. (Dough will be dry and crumbly; use hands to mix completely.)

Roll dough into rectangle, 15×7 1/2 inches, on lightly floured surface. Cut into 1 1/2-inch squares. Place about 1 inch apart on ungreased cookie sheet. Bake about 25 minutes or until set. (These cookies brown very little, and the shape does not change.) Remove from cookie sheet to wire rack.

1 Cookie: Calories 70 (Calories from Fat 35); Fat 4g (Saturated 1g); Cholesterol 0mg; Sodium 70mg; Carbohydrate 8g (Dietary Fiber 0g); Protein 1g.

Butterscotch Shortbread

Chocolate-Glazed Graham Crackers

BAKE: 7 to 9 min per sheet ● YIELD: About 4 dozen cookies

Cookie Tips

These crackers have a wonderful old-fashioned taste created with the use of whole wheat flour. They are sure to please when served with a glass of cold milk.

Make It Your Way

Make **Honey–Graham Cracker Cookies** by leaving out the chocolate and cutting the dough with 2- to 3-inch cookie cutters. Sprinkle the cookies with plain or colored sugar before baking.

1 cup shortening

1/2 cup packed brown sugar

1/4 cup honey

2 cups whole wheat flour

1/2 teaspoon baking powder

1/4 teaspoon salt

1/2 cup semisweet chocolate chips

1 tablespoon shortening

Heat oven to 375°. Beat 1 cup shortening, the brown sugar and honey in large bowl with electric mixer on medium speed, or mix with spoon. Stir in flour, baking powder and salt.

Roll half of dough at a time 1/8 inch thick on lightly floured cloth-covered surface. Cut into 2 1/2-inch rounds. Place 1 inch apart on ungreased cookie sheet. Bake 7 to 9 minutes or until edges are firm. Cool 1 to 2 minutes; remove from cookie sheet to wire rack. Cool completely.

Melt chocolate chips and 1 tablespoon shortening over low heat, stirring occasionally, until smooth. Drizzle over cookies.

1 Cookie: Calories 80 (Calories from Fat 45); Fat 5g (Saturated 1g); Cholesterol 0mg; Sodium 20mg; Carbohydrate 8g (Dietary Fiber 0g); Protein 1g.

Moravian Ginger Cookies

CHILL: 4 hr ● BAKE: 5 or 8 min per sheet
YIELD: About 1 dozen 1/8-inch-thick cookies or about 1 1/2 dozen paper-thin cookies

1/3 cup molasses

1/4 cup shortening

2 tablespoons packed brown sugar

1 1/4 cups all-purpose or whole wheat flour

1/4 teaspoon salt

1/4 teaspoon baking soda

1/4 teaspoon baking powder

1/4 teaspoon ground cinnamon

1/4 teaspoon ground ginger

1/4 teaspoon ground cloves

Dash of ground nutmeg

Dash of ground allspice

Easy Creamy Frosting (below)

Mix molasses, shortening and brown sugar in large bowl with spoon. Stir in remaining ingredients except Easy Creamy Frosting. Cover and refrigerate about 4 hours or until firm.

Heat oven to 375°. Roll half of dough at a time 1/8 inch thick or until paper-thin on floured cloth-covered surface. Cut into 3-inch rounds with floured cutter. Place about 1/2 inch apart on ungreased cookie sheet. Bake 1/8-inch-thick cookies about 8 minutes, paper-thin cookies about 5 minutes, or until light brown. Immediately remove from cookie sheet to wire rack. Cool completely. Frost with Easy Creamy Frosting.

Easy Creamy Frosting

1 cup powdered sugar

1/2 teaspoon vanilla

1 to 2 tablespoons half-and-half

Mix all ingredients until smooth and spreadable.

1 Cookie: Calories 165 (Calories from Fat 45); Fat 5g (Saturated 1g); Cholesterol 0mg; Sodium 90mg; Carbohydrate 29g (Dietary Fiber 0g); Protein 1g.

If you use nonstick cookie sheets, you can prevent the surface from getting scratched by placing large plastic lids or plastic coffee can covers between them when not in use.

Molasses is the concentrated syrup left after sugar has been refined. Either the light or dark variety can be used in recipes.

Frosted Spice Cookies

BAKE: 8 to 10 min per sheet ● YIELD: About 4 dozen cookies

Cookie Tips

Spices should be stored tightly sealed in a cool place. They have a shelf life of about a year and should be replaced when they lose their pungent aroma.

Caramel frosting is often called "penuche" or "penu-chi," which is a name derived from the Mexican word for raw or brown sugar.

2 1/2 cups packed brown sugar

1 cup butter or margarine, softened

1/2 cup shortening

2 eggs

4 1/2 cups all-purpose flour

2 teaspoons baking powder

1 teaspoon ground ginger

1 teaspoon ground cinnamon

1 teaspoon ground cloves

1 teaspoon ground nutmeg

1/2 teaspoon salt

Caramel Frosting (below)

Heat oven to 375°. Beat brown sugar, butter, shortening and eggs in large bowl with electric mixer on medium speed, or mix with spoon. Stir in remaining ingredients except Caramel Frosting.

Roll one fourth of dough at a time 1/4 inch thick on lightly floured surface. Cut into 2 1/2-inch rounds. Place about 2 inches apart on ungreased cookie sheet. Bake 8 to 10 minutes or until light brown. Remove from cookie sheet to wire rack. Cool completely. Frost with Caramel Frosting.

Caramel Frosting

1/2 cup butter or margarine

1 cup packed brown sugar

1/4 cup milk

2 cups powdered sugar

Melt butter in 2-quart saucepan over medium heat. Stir in brown sugar. Heat to boiling, stirring constantly; reduce heat to low. Boil and stir 2 minutes. Stir in milk. Heat to boiling; remove from heat. Place saucepan in bowl of ice or cold water; cool to lukewarm, stirring occasionally. Gradually stir in powdered sugar. Beat until smooth and spreadable. If frosting becomes too stiff, stir in additional milk, 1 teaspoon at a time.

1 Cookie: Calories 175 (Calories from Fat 55); Fat 6g (Saturated 1g); Cholesterol 10mg; Sodium 115mg; Carbohydrate 28g (Dietary Fiber 0g); Protein 2g.

Gingerbread Cookies

CHILL: 2 hr ● BAKE: 10 to 12 min per sheet
YIELD: About 2 1/2 dozen 5-inch cookies or about 5 dozen 2 1/2-inch cookies

1 cup packed brown sugar

1/3 cup shortening

1 1/2 cups dark molasses

2/3 cup cold water

7 cups all-purpose flour

2 teaspoons baking soda

2 teaspoons ground ginger

1 teaspoon salt

1 teaspoon ground allspice

1 teaspoon ground cloves

1 teaspoon ground cinnamon

Creamy White Frosting (below)

Beat brown sugar, shortening, molasses and water in very large bowl with electric mixer on medium speed, or mix with spoon. Stir in remaining ingredients except Creamy White Frosting. Cover and refrigerate about 2 hours or until firm.

Heat oven to 350°. Lightly grease cookie sheet. Roll one fourth of dough at a time 1/4 inch thick on lightly floured surface. Cut with floured gingerbread cookie cutter or other favorite shaped cutter. Place about 2 inches apart on cookie sheet. Bake 10 to 12 minutes or until almost no indentation remains when touched in center. Remove from cookie sheet to wire rack. Cool completely. Frost with Creamy White Frosting.

Creamy White Frosting

4 cups powdered sugar

1 teaspoon vanilla

5 tablespoons half-and-half

Food color, if desired

Mix all ingredients until smooth and spreadable.

1 Cookie: Calories 265 (Calories from Fat 25); Fat 3g (Saturated 1g); Cholesterol 0mg; Sodium 180mg; Carbohydrate 56g (Dietary Fiber 0g); Protein 3g.

Joe Froggers

CHILL: 2 hr ● BAKE: 10 to 12 min per sheet ● YIELD: About 2 1/2 dozen cookies

This is an old-time American cookie named, some say, for a New Englander known as Uncle Joe who made molasses cookies as large as the lily pads in his frog pond.

Serve these wonderfully spicy cookies with hot apple cider.

1 cup sugar

1/2 cup shortening

1 cup dark molasses

1/2 cup water

4 cups all-purpose flour

1 1/2 teaspoons salt

1 1/2 teaspoons ground ginger

1 teaspoon baking soda

1/2 teaspoon ground cloves

1/2 teaspoon ground nutmeg

1/4 teaspoon ground allspice

Sugar

Beat 1 cup sugar, the shortening, molasses and water in large bowl with electric mixer on low speed, or mix with spoon. Stir in remaining ingredients except sugar. Cover and refrigerate about 2 hours or until firm.

Heat oven to 375°. Lightly grease cookie sheet. Roll one fourth of dough at a time 1/4 inch thick on well-floured cloth-covered surface. Cut into 3-inch rounds. Place about 1 1/2 inches apart on cookie sheet. Sprinkle with sugar. Bake 10 to 12 minutes or until almost no indentation remains when touched in center. Remove from cookie sheet to wire rack.

1 Cookie: Calories 150 (Calories from Fat 35); Fat 4g (Saturated 1g); Cholesterol 0mg; Sodium 160mg; Carbohydrate 27g (Dietary Fiber 0g); Protein 2g.

Raspberry Logs

CHILL: 3 hr • BAKE: 8 to 10 min per sheet • YIELD: 4 dozen cookies

1 cup granulated sugar

1/2 cup butter or margarine

1/4 cup shortening

2 teaspoons vanilla

2 eggs

2 1/4 cups all-purpose flour

1/2 cup ground walnuts

1 teaspoon baking powder

1/4 teaspoon salt

1/2 cup raspberry preserves

Powdered sugar

Beat granulated sugar, butter, shortening, vanilla and eggs in large bowl with electric mixer on medium speed, or mix with spoon. Stir in flour, walnuts, baking powder and salt. Cover and refrigerate about 3 hours or until firm.

Heat oven to 375°. Roll half of dough at a time into 12-inch square on floured cloth-covered surface. Cut into rectangles, 2×3 inches. Spoon 1/2 teaspoon preserves along one 3-inch side of each rectangle to within 1/4 inch of edge. Fold dough over preserves, beginning at 3-inch side. Seal edges with fork. Place on ungreased cookie sheet. Bake 8 to 10 minutes or until light brown. Remove from cookie sheet to wire rack. Roll in powdered sugar while warm.

1 Cookie: Calories 90 (Calories from Fat 35); Fat 4g (Saturated 1g); Cholesterol 10mg; Sodium 50mg; Carbohydrate 12g (Dietary Fiber 0g); Protein 1g.

Cookie Tips

Dust the dough, rolling pin and work surface with just enough flour to keep the dough from sticking because excess flour makes cookies tough. Dough that is very sticky can be rolled between sheets of waxed paper.

"I Don't Have That"

You can easily replace raspberry preserves with strawberry preserves, and if you prefer pecans, use them instead of walnuts.

Pecan Crisps

BAKE: 8 to 10 min per sheet • YIELD: About 4 dozen cookies

Cookie Tips

You have several surface choices when rolling out cookie dough. You can use your countertop, a large cutting board, a marble slab, a pastry cloth or waxed paper.

Make It Your Way

Out of pecans? Make **Almond Crisps** by substituting finely chopped almonds and almond extract for the pecans and vanilla extract.

2 cups sugar

3/4 cup very finely chopped pecans

1/3 cup butter or margarine, softened

1 teaspoon vanilla

2 eggs

2 1/4 cups all-purpose flour

2 1/2 teaspoons baking powder

1/4 teaspoon salt

Heat oven to 375°. Mix sugar and pecans in large bowl; reserve 3/4 cup. Beat butter, vanilla and eggs into remaining sugar mixture with electric mixer on low speed, or mix with spoon. Stir in flour, baking powder and salt.

Roll dough into rectangle, 18 × 13 inches, on lightly floured surface. Sprinkle with reserved sugar mixture. Press sugar mixture into dough with rolling pin. Cut dough diagonally every 2 inches in both directions with pastry wheel or knife to form diamonds. Place about 2 inches apart on ungreased cookie sheet. Bake 8 to 10 minutes or until golden brown. Immediately remove from cookie sheet to wire rack.

1 Cookie: Calories 85 (Calories from Fat 25); Fat 3g (Saturated 0g); Cholesterol 10mg; Sodium 55mg; Carbohydrate 13g (Dietary Fiber 0g); Protein 1g.

Cinnamon-Nut Crisps

BAKE: 10 to 12 min per sheet ● YIELD: About 5 dozen cookies

2 cups all-purpose flour

1/2 cup sugar

3/4 cup shortening

2 to 3 tablespoons water

3 tablespoons butter or margarine, softened

2 tablespoons sugar

1 teaspoon ground cinnamon

2 tablespoons very finely chopped nuts

Sugar

Heat oven to 375°. Mix flour and 1/2 cup sugar in large bowl. Cut in shortening, using pastry blender or crisscrossing 2 knives, until particles are size of small peas. Add water, 1 tablespoon at a time, tossing with fork until mixture almost cleans side of bowl.

Roll dough into rectangle, 15×10 inches, on lightly floured cloth-covered surface. Spread butter over dough. Mix 2 tablespoons sugar and the cinnamon; sprinkle evenly over butter. Sprinkle nuts evenly over sugar mixture. Roll up tightly, beginning at 15-inch side. Pinch edge of dough to seal.

Cut roll into 1/4-inch slices. Place about 2 inches apart on ungreased cookie sheet. Sprinkle with sugar. Bake 10 to 12 minutes or until golden brown. Remove from cookie sheet to wire rack.

1 Cookie: Calories 50 (Calories from Fat 25); Fat 3g (Saturated 1g); Cholesterol 0mg; Sodium 5mg; Carbohydrate 6g (Dietary Fiber 0g); Protein 0g.

Cinnamon

Cinnamon is curled, paper-thin slices of dried bark from a laurellike tree. It is America's most popular spice with a sweet and mild taste.

Make It Your Way

To make **Cinnamon-Nut Butterflies**, prepare and cut slices as directed. Put 2 slices side by side on cookie sheet, overlapping slightly; press to seal. Continue as directed except bake 13 to 15 minutes.

Date-Nut Pinwheels

CHILL: 4 hr ● BAKE: 8 to 10 min per sheet ● YIELD: About 6 dozen cookies

Cookie Tips

A quick and easy way to chop dates is to use a food processor. To keep dates from sticking to blade, add about 1 tablespoon sugar from the recipe to the dates before processing.

Make It Your Way

Create attractive red-filled cookies by making **Cherry-Almond Pinwheels**. Replace pitted dates with dried cherries, use 1/2 cup finely chopped blanched almonds and substitute almond extract for the vanilla. These pretty pinwheels are sure to be a hit on a cookie tray.

3/4 pound pitted dates, finely chopped

1/3 cup granulated sugar

1/3 cup water

1/2 cup finely chopped nuts

1 cup packed brown sugar

1/4 cup shortening

1/4 cup butter or margarine, softened

1/2 teaspoon vanilla

1 egg

1 3/4 cups all-purpose flour

1/4 teaspoon salt

Cook dates, granulated sugar and water in 2-quart saucepan over medium heat, stirring constantly, until slightly thickened; remove from heat. Stir in nuts; cool.

Beat brown sugar, shortening, butter, vanilla and egg in large bowl with electric mixer on medium speed, or mix with spoon. Stir in flour and salt.

Roll half of dough at a time on waxed paper into rectangle, 11×7 inches. Spread half of the date-nut filling over each rectangle to within 1/4 inch of 11-inch sides. Roll up tightly, beginning at 11-inch side, using waxed paper to help lift. Pinch edge of dough to seal. Wrap and refrigerate about 4 hours or until firm.

Heat oven to 400°. Cut rolls into 1/4-inch slices. Place about 1 inch apart on ungreased cookie sheet. Bake 8 to 10 minutes or until light brown. Immediately remove from cookie sheet to wire rack.

1 Cookie: Calories 55 (Calories from Fat 20); Fat 2g (Saturated 0g); Cholesterol 5mg; Sodium 20mg; Carbohydrate 8g (Dietary Fiber 0g); Protein 1g.

Mint Ravioli Cookies

CHILL: 1 hr ● BAKE: 7 to 9 min per sheet ● YIELD: 3 dozen cookies

1/2 cup butter or margarine, softened

1/2 cup shortening

1 cup sugar

1 egg

2 1/2 cups all-purpose flour

1 teaspoon baking powder

1/4 teaspoon salt

3 dozen foil-wrapped rectangular chocolate mints, unwrapped

Beat butter, shortening, sugar and egg in large bowl with electric mixer on medium speed, or mix with spoon. Stir in flour, baking powder and salt. Cover and refrigerate about 1 hour or until firm.

Heat oven to 400°. Roll half of dough into rectangle, 13×9 inches, on lightly floured surface. Place mints on dough, forming 6 uniform rows of 6. Roll remaining dough into rectangle, 13×9 inches, on floured waxed paper. Place over mint-covered dough. Cut dough between mints with pastry wheel or knife; press edges of each "ravioli" with fork to seal. Place 2 inches apart on ungreased cookie sheet. Bake 7 to 9 minutes or until light brown. Remove from cookie sheet to wire rack.

1 Cookie: Calories 125 (Calories from Fat 65); Fat 7g (Saturated 2g); Cholesterol 5mg; Sodium 65mg; Carbohydrate 15g (Dietary Fiber 0g); Protein 1g.

Place mints on dough, forming six rows of six.

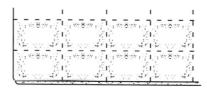

Place remaining dough over mint-covered dough; cut between mints.

Hungarian Poppy Seed Cookies

CHILL: 30 min ● BAKE: 10 to 12 min per sheet ● YIELD: About 3 dozen cookies

Cookie Tips

Lemon peel, clove and poppy seed often flavor Eastern European cookies. Look for commercially prepared poppy seed filling next to canned pie fillings at the supermarket.

Poppy Seed Filling

Poppy seed filling, sold in cans, is a sweet sticky mixture with the texture of thick paste.

1/2 cup butter or margarine

1/4 cup granulated sugar

1 teaspoon grated lemon peel

1 egg

1 1/4 cups all-purpose flour

1/2 teaspoon baking soda

1/4 teaspoon ground cloves

3/4 cup poppy seed filling (from 12 1/2-ounce can)

Powdered sugar

Beat butter and granulated sugar in large bowl with electric mixer on medium speed until light and fluffy, or mix with spoon. Beat in lemon peel and egg. Stir in flour, baking soda and cloves. Roll dough between pieces of waxed paper into 1/4-inch-thick rectangle, 12 × 10 inches. Refrigerate about 30 minutes or until firm.

Heat oven to 350°. Grease cookie sheet. Remove waxed paper from one side of dough. Spread poppy seed filling over dough to within 1/4 inch of edges. Roll up tightly, beginning at 12-inch side, peeling off waxed paper as dough is rolled. Pinch edge of dough to seal.

Cut roll into 1/2-inch slices. Place about 1 inch apart on cookie sheet. Bake 10 to 12 minutes or until edges are light brown. Cool 1 to 2 minutes; remove from cookie sheet to wire rack. Sprinkle with powdered sugar.

1 Cookie: Calories 65 (Calories from Fat 25); Fat 3g (Saturated 1g); Cholesterol 5mg; Sodium 55mg; Carbohydrate 9g (Dietary Fiber 0g); Protein 1g.

Hungarian Poppy Seed Cookies, Mint Ravioli Cookies (page 233)

Glazed Chocolate Pockets

BAKE: 10 to 12 min per sheet ● YIELD: 2 dozen cookies

Cookie Tips

It is easy to glaze all the cookies at one time—set them 1/4 inch apart on a cooling rack over waxed paper and simply pour the glaze over them.

Make It Your Way

Glazed Chocolate Apricot Pockets feature a striking red-speckled filling when you bite into one. To make, replace the coconut with 1/3 cup chopped dried apricots.

1/4 cup powdered sugar

1 package (3 ounces) cream cheese, softened

1/2 teaspoon vanilla

1/3 cup flaked coconut

3/4 cup butter or margarine, softened

2/3 cup granulated sugar

1 egg

2 cups all-purpose flour

1/3 cup baking cocoa

1/4 teaspoon salt

Two-Way Glaze (right)

Heat oven to 375°. Mix powdered sugar and cream cheese with spoon until thoroughly blended. Stir in vanilla and coconut; reserve. Beat butter, granulated sugar and egg in large bowl with electric mixer on medium speed, or mix with spoon. Stir in flour, cocoa and salt.

Roll dough into rectangle, 16×12 inches, on lightly floured cloth-covered surface. Cut into 4-inch squares. Cut squares diagonally in half to form triangles. Place 1 level teaspoon coconut mixture in center of each triangle; flatten slightly. Fold points of triangle to corner, and press edges to seal. Place on ungreased cookie sheet.

Bake 10 to 12 minutes or until set. Remove from cookie sheet to wire rack. Cool completely. Drizzle with Two-Way Glaze.

Two-Way Glaze

1 cup powdered sugar

4 to 6 teaspoons milk

1 tablespoon baking cocoa

1 to 2 teaspoons milk

Mix powdered sugar and 4 to 6 teaspoons milk in 2-cup liquid measuring cup until thin enough to drizzle. Drizzle about half of the glaze over cookies by pouring from measuring cup. (About 3 tablespoons will remain.) Stir cocoa and 1 to 2 teaspoons milk into remaining glaze in cup. Drizzle chocolate glaze over vanilla glaze on cookies.

1 Cookie: Calories 165 (Calories from Fat 70); Fat 8g (Saturated 2g); Cholesterol 15mg; Sodium 110mg; Carbohydrate 21g (Dietary Fiber 0g); Protein 2g.

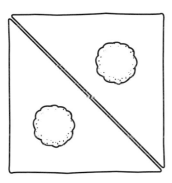

Cut squares in half diagonally to form triangles, and place filling in center of each triangle.

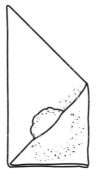

Fold points of triangle to corner.

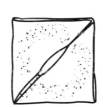

Press edges to seal.

Sunshine Cookies

BAKE: 6 to 8 min per sheet ● YIELD: About 4 dozen cookies

Cookie Tips

These bright yellow cookies have a crunchy texture from the cornmeal and are delicious served with fresh fruit.

Did you know that the Dutch get credit for giving us the word *cookie*? It comes from the Dutch word *koekje* and means "little cake."

1 cup sugar

1/2 cup butter or margarine, softened

1/4 cup shortening

1/2 teaspoon almond extract

2 egg yolks

1 1/4 cups yellow cornmeal

1 cup all-purpose flour

1 teaspoon baking powder

1/4 teaspoon salt

Heat oven to 400°. Beat sugar, butter, shortening, almond extract and egg yolks in large bowl with electric mixer on medium speed, or mix with spoon. Stir in remaining ingredients.

Roll half of dough at a time 1/8 inch thick on lightly floured surface. Cut into desired shapes with 3-inch cutter. Place about 1 inch apart on ungreased cookie sheet. Bake 6 to 8 minutes or until very light brown. Immediately remove from cookie sheet to wire rack.

1 Cookie: Calories 65 (Calories from Fat 25); Fat 3g (Saturated 1g); Cholesterol 10mg; Sodium 45mg; Carbohydrate 9g (Dietary Fiber 0g); Protein 1g.

Almond-Filled Crescents

CHILL: 1 hr ● BAKE: 14 to 16 min per sheet ● YIELD: 4 dozen cookies

1 cup powdered sugar

1 cup whipping (heavy) cream

2 eggs

3 3/4 cups all-purpose flour

1 teaspoon baking powder

1/2 teaspoon salt

1 package (7 or 8 ounces) almond paste

3/4 cup butter or margarine, softened

Easy Glaze (below)

Mix powdered sugar, whipping cream and eggs in large bowl with spoon. Stir in flour, baking powder and salt (dough will be stiff). Cover and refrigerate about 1 hour or until firm.

Heat oven to 375°. Break almond paste into small pieces in medium bowl; add butter. Beat with electric mixer on low speed until blended. Beat on high speed until fluffy (tiny bits of almond paste will remain).

Roll one fourth of dough at a time into 10-inch circle on lightly floured surface. Spread one fourth of almond paste mixture (about 1/2 cup) over circle. Cut into 12 wedges. Roll up wedges, beginning at rounded edge. Place on ungreased cookie sheet with points underneath. Repeat with remaining dough and almond paste mixture. Bake 14 to 16 minutes or until golden brown. Remove from cookie sheet to wire rack. Cool completely. Drizzle with Easy Glaze.

Easy Glaze

1 cup powdered sugar

6 to 7 teaspoons milk

Mix ingredients until smooth and thin enough to drizzle.

1 Cookie: Calories 120 (Calories from Fat 55); Fat 6g (Saturated 2g); Cholesterol 15mg; Sodium 75mg; Carbohydrate 15g (Dietary Fiber 0g); Protein 2g.

Cookie Tips

Use a metal pie server to pull the cut wedges of dough away from the circle.

Make It Your Way

An 8-ounce can of poppy seed filling can be used instead of almond paste to make **Poppy Seed-Filled Crescents**.

Peach Triangles

BAKE: 9 to 12 min per sheet ● YIELD: About 4 dozen cookies

Cookie Tips

When using fruit preserves as a filling, the thicker the better to prevent the filling from running out while the cookies are baking.

Make It Your Way

Cherry Triangles are a special treat for Valentine's Day. Substitute cherry preserves for the peach.

1 cup sugar

1/2 cup shortening

2 eggs

2 cups all-purpose flour

1 1/2 teaspoons baking powder

1/4 teaspoon salt

Peach Filling (below)

Sugar

Heat oven to 375°. Beat 1 cup sugar, the shortening and eggs in large bowl with electric mixer on medium speed, or mix with spoon. Stir in flour, baking powder and salt. Prepare Peach Filling.

Roll half of dough at a time 1/8 inch thick on lightly floured cloth-covered surface. Cut into 3-inch rounds. Place 1 level teaspoon filling on center of each round. Bring three sides of each round together at center to form triangle. Pinch edges together to form 3 slight ridges. Place on ungreased cookie sheet. Sprinkle with sugar. Bake 9 to 12 minutes or until golden brown. Cool 1 to 2 minutes; remove from cookie sheet to wire rack.

Peach Filling

2/3 cup peach preserves

1/2 cup finely chopped dried peaches

Mix ingredients until spreadable.

1 Cookie: Calories 75 (Calories from Fat 20); Fat 2g (Saturated 1g); Cholesterol 10mg; Sodium 30mg; Carbohydrate 13g (Dietary Fiber 0g); Protein 1g.

Toffee Meringue Sticks

CHILL: 1 hr ● BAKE: 12 to 14 min per sheet ● YIELD: About 4 dozen cookies

1 cup packed brown sugar

1/3 cup butter or margarine, softened

1 teaspoon vanilla

1 egg yolk

1/2 cup whipping (heavy) cream

2 1/2 cups all-purpose flour

1/4 teaspoon salt

2 egg whites

1/2 cup granulated sugar

1 package (6 ounces) almond brickle chips (1 cup)

Beat brown sugar, butter, vanilla and egg yolk in large bowl with electric mixer on medium speed, or mix with spoon. Stir in whipping cream. Stir in flour and salt. Cover and refrigerate about 1 hour or until firm.

Heat oven to 375°. Roll one fourth of dough at a time into strip, 12×3 inches, on lightly floured surface. Place 2 strips about 2 inches apart on ungreased cookie sheet.

Beat egg whites in medium bowl on high speed until foamy. Beat in granulated sugar, 1 tablespoon at a time, continue beating until stiff and glossy. Fold in brickle chips. Spread one fourth of the meringue over each strip of dough. Bake 12 to 14 minutes or until edges are light brown. Cool 10 minutes. Cut each strip crosswise into 1-inch sticks. Remove from cookie sheet to wire rack.

1 Cookie: Calories 85(Calories from Fat 25); Fat 3g (Saturated 1g); Cholesterol 10mg; Sodium 45mg; Carbohydrate 14g (Dietary Fiber 0g); Protein 1g.

Cookie Tips

Shape the dough strips easily this way: Roll one fourth of the dough about 10 inches long, then roll and flatten it into a 12×3-inch rectangle.

Make It Your Way

To make **Hazelnut Meringue Sticks**, substitute granulated sugar for the brown sugar and 3/4 cup (2.5 ounces) ground hazelnuts for the almond brickle pieces.

CHAPTER 7

The Ultimate Spritz *244*
Date-Filled Spritz *246*
Key Lime Coolers *247*
Ladyfingers *248*
Almond Macaroons *250*
Swedish Half-Moon
   Cookies *251*
Palmiers *252*
Springerle *254*
Pizzelles *254*
Krumkake *256*
Orange Madeleines *257*
Cookie-Mold Cookies *258*
Chocolate-Cherry Sand
   Tarts *259*
Brandy Snap Cups *260*
Snowflakes *261*
Rosettes *262*

The Ultimate Valentine's Day
   Cookie *264*
Chocolate Linzer Hearts *266*
Orange-Almond Pillows *267*
Lebkuchen *268*
Miniature Florentines *269*
Sugar Cookie Stockings *270*
Gingerbread Village *272*
Hamantaschen *274*
Esther's Bracelets *276*
Cranberry-Orange
   Cookies *278*
Frosted Pumpkin-Pecan
   Cookies *279*
Hazelnut Sablés *280*
Lemon Tea Biscuits *281*
Spicy Seascape Cookies *282*
Orange Slices *283*

Celebrate with Cookies

Key Lime Coolers (page 247),
Brandy Snap Cups (page 260)

Wonderful, warm memories and family traditions are often centered around the holidays. We often go the extra mile and do something just a little more special. For many of us, that means making spritz cookies. This tender, little butter cookie has passed the test of time.

The Ultimate Spritz

BAKE: 5 to 8 min per sheet ● YIELD: About 6 1/2 dozen cookies

Cookie Tips

These cookies are delicate and crisp with a rich, buttery flavor that is perfect for any occasion.

The name for these cookies comes from the German word *spritzen*, meaning "to squirt" because the soft dough is squirted or pushed through a cookie press to make fancy designs.

Make It Your Way

Chocolate Spritz are easily made by stirring 2 ounces unsweetened chocolate, melted and cooled, into the margarine-sugar mixture.

To make **Spice Spritz**, stir in 1 teaspoon ground cinnamon, 1/2 teaspoon ground nutmeg and 1/4 teaspoon ground allspice with the flour.

1 cup butter or margarine, softened

1/2 cup sugar

2 1/4 cups all-purpose flour

1/4 teaspoon salt

1 egg

1/4 teaspoon almond extract or vanilla

Currants, raisins, candies, colored sugar, finely chopped nuts, candied fruit or fruit peel, if desired

Heat oven to 400°. Beat butter and sugar in large bowl with electric mixer on medium speed, or mix with spoon. Stir in remaining ingredients.

Place dough in cookie press. Form desired shapes on ungreased cookie sheet. Decorate with currants.

Bake 5 to 8 minutes or until set but not brown. Immediately remove from cookie sheet to wire rack. To decorate cookies after baking, use a drop of corn syrup to attach decorations to cookies.

1 Cookie: Calories 45 (Calories from Fat 25); Fat 3g (Saturated 1g); Cholesterol 5mg; Sodium 40mg; Carbohydrate 4g (Dietary Fiber 0g); Protein 1g.

The Ultimate Spritz, Date-Filled Spritz (page 246)

Date-Filled Spritz

BAKE: 12 to 15 min per sheet ● YIELD: About 4 dozen cookies

The Ultimate Spritz (page 244)

The Ultimate Spritz (page 244)

1 package (8 ounces) pitted dates (about 1 1/4 cups)

1 cup walnut pieces (about 4 ounces)

1/4 cup sugar

1/4 cup honey

1 teaspoon grated orange peel

2 tablespoons orange juice

Cookie Tips

Citrus fruits will produce more juice if first microwaved on the High setting for 15 to 20 seconds before squeezing.

Make It Your Way

A bright-red filling is what you will see in **Cranberry-Filled Spritz**. Replace the dates with dried cranberries.

Heat oven to 375°. Prepare dough for The Ultimate Spritz, using vanilla. Place remaining ingredients in food processor. Cover and process about 20 seconds, using quick on-and-off motions, until mixture is ground and resembles thick paste.

Place dough in cookie press with ribbon tip. Form 10-inch ribbons about 2 inches apart on ungreased cookie sheet. Spoon date mixture down center of each ribbon to form 1/2-inch-wide strip. Top with another ribbon of dough. Gently press edges with fork to seal.

Bake 12 to 15 minutes or until light brown. Immediately cut ribbons into 2-inch lengths. Remove from cookie sheet to wire rack.

1 Cookie: Calories 100 (Calories from Fat 45); Fat 5g (Saturated 1g); Cholesterol 5mg; Sodium 60mg; Carbohydrate 13g (Dietary Fiber 0g); Protein 1g.

Key Lime Coolers

BAKE: 9 to 11 min per sheet • YIELD: About 4 dozen cookies

1 cup butter or margarine

1/2 cup powdered sugar

1 3/4 cups all-purpose flour

1/4 cup cornstarch

1 tablespoon grated lime peel

1/2 teaspoon vanilla

Granulated sugar

Key Lime Glaze (below)

Heat oven to 350°. Beat butter and powdered sugar in large bowl with electric mixer on medium speed until light and fluffy, or mix with spoon. Stir in flour, cornstarch, lime peel and vanilla until well blended.

Shape dough into 1-inch balls. Place about 2 inches apart on ungreased cookie sheet. Press bottom of glass into dough to grease, then dip into granulated sugar; press on shaped dough until 1/4 inch thick. Bake 9 to 11 minutes or until edges are light golden brown. Remove from cookie sheet to wire rack. Cool completely. Brush with Key Lime Glaze.

Key Lime Glaze

1/2 cup powdered sugar

2 teaspoons grated lime peel

4 teaspoons Key lime or regular lime juice

Mix all ingredients until smooth.

1 Cookie: Calories 70 (Calories from Fat 35); Fat 4g (Saturated 1g); Cholesterol 0mg; Sodium 45mg; Carbohydrate 7g (Dietary Fiber 0g); Protein 1g.

Cookie Tips

Powdered sugar and cornstarch create the "melt-in-your-mouth" quality of these cookies.

Florida residents will find Key lime juice makes these refreshing cookies even more special.

Make It Your Way

If you like using a cookie press, try making **Key Lime Ribbons.** Prepare dough as directed, but do not shape into balls. Place dough in cookie press with ribbon tip. Form long ribbons of dough on ungreased cookie sheet. Cut into 3-inch lengths. Continue as directed above.

Ladyfingers

BAKE: 10 to 12 min per sheet ● YIELD: About 3 1/2 dozen cookies

Cookie Tips

To create the cookies as seen in the picture, spread lemon curd or chocolate frosting between two Ladyfingers.

Make It Your Way

Make **Chocolate-Dipped Ladyfingers** by dipping cookies halfway into melted chocolate. Place on waxed paper to set.

3 eggs, separated

1/4 teaspoon cream of tartar

1/4 cup granulated sugar

1/3 cup granulated sugar

3/4 cup all-purpose flour

3 tablespoons water

1/2 teaspoon vanilla

1/4 teaspoon baking powder

1/4 teaspoon lemon extract, if desired

1/8 teaspoon salt

Powdered sugar, if desired

Heat oven to 350°. Grease and flour cookie sheet. Beat egg whites and cream of tartar in large bowl with electric mixer on medium speed until foamy. Beat in sugar, 1 tablespoon at a time; continue beating until stiff peaks form.

Beat egg yolks and 1/3 cup granulated sugar in medium bowl on medium speed about 3 minutes or until thick and lemon colored. Stir in remaining ingredients except powdered sugar. Fold egg yolk mixture into egg white mixture.

Place batter in decorating bag with #9 tip or in cookie press with #32 tip. Form 3-inch fingers about 2 inches apart on cookie sheet. Bake 10 to 12 minutes or until set and light brown. Immediately remove from cookie sheet to wire rack. Sprinkle tops with powdered sugar while warm.

1 Cookie: Calories 25 (Calories from Fat 0); Fat 0g (Saturated 0g); Cholesterol 15mg; Sodium 15mg; Carbohydrate 5g (Dietary Fiber 0g); Protein 1g.

Ladyfingers, Almond Macaroons (page 250)

Almond Macaroons

CHILL: 30 min ● BAKE: 12 min per sheet ● YIELD: About 3 dozen cookies

Cookie Tips

Don't waste those egg yolks! Place them in a small container, adding enough water to cover yolks completely (to prevent drying). Cover tightly and refrigerate up to 24 hours. Drain water before using.

Make It Your Way

Add 2 teaspoons finely grated orange peel and 3 drops each red and yellow food color to create **Orange-Almond Macaroons**.

1 package (7 or 8 ounces) almond paste
1/4 cup all-purpose flour
1 1/4 cups powdered sugar
1/4 teaspoon almond extract
2 egg whites
3 dozen blanched whole almonds

Grease cookie sheet. Break almond paste into small pieces in large bowl. Stir in flour, powdered sugar and almond extract. Add egg whites. Beat with electric mixer on medium speed about 2 minutes, scraping bowl occasionally, until smooth.

Place dough in decorating bag fitted with #9 rosette tip. Pipe 1 1/2-inch cookies about 2 inches apart onto cookie sheet. Top each with almond. Refrigerate 30 minutes.

Heat oven to 325°. Bake about 12 minutes or until edges are light brown. Immediately remove from cookie sheet to wire rack. Cool completely. Store in airtight container.

1 Cookie: Calories 60 (Calories from Fat 20); Fat 2g (Saturated 0g); Cholesterol 0mg; Sodium 5mg; Carbohydrate 9g (Dietary Fiber 0g); Protein 1g.

Swedish Half-Moon Cookies

CHILL: 1 hr ● BAKE: 10 to 12 min per sheet ● YIELD: About 3 dozen cookies

1 3/4 cups all-purpose flour

1/2 cup potato flour or cornstarch

1/2 cup powdered sugar

1 cup butter or margarine, well chilled and cut into cubes

1/8 teaspoon almond extract

1 egg

1/2 cup cherry preserves

1 egg white, beaten

1/4 cup white coarse sugar crystals (decorating sugar)

1/4 cup finely chopped blanched almonds

Mix flours and powdered sugar in large bowl. Cut in butter, using pastry blender or crisscrossing 2 knives, until mixture resembles fine crumbs. Stir in almond extract and egg until dough leaves side of bowl. Cover and refrigerate 1 hour.

Heat oven to 350°. Cover cookie sheet with baking parchment paper. Roll one fourth of dough at a time between pieces of waxed paper until 1/8 inch thick. (Keep remaining dough refrigerated until ready to roll.) Cut with fluted 3-inch round biscuit cutter. Spoon 1/2 teaspoon cherry preserves onto half of each cookie. Fold dough over preserves to form half-moon shape. Pinch edges to seal. Place on cookie sheet.

Brush dough with egg white. Sprinkle with sugar crystals and almonds. Bake 10 to 12 minutes or until edges are light brown. Remove from cookie sheet to wire rack.

1 Cookie: Calories 105 (Calories from Fat 55); Fat 6g (Saturated 1g); Cholesterol 5mg; Sodium 65mg; Carbohydrate 12g (Dietary Fiber 0g); Protein 1g.

Potato Flour

This tender cookie is made with potato flour (sometimes called "potato starch"). It is often found in stores near the cornstarch, in a section with gluten-free products and in health food stores.

"I Don't Have That"

Replace cherry preserves with peach preserves. The peach flavor blends well with the flavor of almonds.

Palmiers

BAKE: 8 to 10 min per sheet • YIELD: About 2 1/2 dozen cookies

Sugar

1/2 package (17 1/4-ounce size) frozen puff pastry (1 sheet), thawed

1/2 cup sugar

1 ounce semisweet baking chocolate, melted

Heat oven to 375°. Lightly grease cookie sheet. Sprinkle sugar over kitchen counter or breadboard. Roll pastry into 1/8-inch-thick rectangle, 12×9 1/2 inches, on sugared surface. Mark a line lengthwise down center of rectangle. Fold long sides of rectangle toward center line, leaving 1/4 inch uncovered at center. Fold rectangle lengthwise in half to form strip, 12×2 1/2 inches, lightly pressing pastry together.

Cut strip crosswise into 1/4-inch slices. Coat both sides of slices with 1/2 cup sugar. Place about 2 inches apart on cookie sheet. Bake 8 to 10 minutes, turning after 5 minutes, until cookies begin to turn golden brown. Immediately remove from cookie sheet to wire rack. Cool completely. Dip ends of cookies into melted chocolate. Place on waxed paper until chocolate is firm.

1 Cookie: Calories 60 (Calories from Fat 20); Fat 2g (Saturated 1g); Cholesterol 0mg; Sodium 25mg; Carbohydrate 9g (Dietary Fiber 0g); Protein 1g.

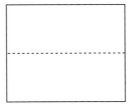

Mark a line lengthwise down center of dough.

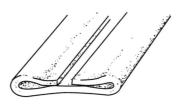

Fold long sides toward center line, leaving 1/4 inch at center.

Fold dough in half lengthwise to form strip.

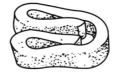

Cut dough strip crosswise into slices.

Palmiers, Anise Biscotti (page 204)

Springerle

BAKE: 12 to 15 min per sheet ● YIELD: About 3 dozen cookies

Anise seed is one of the oldest cultivated spices and was enjoyed by the early Egyptians. It has a sweet mildly licorice taste and is used for flavoring candy, baked products and seafood.

1 cup sugar

2 eggs

2 cups all-purpose flour

2 teaspoons anise seed

Heat oven to 325°. Beat sugar and eggs with electric mixer on medium speed about 5 minutes or until thick and lemon colored. Stir in flour and anise seed.

Roll half of dough at a time 1/4 inch thick on floured cloth-covered surface. Roll well-floured springerle rolling pin over dough to emboss with designs. Cut out cookies around designs. Place about 1 inch apart on ungreased cookie sheet. Bake 12 to 15 minutes or until light brown. Immediately remove from cookie sheet to wire rack.

1 Cookie: Calories 50 (Calories from Fat 0); Fat 0g (Saturated 0g); Cholesterol 10mg; Sodium 5mg; Carbohydrate 11g (Dietary Fiber 0g); Protein 1g.

Pizzelles

COOK: 30 seconds per cookie ● YIELD: About 3 1/2 dozen cookies

These Italian cookies are wafer-thin and lightly flavored with anise. They are cooked in a hot pizzelle iron, also known as a "cialde" iron.

If you work quickly, pizzelles can be rolled into a cone shape and used as ice-cream cones. Or if you prefer, roll the cookies into cylinders and fill with pastry or whipped cream.

2 cups all-purpose flour

1 cup sugar

3/4 cup butter or margarine, melted and cooled

1 tablespoon anise extract or vanilla

4 eggs, slightly beaten

Heat pizzelle iron according to manufacturer's directions. Mix all ingredients in a medium bowl. Drop 1 tablespoon batter onto heated pizzelle iron; close. Cook about 30 seconds or until golden brown. Carefully remove pizzelle from iron. Cool on wire rack. Repeat for each cookie.

1 Cookie: Calories 75 (Calories from Fat 35); Fat 4g (Saturated 1g); Cholesterol 20mg; Sodium 45mg; Carbohydrate 9g (Dietary Fiber 0g); Protein 1g.

Springerle, Pizzelles, Krumkake (page 256)

Krumkake

COOK: 30 seconds per cookie ● YIELD: About 4 dozen cookies

1 cup sugar

3/4 cup all-purpose flour

1/2 cup butter or margarine, melted

1/3 cup whipping (heavy) cream

1 teaspoon vanilla

2 teaspoons cornstarch

4 eggs

Beat all ingredients with spoon until smooth. Heat krumkake iron over small electric or gas unit on medium-high heat until hot (grease lightly if necessary). Pour scant tablespoon batter onto iron; close gently. Heat each side about 15 seconds or until light golden brown. Keep iron over heat at all times. Carefully remove cookie. Immediately roll around cone-shape roller. Remove roller when cookie is set. Cool on wire rack.

1 Cookie: Calories 55 (Calories from Fat 25); Fat 3g (Saturated 1g); Cholesterol 20mg; Sodium 30mg; Carbohydrate 6g (Dietary Fiber 0g); Protein 1g.

Orange Madeleines

BAKE: 10 to 12 min per pan ● YIELD: About 2 dozen cookies

1 egg, separated
1/2 cup granulated sugar
1 cup all-purpose flour
1/2 cup milk
2 tablespoons vegetable oil
1 tablespoon orange-flavored liqueur
1 1/2 teaspoons baking powder
1 1/2 teaspoons grated orange peel
1/4 teaspoon salt
Powdered sugar

Heat oven to 375°. Grease and flour twenty-four 3-inch* madeleine mold pan. Beat egg white in small bowl with electric mixer on medium speed until foamy. Beat in 1/4 cup of the granulated sugar, 1 tablespoon at a time; continue beating until very stiff and glossy. Set aside.

Beat remaining 1/4 cup granulated sugar, the egg yolk and remaining ingredients except powdered sugar in medium bowl on high speed 2 minutes, scraping bowl occasionally. Fold in egg white mixture.

Fill molds two thirds full. Tap pan firmly on counter to remove air bubbles. Bake 10 to 12 minutes or until edges are light brown. Cool 1 to 2 minutes; remove from molds to wire rack. Cool completely. Sprinkle with powdered sugar just before serving.

1 Cookie: Calories 50 (Calories from Fat 10); Fat 1g (Saturated 0g); Cholesterol 10mg; Sodium 60mg; Carbohydrate 9g (Dietary Fiber 0g); Protein 1g.

One 12-mold pan can be used. Bake half of batter; wash, grease and flour pan. Bake remaining batter. Twenty-four-mold pans are also available.

Cookie Tips

Sponge cakes in miniature, French madeleines are baked in shell-shape molds. If you must bake the recipe in 2 batches, don't let the batter sit any longer than it has to, or the second batch will not be a tender as the first.

Make It Your Way

Attractive pink-colored **Cherry Madeleines** or **Berry Madeleines** are made by using maraschino cherry juice or raspberry-flavored liqueur for the orange-flavored liqueur.

Cookie-Mold Cookies

CHILL: 2 hr ● BAKE: 8 to 10 min per sheet of molds for 2-inch cookies, 10 to 12 min for 5-inch cookies
YIELD: About 4 1/2 dozen 2-inch cookies or 2 dozen 5-inch cookies

Cookie Tips

Slightly spicy with a hint of almond, these cookies are reminiscent of the Dutch-heritage, store-bought cookies in the shape of windmills. If you have windmill molds, use them, but any cookie mold will do. Molds have been used to shape cookies in China and Europe for hundreds of years, and some American molds date to the eighteenth century.

Make It Your Way

To make cookies in a cast-iron cookie mold, first grease and flour the mold(s). Press dough into mold as directed. Bake smaller molds about 15 minutes, larger molds about 20 minutes. Cool cookies 10 minutes before removing from molds.

3/4 cup packed brown sugar
1/2 cup butter or margarine, softened
1/4 cup molasses
1/2 teaspoon vanilla
1 egg
2 1/4 cups all-purpose flour
1/2 teaspoon ground allspice
1/4 teaspoon salt
1/4 teaspoon baking soda
3/4 cup coarsely chopped sliced almonds

Beat brown sugar, butter, molasses, vanilla and egg in large bowl with electric mixer on medium speed, or mix with spoon. Stir in remaining ingredients except almonds. Stir in almonds. Cover and refrigerate about 2 hours or until firm.

Heat oven to 350°. Lightly grease cookie sheet. Flour wooden or ceramic cookie mold(s). Tap mold to remove excess flour. Firmly press small amounts of dough into mold, adding more dough until mold is full and making sure dough is a uniform thickness across mold. Hold mold upright and tap edge firmly several times on hard surface (such as a counter or cutting board). If cookie does not come out, turn mold and tap another edge until cookie comes out of mold. Place cookies on cookie sheet.

Bake 8 to 10 minutes for 2-inch cookies, 10 to 12 minutes for 5-inch cookies, or until edges are light brown. (Time depends on thickness of cookies; watch carefully.) Remove from cookie sheet to wire rack.

1 Cookie: Calories 65 (Calories from Fat 25); Fat 3g (Saturated 0g); Cholesterol 5mg; Sodium 40mg; Carbohydrate 8g (Dietary Fiber 0g); Protein 1g.

Chocolate-Cherry Sand Tarts

CHILL: 2 hr ● BAKE: 12 to 15 min per sheet of molds ● YIELD: About 4 1/2 dozen cookies

3/4 cup sugar

3/4 cup butter or margarine, softened

1 egg white

1 3/4 cups all-purpose flour

1/4 cup baking cocoa

About 1 3/4 cups cherry preserves

Chocolate Drizzle (below)

Beat sugar, butter and egg white in large bowl with electric mixer on medium speed, or mix with spoon. Stir in flour and cocoa. Cover and refrigerate about 2 hours or until firm.

Heat oven to 350°. Shape dough into 1 inch balls. Press each ball in bottom and up side of each ungreased sandbakelse mold, about 1 3/4 × 1/2 inch. Spoon about 1 1/2 teaspoons cherry preserves into each mold. Place on cookie sheet.

Bake 12 to 15 minutes or until crust is set. Cool 10 minutes; carefully remove from molds to wire rack. Cool completely. Drizzle with Chocolate Drizzle.

Chocolate Drizzle

2/3 cup semisweet chocolate chips

1 tablespoon shortening

Melt ingredients over low heat, stirring occasionally, until smooth.

1 Cookie: Calories 95 (Calories from Fat 35); Fat 4g (Saturated 1g); Cholesterol 0mg; Sodium 35mg; Carbohydrate 14g (Dietary Fiber 0g); Protein 1g.

Cookie Tips

To quickly make Chocolate Glaze, place chocolate chips and shortening in a microwavable bowl. Microwave uncovered on Medium (50%) 1 to 2 minutes or until mixture can be stirred smooth.

Sandbakelse Mold

A sandbakelse mold is a metal pan designed with tiny fluted cups and is used to bake tiny cookies with a filling. These molds can be found at kitchenware specialty stores.

Brandy Snap Cups

BAKE: 4 min ● YIELD: About 15 cookies

Cookie Tips

These crispy, thin cookies have a delicate, crisp texture and a subtle flavor that complements fruit.

Make It Your Way

Delight and dazzle your guests with an extra fancy dessert, **Chocolate Berry Cups**. First, drizzle chocolate syrup on the dessert plate in any pattern you desire. Next, fill the cookie cup with ice cream and top with fresh berries. Pass the chocolate syrup for those wanting just a little more to top their dessert!

1/4 cup butter or margarine

1/4 cup dark corn syrup

2 tablespoons plus 2 teaspoons brown sugar

1 teaspoon brandy

6 tablespoons all-purpose flour

1/4 teaspoon ground ginger

4 cups mixed fresh strawberries and raspberries

2/3 cup raspberry jam, melted

Heat oven to 350°. Heat butter, corn syrup and brown sugar to boiling in 1 1/2-quart saucepan, stirring frequently; remove from heat. Stir in brandy. Mix flour and ginger; gradually stir into syrup mixture. Drop dough by heaping teaspoonfuls at least 5 inches apart onto lightly greased cookie sheets or line sheets with baking parchment paper. Bake until cookies have spread into 4- or 5-inch rounds and are golden brown, 3 to 4 minutes (watch carefully as these cookies brown quickly).

Cool cookies 1 to 3 minutes before removing from cookie sheets. Working quickly, shape over inverted drinking glass about 2 to 2 1/2 inches in diameter. Allow cookies to harden; remove gently and place on wire racks. Cool completely. If cookies become too crisp to shape, return to oven to soften about 1 minute. Fill each cookie cup with 1/4 cup berries. Drizzle with jam.

1 Cookie: Calories 105 (Calories from Fat 25); Fat 3g (Saturated 2g); Cholesterol 20mg; Sodium 35mg; Carbohydrate 10g (Dietary Fiber 2g); Protein 1g.

Snowflakes

FRY: 1 min per cookie ● YIELD: About 3 1/2 dozen cookies

3 eggs, beaten

2 tablespoons vegetable oil

1/2 teaspoon baking powder

1/4 teaspoon salt

1 3/4 to 2 cups all-purpose flour

Vegetable oil

Powdered sugar

Mix eggs, 2 tablespoons oil, the baking powder and salt in large bowl with spoon. Gradually stir in enough flour to make a very stiff dough. Turn onto lightly floured surface. Knead 5 minutes.

Heat oil (at least 1 inch deep) in Dutch oven to 375°. Roll half of dough at a time as thin as possible on generously floured surface, turning dough frequently to prevent sticking. (Dough will bounce back; continue rolling until it stays stretched out.)

Cut dough into 3-inch squares, hexagons or circles, using pastry wheel, knife or cookie cutter. Fold pieces into fourths. Cut random designs into edges.* Open folded dough. Fry 2 or 3 opened dough pieces at a time about 30 seconds or until light brown. Turn quickly and fry about 30 seconds or until light brown on other side. Drain on paper towels. Cool completely. Sprinkle with powdered sugar just before serving.

1 Cookie: Calories 40 (Calories from Fat 20); Fat 2g (Saturated 0g); Cholesterol 15mg; Sodium 25mg; Carbohydrate 4g (Dietary Fiber 0g); Protein 1g.

Cut all pieces before starting to fry, placing them on lightly floured surface.

Cookie Tips

Cut these snowflake cookies just as you would fold paper snowflakes. Canape cutters can also be used to cut designs in the dough.

For a quick and easy way to sprinkle cookies, keep a salt shaker filled with powdered sugar in your cupboard.

Rosettes

FRY: 30 seconds per cookie ● YIELD: About 2 dozen cookies

Cookie Tips

Be sure the rosette iron is hot enough or the batter will stick. Test the first rosette for crispness. If it isn't crisp enough, the batter is too thick; stir in a small amount of water or milk, about 1 or 2 tablespoons.

These delicate, lacy cookies are easily broken, so store them carefully in a loosely covered, flat container.

1 tablespoon granulated sugar

1/2 teaspoon salt

1 egg

1/2 cup all-purpose flour

1/2 cup water or milk

1 tablespoon vegetable oil

Vegetable oil

Rosette Glaze (below) or powdered sugar

Beat granulated sugar, salt and egg in deep 1 1/2-quart bowl with electric mixer on medium speed. Beat in flour, water and 1 tablespoon oil until smooth. Heat oil (2 to 3 inches) in 3-quart saucepan over medium-high heat to 400°.

Heat rosette iron before making each cookie by placing in hot oil 1 minute. Tap excess oil from iron onto paper towel. Dip hot iron into batter just to top edge (do not go over top). Fry about 30 seconds or until golden brown. Immediately remove rosette. Invert onto paper towel to cool. Just before serving, dip rosettes into Rosette Glaze, or sprinkle with powdered sugar.

Rosette Glaze

1 1/2 cups powdered sugar

3 tablespoons milk

1/2 teaspoon grated orange or lemon peel or 1/2 teaspoon vanilla or 1/4 teaspoon almond extract

Food color, if desired

Mix all ingredients until smooth.

1 Cookie: Calories 60 (Calories from Fat 20); Fat 2g (Saturated 0g); Cholesterol 10mg; Sodium 50mg; Carbohydrate 10g (Dietary Fiber 0g); Protein 1g.

Rosettes, Snowflakes (page 261)

The Ultimate Valentine's Day Cookie

BAKE: 5 to 7 min per sheet ● YIELD: About 4 dozen cookies

1 cup powdered sugar

1 cup butter or margarine, softened

1 tablespoon white vinegar

2 1/4 cups all-purpose flour

1 1/2 teaspoons ground ginger

3/4 teaspoon baking soda

1/4 teaspoon salt

6 drops red food color

Heat oven to 400°. Beat powdered sugar, butter and vinegar in large bowl with electric mixer on medium speed, or mix with spoon. Stir in remaining ingredients except food color. Divide dough in half. Mix food color into one half. (If dough is too dry, stir in milk, 1 teaspoon at a time.)

Roll dough 1/8 inch thick on lightly floured cloth-covered surface. Cut into heart shapes with various sizes of cookie cutters. Place smaller hearts on larger hearts of different color dough if desired. Place about 2 inches apart on ungreased cookie sheet.

Bake 5 to 7 minutes or until set but not brown. Cool 1 to 2 minutes; carefully remove from cookie sheet to wire rack. Cool completely. Decorate with white and pink Decorator's Frosting (page 210) if desired.

1 Cookie: Calories 70 (Calories from Fat 35); Fat 4g (Saturated 1g); Cholesterol 0mg; Sodium 75mg; Carbohydrate 7g (Dietary Fiber 0g); Protein 1g.

The Ultimate Valentine's Day Cookie, Chocolate Linzer Hearts (page 266)

Chocolate Linzer Hearts

CHILL: 1 hr ● BAKE: 7 to 9 min per sheet ● YIELD: 3 dozen cookies

Cookie Tips

These cookies are a variation of the famous Austrian Linzer Torte. The toasted hazelnuts, raspberry jam and chocolate provide a unique taste sensation.

Hazelnuts

Hazelnuts, also called "filberts," are the nuts of the hazel tree, which is a member of the birch family.

1 cup butter or margarine, softened

1/2 cup sugar

1 teaspoon vanilla

2 eggs

1 cup hazelnuts, toasted (page 64), skinned and ground

1/2 ounce semisweet baking chocolate, finely chopped

2 1/2 cups all-purpose flour

1 1/2 teaspoons ground cinnamon

1/2 teaspoon ground nutmeg

1/2 cup raspberry jam

1 ounce semisweet baking chocolate, melted

Beat butter and sugar in large bowl with electric mixer on medium speed until light and fluffy, or mix with spoon. Beat in vanilla and eggs until smooth. Add remaining ingredients except jam and melted chocolate. Beat until well blended. Cover and refrigerate 1 hour (dough will be sticky).

Heat oven to 375°. Roll one fourth of dough at a time between pieces of waxed paper until 1/8 inch thick. (Keep remaining dough refrigerated until ready to roll.) Cut with 2-inch heart-shape cookie cutter. Cut small heart shape from center of half of the 2-inch hearts, if desired. Place on ungreased cookie sheet.

Bake 7 to 9 minutes or until light brown. Remove from cookie sheet to wire rack. Cool completely. Spread about 1/2 teaspoon raspberry jam on bottom of whole heart cookies; top with cut-out heart cookie. Drizzle with melted chocolate. Let stand until chocolate is firm.

1 Cookie: Calories 125 (Calories from Fat 65); Fat 7g (Saturated 1g); Cholesterol 10mg; Sodium 65mg; Carbohydrate 14g (Dietary Fiber 0g); Protein 2g.

Orange-Almond Pillows

BAKE: 10 to 12 min per sheet ● YIELD: About 2 dozen cookies

1 1/2 cups blanched whole almonds, ground
1 tablespoon grated orange peel
1 egg white
1/2 cup powdered sugar
Orange Glaze (below)

Heat oven to 350°. Grease and flour cookie sheet, or cover with cooking parchment paper. Mix ground almonds and orange peel; set aside. Beat egg white in medium bowl with electric mixer on high speed until stiff but not dry. Gradually beat in powdered sugar. Beat on high speed about 3 minutes or until slightly stiff. Fold almond mixture into egg white mixture (mixture will be stiff).

Roll dough into rectangle, 9×6 inches, on cloth-covered surface generously dusted with powdered sugar. Cut into 1 1/2-inch squares. Place 1 inch apart on cookie sheet. Bake 10 to 12 minutes or until set and very light brown. Remove from cookie sheet to wire rack. Cool completely. Drizzle with Orange Glaze.

Orange Glaze

3/4 cup powdered sugar
1/4 teaspoon grated orange peel
3 to 4 teaspoons orange juice

Mix all ingredients until smooth and thin enough to drizzle.

1 Cookie: Calories 80 (Calories from Fat 45); Fat 5g (Saturated 0g); Cholesterol 0mg; Sodium 5mg; Carbohydrate 8g (Dietary Fiber 1g); Protein 2g.

Cookie Tips

These little puffs really look like pillows. For crisp cookies, bake until light brown. For chewy cookies, bake until just set, but not brown.

"I Don't Have That"

The cookies are just as delicious when grated lemon peel and lemon juice are used instead of orange peel and orange juice in the cookies and glaze.

Lebkuchen

CHILL: 8 hr ● BAKE: 10 to 12 min per sheet ● YIELD: About 5 dozen cookies

1/2 cup honey

1/2 cup molasses

3/4 cup packed brown sugar

1 teaspoon grated lemon peel

1 tablespoon lemon juice

1 egg

2 3/4 cups all-purpose flour

1 teaspoon ground allspice

1 teaspoon ground cinnamon

1 teaspoon ground cloves

1 teaspoon ground nutmeg

1/2 teaspoon baking soda

1/3 cup cut-up citron

1/3 cup chopped nuts

Glazing Icing (below)

Heat honey and molasses to boiling in 1-quart saucepan; remove from heat and cool completely. Mix honey-molasses mixture, brown sugar, lemon peel, lemon juice and egg in large bowl with spoon. Stir in remaining ingredients except citron, nuts and Glazing Icing. Stir in citron and nuts. Cover and refrigerate at least 8 hours but no longer than 24 hours.

Prepare Glazing Icing. Heat oven to 400°. Grease cookie sheet. Roll one fourth of dough at a time 1/4 inch thick on lightly floured cloth-covered surface. Cut into rectangles, 2 1/2 × 1 1/2 inches. Place 1 inch apart on cookie sheet. Bake 10 to 12 minutes or until no indentation remains when touched in center.

Brush Glazing Icing lightly over hot cookies. Immediately remove from cookie sheet to wire rack. Cool completely.

Glazing Icing

1 cup granulated sugar

1/2 cup water

1/4 cup powdered sugar

Mix granulated sugar and water in 1-quart saucepan. Cook over medium heat to 230°. Stir in powdered sugar. If icing becomes sugary while brushing on cookies, reheat slightly, adding a small amount of water until clear again.

1 Cookie: Calories 75 (Calories from Fat 10); Fat 1g (Saturated 0g); Cholesterol 5mg; Sodium 15mg; Carbohydrate 16g (Dietary Fiber 0g); Protein 1g.

Miniature Florentines

BAKE: 4 to 6 min per sheet ● YIELD: About 6 dozen cookies

1/2 cup sugar

1/4 cup butter or margarine

1/4 cup whipping (heavy) cream

2 tablespoons honey

1/2 cup sliced almonds

1/4 cup candied orange peel, finely chopped

1 tablespoon grated orange peel

1 package (4 ounces) sweet baking chocolate, melted

Heat oven to 375°. Cover cookie sheet with cooking parchment paper. Mix sugar, butter, whipping cream and honey in 2 1/2-quart saucepan. Heat to boiling, stirring constantly. Boil 5 minutes, stirring constantly; remove from heat. Stir in remaining ingredients. Let stand 5 minutes.

Drop mixture by 1/2 teaspoonfuls 2 inches apart onto cookie sheet. Bake 4 to 6 minutes or until golden brown and bubbly. Cool 2 minutes or until firm; remove from cookie sheet to wire rack. Cool completely.

Turn cookies upside down; brush with melted chocolate. Let stand at room temperature until chocolate is firm.

1 Cookie: Calories 30 (Calories from Fat 20); Fat 2g (Saturated 1g); Cholesterol 0mg; Sodium 10mg; Carbohydrate 3g (Dietary Fiber 0g); Protein 0g.

Cookie Tips

Watch these little cookies carefully because they darken quickly.

Florentines were invented by Austrian bakers and usually contain butter, sugar, cream, honey and candied fruit. They often have one side dipped in chocolate.

Sugar Cookie Stockings

CHILL: 2 hr ● BAKE: 9 min per sheet ● YIELD: 7 to 12 cookies

Cookie Tips

Feel free to make any shape you like. Draw a Santa's hat, Christmas tree or bell and use that as the pattern to make a host of holiday cookies.

Start a tradition by making these cookies with your family to enjoy during the holidays or to give as gifts.

Mary's Sugar Cookies (page 208)
Food colors, if desired
Thin Cookie Glaze (below) or Decorator's Frosting (page 210)

Prepare and refrigerate dough for Mary's Sugar Cookies as directed, tinting dough with desired food colors.

Heat oven to 375°. Roll one third of dough at a time 3/16 inch thick on lightly floured cloth-covered surface. Cut into 6- to 8-inch stockings. (To enlarge pattern, see directions (page 271). If desired, cut toy-shape cookies to stick out of tops of stockings.

Place stockings on ungreased cookie sheet. Cut accent dough (toes, heels, cuffs) to place on stockings if desired. Bake about 9 minutes or until light brown. Cool 1 to 2 minutes; remove from cookie sheet to wire rack. Cool completely. Spread with Thin Cookie Glaze.

Thin Cookie Glaze

2 cups powdered sugar
2 tablespoons milk
1/4 teaspoon almond extract
4 or 5 drops red or green food color
About 1/3 cup powdered sugar

Mix 2 cups powdered sugar, the milk, and almond extract. Tint half of the mixture with food color. Add additional milk, a few drops at a time, if necessary, or until desired spreading consistency. Place baked cookies on wire rack. Pour small amount of tinted glaze over each cookie; spread to edge with spatula. Add enough powdered sugar to remaining glaze to make frosting that can be used in a decorating bag and will hold its shape. Place in decorating bag with #2 writing tip. Decorate cookies as desired. Makes enough to glaze and decorate 8 to 10 stockings

1 Cookie: Calories 645 (Calories from Fat 245); Fat 27g (Saturated 6g); Cholesterol 30mg; Sodium 500mg; Carbohydrate 95g (Dietary Fiber 1g); Protein 6g.

Sugar Cookie Stockings

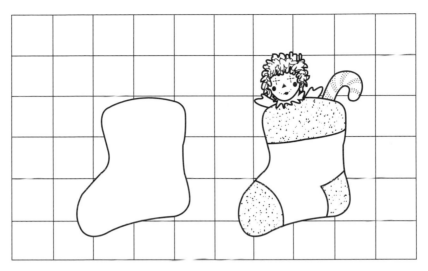

1. Enlarge grid to desired size and draw in stocking pattern.

2. Add toy-shape cookies to top of stocking and accent dough to toes, heels and cuffs if desired.

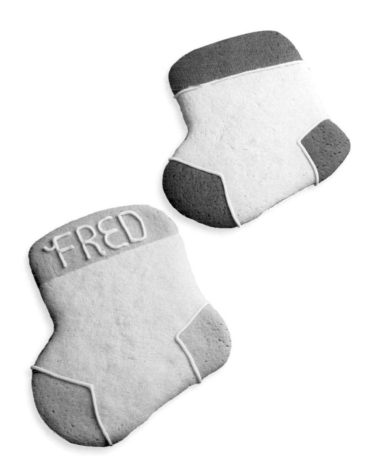

Gingerbread Village

BAKE: 15 min per pan ● YIELD: One 4-building village

Cookie Tips

Decorate the buildings any way you like. Use red cinnamon candies, licorice bits and whips, jelly candies, jelly beans, pillow mints, peppermints and whatever else strikes your fancy. Sliced almonds are wonderful masonry or paving stones. Make an old-fashioned lamppost from a peppermint stick with small gingerbread squares as the lantern top.

Gingerbread

Gingerbread is a type of cake or shaped cookie flavored with molasses and ginger. It was one of the favorites of early Americans when molasses was often the only sweetener available.

1/2 cup packed brown sugar
1/4 cup shortening
3/4 cup dark molasses
1/3 cup cold water
3 1/2 cups all-purpose flour
1 teaspoon baking soda
1 teaspoon ground ginger
1/2 teaspoon salt
1/2 teaspoon ground allspice
1/2 teaspoon ground cinnamon
1/2 teaspoon ground cloves
Gingerbread Frosting (below)
Assorted candies and nuts

Heat oven to 350°. Grease square pan, 9×9×2 inches, and jelly roll pan, 15 1/2×10 1/2×1 inch. Beat brown sugar, shortening and molasses in large bowl with electric mixer on medium speed, or mix with spoon. Stir in water. Stir in remaining ingredients except Frosting and assorted candies.

Press one third of dough into square pan. Press remaining dough into jelly roll pan. Bake 1 pan at a time about 15 minutes or until no indentation remains when touched in center. Cool 5 minutes. Invert onto large cutting surface. Immediately cut jelly roll into fourths and then into buildings as shown on page 273. Cut square into braces as shown. Cool completely.

Cover piece of cardboard, about 28×10 inches, with aluminum foil. Decorate front of buildings as desired with Frosting and assorted candies and nuts. Use frosting to attach supports to backs of buildings, buildings to cardboard and sidewalk to cardboard. Complete by decorating as desired.

Gingerbread Frosting

2 cups powdered sugar
1/3 cup shortening
2 tablespoons light corn syrup
5 to 6 teaspoons milk

Mix all ingredients until smooth and spreadable.

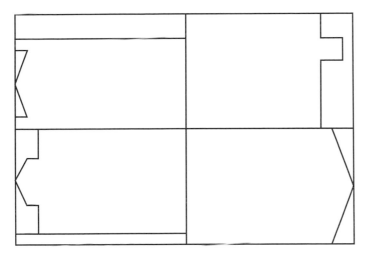
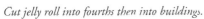

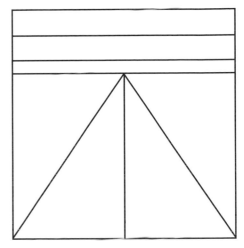

Cut jelly roll into fourths then into buildings.

Cut square into braces.

Gingerbread Village

Hamantaschen

CHILL: 2 hr ● BAKE: 12 to 15 min per sheet ● YIELD: About 4 dozen cookies

Cookie Tips

These rich, filled cookies celebrate the holiday of Purim, which honors the victory of the Jews of ancient Persia over Haman's plot to destroy them. Haman was an adviser to King Ahasuerus, and Hamantaschen are "Haman's pockets." Some Hamantaschen recipes call for a yeast-raised or sour cream dough; we use a short crust dough for tender results.

To speed up the making of these cookies, use canned apricot or poppy seed filling.

2 1/2 cups all-purpose flour

1/2 cup sugar

1 teaspoon baking powder

3/4 cup butter or margarine

1 teaspoon grated lemon peel

1/2 teaspoon vanilla

2 eggs

Prune Filling (below), Apricot or Plum Filling or Poppy Seed Filling (right)

Mix flour, sugar and baking powder in large bowl. Cut in butter, using pastry blender or crisscrossing 2 knives, until mixture resembles fine crumbs. Mix lemon peel, vanilla and eggs. Stir into flour mixture until dough forms a ball. (Use hands to mix all ingredients if necessary; add up to 1/4 cup additional flour if dough is too sticky to handle.) Cover and refrigerate about 2 hours or until firm.

Prepare desired filling. Heat oven to 350°. Roll half of dough at a time 1/8 inch thick on lightly floured cloth-covered surface. Cut into 3-inch rounds. Spoon 1 level teaspoon filling onto each round. Bring up 3 sides, using metal spatula to lift, to form triangle around filling. Pinch edges together firmly. Place about 2 inches apart on ungreased cookie sheet. Bake 12 to 15 minutes or until light brown. Immediately remove from cookie sheet to wire rack.

Prune Filling

1 package (12 ounces) pitted prunes

1 cup chopped walnuts

2 tablespoons honey

1 tablespoon lemon juice

Heat prunes and enough water to cover to boiling in 2-quart saucepan; reduce heat. Cover and simmer 10 minutes; drain well. Mash prunes. Stir in remaining ingredients.

Apricot or Plum Filling

1 1/2 cups apricot or plum jam

1/2 cup finely chopped almonds or walnuts

1 teaspoon grated lemon peel

1 tablespoon lemon juice

About 1/2 cup dry bread crumbs

Mix jam, almonds, lemon peel and lemon juice. Stir in just enough bread crumbs until thickened.

Poppy Seed Filling

1 cup poppy seed

1/4 cup walnut pieces

1 tablespoon butter or margarine

1 tablespoon honey

1 teaspoon lemon juice

1 egg white

Place all ingredients in blender or food processor. Cover and blend until smooth.

1 Cookie: Calories 105 (Calories from Fat 45); Fat 5g (Saturated 1g); Cholesterol 10mg; Sodium 45mg; Carbohydrate 13g (Dietary Fiber 0g); Protein 2g.

Esther's Bracelets

BAKE: 9 to 11 min per sheet ● YIELD: About 6 dozen cookies

Cookie Tips

Queen Esther revealed the evil plot of Haman to King Ahasuerus of ancient Persia, thereby saving the Persian Jews. These almond cookies honor her. Serve these cookies at a Purim celebration.

"I Don't Have That"

Walnuts can be used to replace the almonds in this recipe. When you make this substitution, be sure to use vanilla instead of almond extract.

1 cup sugar

3/4 cup butter or margarine, softened

3/4 cup shortening

1/2 teaspoon almond extract

2 eggs

4 cups all-purpose flour

1/2 cup finely chopped almonds

Glaze (below)

Finely chopped almonds, if desired

Heat oven to 375°. Beat sugar, butter, shortening, almond extract and eggs in large bowl with electric mixer on medium speed, or mix with spoon. Stir in flour and 1/2 cup almonds.

Shape dough into 1 1/4-inch balls. Roll each ball into rope, 6 inches long. Form each rope into circle, crossing ends and tucking under. Place on ungreased cookie sheet. Bake 9 to 11 minutes or until set but not brown. Remove from cookie sheet to wire rack. Cool completely. Drizzle with Glaze. Sprinkle with finely chopped almonds.

Glaze

3 cups powdered sugar

4 to 5 tablespoons milk

Mix ingredients until thin enough to drizzle.

1 Cookie: Calories 100 (Calories from Fat 45); Fat 5g (Saturated 1g); Cholesterol 5mg; Sodium 25mg; Carbohydrate 13g (Dietary Fiber 0g); Protein 1g.

Esther's Bracelets, Hamantaschen (page 274)

Cranberry-Orange Cookies

BAKE: 12 to 14 min per sheet • YIELD: About 4 dozen cookies

Cookie Tips

With all the lovely flavors of a holiday cranberry quick-bread, these cookies are soft-centered with slightly crunchy edges.

Cranberries

This indigenous American fruit was first called "crane berries" after the shape of the shrub's pale pink blossoms, which look like the heads of cranes. Also, cranes were often seen wading in the cranberry bogs. Cranberries are harvested in the autumn but can be found year-round in supermarkets. They have become a staple in celebrating the Thanksgiving holiday.

1 cup granulated sugar

1/2 cup packed brown sugar

1 cup butter or margarine, softened

1 teaspoon grated orange peel

2 tablespoons orange juice

1 egg

2 1/2 cups all-purpose flour

1/2 teaspoon baking soda

1/2 teaspoon salt

2 cups coarsely chopped fresh or frozen cranberries

1/2 cup chopped nuts, if desired

Orange Frosting (below)

Heat oven to 375°. Beat sugars, butter, orange peel, orange juice and egg in large bowl with electric mixer on medium speed, or mix with spoon. Stir in flour, baking soda and salt. Stir in cranberries and nuts.

Drop dough by rounded tablespoonfuls about 2 inches apart onto ungreased cookie sheet. Bake 12 to 14 minutes or until light brown. Remove from cookie sheet to wire rack. Cool completely. Spread with Orange Frosting.

Orange Frosting

1 1/2 cups powdered sugar

1/2 teaspoon grated orange peel

3 tablespoons orange juice

Mix all ingredients until smooth and spreadable.

1 Cookie: Calories 105 (Calories from Fat 35); Fat 4g (Saturated 1g); Cholesterol 5mg; Sodium 85mg; Carbohydrate 16g (Dietary Fiber 0g); Protein 1g.

Frosted Pumpkin-Pecan Cookies

BAKE: 12 to 15 min ● YIELD: About 5 dozen cookies

1 1/2 cups packed brown sugar

1/2 cup butter or margarine, softened

1/2 cup shortening

1 cup canned pumpkin

1 egg

2 1/3 cups all-purpose flour

1 teaspoon baking powder

1/2 teaspoon salt

1/2 teaspoon ground cinnamon

2 cups chopped pecans

Spiced Frosting (below)

Heat oven to 350°. Beat brown sugar, butter and shortening in large bowl with electric mixer on medium speed, or mix with spoon. Stir in pumpkin and egg. Stir in flour, baking powder, salt and cinnamon. Stir in pecans.

Drop dough by rounded tablespoonfuls about 2 inches apart onto ungreased cookie sheet; flatten slightly. Bake 12 to 15 minutes or until no indentation remains when touched lightly in center. Remove from cookie sheet to wire rack. Cool completely. Frost with Spiced Frosting.

Spiced Frosting

3 cups powdered sugar

1/4 cup butter or margarine, softened

1/4 teaspoon ground cinnamon

3 to 4 tablespoons milk

Mix all ingredients until smooth and spreadable.

1 Cookie: Calories 130 (Calories from Fat 65); Fat 7g (Saturated 1g); Cholesterol 5mg; Sodium 60mg; Carbohydrate 16g (Dietary Fiber 0g); Protein 1g.

Hazelnut Sablés

CHILL: 1 hr ● BAKE: 8 to 10 min per sheet ● YIELD: About 3 dozen cookies

Cookie Tips

Sablés (pronounced "sah blay") is the French word for "sandies," which are rich, short cookies.

"I Don't Have That"

Pecans can be substituted for the hazelnuts.

3/4 cup butter or margarine, softened

3/4 cup powdered sugar

1/2 teaspoon vanilla

1 egg yolk

1 1/4 cups all-purpose flour

1/2 cup hazelnuts, toasted (page 64) and ground

1 egg, beaten

1/4 cup chopped hazelnuts

1/4 cup white coarse sugar crystals (decorating sugar)

Beat butter and powdered sugar in large bowl with electric mixer on medium speed until light and fluffy, or mix with spoon. Stir in vanilla and egg yolk. Stir in flour and ground hazelnuts until well blended. Cover tightly and refrigerate 1 hour.

Heat oven to 350°. Roll one fourth of dough at a time 1/4 inch thick on lightly floured surface. (Keep remaining dough refrigerated until ready to roll.) Cut into 2 1/2-inch rounds. Place about 2 inches apart on ungreased cookie sheet.

Brush with egg. Sprinkle with chopped hazelnuts and sugar crystals. Bake 8 to 10 minutes or until edges are light brown. Remove from cookie sheet to wire rack.

1 Cookie: Calories 80 (Calories from Fat 45); Fat 5g (Saturated 1g); Cholesterol 10mg; Sodium 45mg; Carbohydrate 8g (Dietary Fiber 0g); Protein 1g.

Lemon Tea Biscuits

CHILL: 1 hr ● BAKE: 7 to 9 min per sheet ● YIELD: 4 dozen cookies

1 cup butter or margarine, softened

1/2 cup sugar

1 tablespoon grated lemon peel

1/4 teaspoon salt

1 egg

2 cups all-purpose flour

1/2 cup ground pecans

1 cup lemon curd

Tart Lemon Glaze (below)

Beat butter, sugar, lemon peel, salt and egg in large bowl with electric mixer on medium speed, or mix with spoon. Stir in flour and pecans. Cover and refrigerate about 1 hour or until firm.

Heat oven to 350°. Roll half of dough at a time about 1/8 inch thick on lightly floured surface. Cut into 2-inch rounds. Place on ungreased cookie sheet. Bake 7 to 9 minutes or just until edges are starting to brown. Remove from cookie sheet to wire rack. Cool completely. Spread 1 rounded teaspoonful lemon curd between bottoms of pairs of cookies. Brush tops with Tart Lemon Glaze.

Tart Lemon Glaze

1/4 cup powdered sugar

1 teaspoon grated lemon peel

2 teaspoons lemon juice

Mix all ingredients until smooth and spreadable.

1 Cookie: Calories 85 (Calories from Fat 45); Fat 5g (Saturated 1g); Cholesterol 10mg; Sodium 65mg; Carbohydrate 9g (Dietary Fiber 0g); Protein 1g.

Spicy Seascape Cookies

BAKE: 7 to 9 min per sheet ● YIELD: About 4 1/2 dozen cookies

Cookie Tips

Cookie Tips

Generous amounts of cardamom and cinnamon give these cookies their spicy kick. If you prefer a milder flavor, cut the amount of spices in half.

Cardamom

Cardamom is an exotic spice with a warm, slightly pungent flavor. It's best to purchase the whole pods and crush the seeds as needed because the ground seeds quickly lose their flavor and aroma.

3/4 cup butter or margarine, softened

2/3 cup powdered sugar

2 tablespoons light molasses

1 egg

2 cups all-purpose flour

2 teaspoons ground cardamom

1 1/2 teaspoons ground cinnamon

1 teaspoon baking soda

Thin Glaze (below)

Heat oven to 325°. Grease cookie sheet. Beat butter, powdered sugar, molasses and egg in large bowl with electric mixer on medium speed, or mix with spoon. Stir in flour, cardamom, cinnamon and baking soda.

Roll one third of dough at a time 1/8 inch thick on lightly floured surface. Cut into sand dollars, starfish and scallops as directed below. Bake 7 to 9 minutes or until light brown. Remove from cookie sheet to wire rack. Cool completely. Prepare Thin Glaze; decorate cookies as directed.

1 Cookie: Calories 60 (Calories from Fat 25); Fat 3g (Saturated 1g); Cholesterol 5mg; Sodium 55mg; Carbohydrate 7g (Dietary Fiber 0g); Protein 1g.

Thin Glaze

3/4 cup powdered sugar

1 tablespoon plus 1 1/2 teaspoons hot water

Peach or coral paste food color

Mix all ingredients until smooth. If glaze becomes too stiff, add additional hot water, 1/2 teaspoon at a time.

Sand Dollars: Cut dough with round 3-inch cutter. Place on cookie sheet. Draw five-pointed star in middle of circle. Make small hole in center and indentations at edge of circle. After baking, brush with uncolored Thin Glaze; sprinkle with granulated sugar if desired.

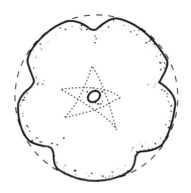

Starfish: Cut dough with five-pointed star-shape cutter. Place on cookie sheet. Curve tips of stars and make indentations down center of each starfish "arm" with knife. After baking, brush with tinted Thin Glaze.

Scallops: Cut dough with scalloped 2 1/2-inch round cutter. Cut 2 small wedges off bottom of circle to form base of shell. Draw curved lines across top, using knife, to form shell pattern. After baking, brush with tinted Thin Glaze. While glaze is still wet, lightly sprinkle with baking cocoa; brush to make marbled effect.

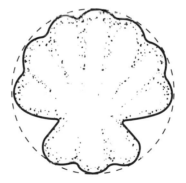

Orange Slices

CHILL: 1 hr • BAKE: 7 to 8 min per sheet • YIELD: About 6 dozen cookies

1 1/2 cups powdered sugar

1 cup butter or margarine, softened

1 tablespoon grated orange peel

1 teaspoon vanilla

1 egg

2 3/4 cups all-purpose flour

1 teaspoon baking soda

1 teaspoon cream of tartar

Orange sugar (in Cookie Tips)

Frosting (below)

Beat powdered sugar and butter in large bowl with electric mixer on medium speed, or mix with spoon. Stir in orange peel, vanilla and egg. Stir in flour, baking soda and cream of tartar. Cover and refrigerate about 1 hour or until firm.

Heat oven to 375°. Roll half of dough at a time 1/8 inch thick on lightly floured surface. Cut into 3-inch rounds; cut rounds in half. Place on ungreased cookie sheet. Sprinkle with orange sugar. Bake 7 to 8 minutes or until light brown. Remove from cookie sheet to wire rack. Cool completely. Place Frosting in decorating bag with #3 writing tip. Pipe on cookies to outline orange segments.

Frosting

2 cups powdered sugar

1/2 teaspoon vanilla

About 2 tablespoons half-and-half

Mix all ingredients until smooth and spreadable.

1 Cookie: Calories 70 (Calories from Fat 25); Fat 3g (Saturated 1g); Cholesterol 5mg; Sodium 50mg; Carbohydrate 10g (Dietary Fiber 0g); Protein 1g.

Orange Slices, Spicy Seascape Cookies (page 282)

CHAPTER 8

Jumbo Molasses Cookies *288*
Coconut-Almond
 Macaroons *290*
Frosted Banana Bars *291*
Peanut Butter–Marshmallow
 Treats *292*
Oatmeal Raisin Cookies *293*
Brownie Crinkles *294*
Walnut Biscotti *296*
Chocolaty Meringue Stars *298*
Chocolate Mini-Chippers *299*

No-Roll Coconut-Sugar
 Cookies *300*
Ginger-Almond Cookies *302*
Glazed Lemon Bars *303*
Raspberry-Chocolate Bars *304*
Chocolate-Pecan Squares *306*
Cardamom-Cashew Bars *308*
Golden Cereal-Nut
 Clusters *309*
Butter Crunch Clusters *310*

Special Cookies for Special Diets

Coconut-Almond Macaroons (page 290),
Chocolaty Meringue Stars (page 298)

Eggless, wheat-free and low-fat are just some of the special recipes often requested, so picking just one is difficult. Jumbo Molasses Cookies wins on two points: The cookies don't contain eggs, and they're low in fat.

Jumbo Molasses Cookies

CHILL: 3 hr   ●   BAKE: 10 to 12 min per sheet   ●   YIELD: About 3 dozen cookies

Cookie Tips

These oversize cookies are cakelike and tender, even without any eggs. They have an added bonus of being low in fat too.

Make It Your Way

Frosted Jumbo Molasses Cookies are an old-fashioned favorite. Frost them with Vanilla Frosting on page 21.

1 cup sugar

1/2 cup shortening

1 cup dark molasses

1/2 cup water

4 cups all-purpose flour

1 1/2 teaspoons salt

1 1/2 teaspoons ground ginger

1 teaspoon baking soda

1/2 teaspoon ground cloves

1/2 teaspoon ground nutmeg

1/4 teaspoon ground allspice

Sugar

Beat 1 cup sugar and the shortening in large bowl with electric mixer on medium speed, or mix with spoon. Stir in remaining ingredients except sugar. Cover and refrigerate at least 3 hours until dough is firm.

Heat oven to 375°. Generously grease cookie sheet. Roll dough 1/4 inch thick on generously floured cloth-covered surface. Cut into 3-inch circles. Sprinkle with sugar. Place about 1 1/2 inches apart on cookie sheet. Bake 10 to 12 minutes or until almost no indentation remains when touched lightly in center. Cool 2 minutes; remove from cookie sheet to wire rack.

1 Cookie: Calories 125 (Calories from Fat 25); Fat 3g (Saturated 1g); Cholesterol 0mg; Sodium 135mg; Carbohydrate 23g (Dietary Fiber 0g); Protein 1g
Diet Exchanges: 1 1/2 starch.

Jumbo Molasses Cookies

Coconut-Almond Macaroons

BAKE: 20 to 25 min per sheet • YIELD: About 3 1/2 dozen cookies

Cookie Tips

Egg whites beat much more quickly if they are at room temperature. Egg whites can be left on the counter for up to 30 minutes to warm.

Make It Your Way

Make **Peppermint-Coconut-Almond Macaroons** by substituting peppermint for the almond extract.

3 egg whites

1/4 teaspoon cream of tartar

1/8 teaspoon salt

3/4 cup sugar

1/4 teaspoon almond extract

2 cups flaked coconut

9 candied cherries, each cut into fourths

Heat oven to 300°. Cover cookie sheet with aluminum foil or cooking parchment paper. Beat egg whites, cream of tartar and salt in small bowl with electric mixer on high speed until foamy. Beat in sugar, 1 tablespoon at a time; continue beating until stiff and glossy. Do not underbeat. Pour into medium bowl. Fold in almond extract and coconut.

Drop mixture by teaspoonfuls about 1 inch apart onto cookie sheet. Place 1 cherry piece on each cookie. Bake 20 to 25 minutes or just until edges are light brown. Cool 10 minutes; remove from foil to wire rack.

1 Cookie: Calories 35 (Calories from Fat 10); Fat 1g (Saturated 1g); Cholesterol 0mg; Sodium 20mg; Carbohydrate 6g (Dietary Fiber 0g); Protein 0g.
Diet Exchanges: 1/2 fruit.

Frosted Banana Bars

BAKE: 20 to 25 min per pan ● YIELD: 24 bars

2/3 cup sugar

1/2 cup reduced-fat sour cream

2 tablespoons butter or margarine, softened

2 egg whites or 1/4 cup fat-free cholesterol-free egg product

3/4 cup mashed very ripe bananas (2 medium)

1 teaspoon vanilla

1 cup all-purpose flour

1/2 teaspoon baking soda

1/4 teaspoon salt

2 tablespoons finely chopped walnuts

White Frosting (below)

Ground nutmeg, if desired

Cookie Tips

Put overripe bananas in the freezer, unpeeled, for later use. When you're ready to use them, just thaw them, cut off the top of the peel and squeeze the banana into your mixing bowl.

Frosting and glazes made with skim milk are more translucent-looking than those made with whole milk.

Heat oven to 375°. Spray square pan, 9×9×2 inches, with cooking spray. Beat sugar, sour cream, butter and egg whites in large bowl with electric mixer on low speed 1 minute, scraping bowl occasionally. Beat in bananas and vanilla on low speed 30 seconds. Beat in flour, baking soda and salt on medium speed 1 minute, scraping bowl occasionally. Stir in walnuts. Spread in pan.

Bake 20 to 25 minutes or until light brown; cool. Frost with White Frosting. Sprinkle with nutmeg. Cut into 6 rows by 4 rows.

White Frosting

1 1/4 cups powdered sugar

1 tablespoon butter or margarine, softened

1/2 teaspoon vanilla

1 to 2 tablespoons skim milk

Mix all ingredients until smooth and spreadable.

1 Bar: Calories 95 (Calories from Fat 20); Fat 2g (Saturated 1g); Cholesterol 0mg; Sodium 75mg; Carbohydrate 18g (Dietary Fiber 0g); Protein 1g.
Diet Exchanges: 1 starch.

Peanut Butter–
Marshmallow Treats

PREP: 12 min per pan ● YIELD: 36 squares

Cookie Tips

Not only are these treats egg-less, but they're low in fat too!

Make It Your Way

Just for fun, roll the cereal mixture into balls instead of putting it into a pan.

32 large marshmallows or 3 cups miniature marshmallows

1/4 cup butter or margarine

1/2 teaspoon vanilla

5 cups Reese's® Peanut Butter Puffs® cereal

Spray square pan, 9×9×2 inches, with cooking spray. Heat marshmallows and butter in 3-quart saucepan over low heat, stirring constantly, until marshmallows are melted and mixture is smooth; remove from heat. Stir in vanilla.

Stir in half of the cereal at a time until evenly coated. Press in pan; cool. Cut into 6 rows by 6 rows.

1 Square: Calories 45 (Calories from Fat 10); Fat 1g (Saturated 0g); Cholesterol 0mg; Sodium 60mg; Carbohydrate 9g (Dietary Fiber 0g); Protein 0g.
Diet Exchanges: 1/2 starch.

Oatmeal-Raisin Cookies

BAKE: 9 to 11 min per sheet ● YIELD: About 3 dozen cookies

2/3 cup granulated sugar

2/3 cup packed brown sugar

1/2 cup butter or margarine, softened

1/2 cup unsweetened applesauce

1/2 cup fat-free, cholesterol-free egg product or 2 eggs

1 1/2 teaspoons ground cinnamon

1 teaspoon baking soda

1/2 teaspoon baking powder

1/2 teaspoon salt

1 1/2 teaspoons vanilla

3 cups quick-cooking or old-fashioned oats

1 cup all-purpose flour

2/3 cup raisins

Heat oven to 375°. Mix all ingredients except oats, flour and raisins in large bowl with spoon. Stir in oats, flour and raisins.

Drop dough by rounded tablespoonfuls about 2 inches apart onto ungreased cookie sheet. Bake 9 to 11 minutes or until light brown. Immediately remove from cookie sheet to wire rack.

1 Cookie: Calories 105 (Calories from Fat 25); Fat 3g (Saturated 1g); Cholesterol 0mg; Sodium 110mg; Carbohydrate 18g (Dietary Fiber 1g); Protein 2g.
Diet Exchanges: 1 starch, 1/2 fat.

Brownie Crinkles

BAKE: 10 to 12 min per sheet ● YIELD: About 3 1/2 dozen cookies

Cookie Tips

You're not going to believe how rich, fudgy and chewy these cookies really are.

Make It Your Way

Serve these cookies with fat-free vanilla yogurt and fat-free chocolate fudge ice-cream topping.

1 package Betty Crocker Sweet Rewards low-fat fudge brownie mix

1/4 cup water

1/4 cup fat-free, cholesterol-free egg product or 1 egg

1/2 cup powdered sugar

Heat oven to 350°. Grease cookie sheet. Mix brownie mix (dry), water and egg product with spoon about 50 strokes or until well blended.

Shape dough by rounded teaspoonfuls into balls. Roll in powdered sugar. Place about 2 inches apart on cookie sheet. Bake 10 to 12 minutes or until almost no indentation remains when touched lightly in center. Immediately remove from cookie sheet to wire rack.

1 Cookie: Calories 65 (Calories from Fat 10); Fat 1g (Saturated 0g); Cholesterol 0mg; Sodium 50mg; Carbohydrate 13g (Dietary Fiber 0g); Protein 1g.
Diet Exchanges: 1 starch.

Brownie Crinkles

Walnut Biscotti

BAKE: 25 to 30 min per sheet ● YIELD: About 2 1/2 dozen cookies

3/4 cup walnut halves, toasted (page 64)

1 cup all-purpose flour

3/4 cup whole wheat flour

1/2 cup packed brown sugar

1 teaspoon baking soda

1/2 teaspoon ground cinnamon

Dash of salt

3 egg whites or 1/2 cup fat-free, cholesterol-free egg product

Heat oven to 350°. Spray nonstick cookie sheet with cooking spray. Place walnuts in food processor or blender. Cover and process, using quick on-and-off motions, until walnuts are consistency of coarse meal. Mix 1/2 cup of the ground walnuts and the remaining ingredients except egg whites in large bowl. Stir in egg whites thoroughly until stiff dough forms.

Sprinkle remaining ground walnuts on cutting board or waxed paper. Divide dough in half. Shape each half into rectangle, 7×3 inches, on walnuts. Carefully transfer rectangles onto ungreased cookie sheet. Bake 15 minutes. Cut crosswise into 1/2-inch slices. Turn slices cut sides down on cookie sheet.

Bake 10 to 15 minutes or until crisp and browned. Remove from cookie sheet to wire rack. Store tightly covered.

1 Cookie: Calories 70 (Calories from Fat 20); Fat 2g (Saturated 0g); Cholesterol 0mg; Sodium 60mg; Carbohydrate 10g (Dietary Fiber 0g); Protein 1g.
Diet Exchanges: 1 starch.

Walnut Biscotti

Chocolaty Meringue Stars

BAKE: 33 to 35 min per sheet • YIELD: About 4 dozen cookies

Cookie Tips

These yummy little cookies are perfect to serve to anyone who is allergic to wheat.

Plastic containers with tight-fitting lids or resealable freezer bags are perfect for storing cookies.

3 egg whites

1/2 teaspoon cream of tartar

2/3 cup sugar

2 tablespoons plus 1 teaspoon baking cocoa

About 1/3 cup ground walnuts

Heat oven to 275°. Cover cookie sheet with aluminum foil or baking parchment paper. Beat egg whites and cream of tartar in medium bowl with electric mixer on medium speed until foamy. Beat in sugar, 1 tablespoon at a time; continue beating until stiff and glossy. Do not underbeat. Fold in cocoa. (Batter will not be mixed completely; there will be some streaks of cocoa.)

Place meringue in decorating bag fitted with large star tip (#4). Pipe 1 1/4-inch stars onto cookie sheet. Sprinkle lightly with walnuts; brush excess nuts from cookie sheet.

Bake 33 to 35 minutes or until outside is crisp and dry (meringues will be soft inside). Cool 5 minutes; remove from cookie sheet to wire rack. Store in airtight container.

1 Cookie: Calories 10 (Calories from Fat 0); Fat 0g (Saturated 0g); Cholesterol 0mg; Sodium 5mg; Carbohydrate 3g (Dietary Fiber 0g); Protein 0g.
Diet Exchanges: no exchanges.

Chocolate Mini-Chippers

BAKE: 8 to 10 min per sheet ● YIELD: About 2 1/2 dozen cookies

1/2 cup granulated sugar

1/4 cup packed brown sugar

1/4 cup butter or margarine, softened

1 teaspoon vanilla

1 egg white or 2 tablespoons fat-free, cholesterol-free egg product

1/2 cup all-purpose flour

1/2 cup whole wheat flour

1/2 teaspoon baking soda

1/4 teaspoon salt

1/2 cup miniature semisweet chocolate chips

Heat oven to 375°. Beat sugars, butter, vanilla and egg white in large bowl with electric mixer on medium speed, or mix with spoon. Stir in flours, baking soda and salt. Stir in chocolate chips.

Drop dough by rounded teaspoonfuls about 2 inches apart onto ungreased cookie sheet. Bake 8 to 10 minutes or until golden brown. Cool 1 to 2 minutes; remove from cookie sheet to wire rack.

1 Cookie: Calories 60 (Calories from Fat 20); Fat 2g (Saturated 1g); Cholesterol 0mg; Sodium 60mg; Carbohydrate 10g (Dietary Fiber 0g); Protein 1g.
Diet Exchanges: 1/2 starch, 1/2 fat

Cookie Tips

You can have your favorite cookie and not miss out on the taste. One little trick is to use miniature chocolate chips—their size allows them to be distributed more evenly through the dough, giving you chocolate in each bite!

Make It Your Way

You can eliminate the whole wheat flour and use all-purpose flour in its place.

No-Roll Coconut-Sugar Cookies

BAKE: 8 to 10 min per sheet ● YIELD: About 8 dozen cookies

Cookie Tips

Can't eat eggs? You'll love this delightful, eggless sugar cookie.

Make It Your Way

Here's how to make **Soft No-Roll Sugar Cookies**: Decrease sugar to 1 1/2 cups and butter to 1 1/2 cups. Add 1 egg with the sugar. Substitute 1 teaspoon baking powder for the baking soda. Flatten cookies to 2 inches in diameter. Bake 7 to 9 minutes or until set (cookies will be pale). Cool 1 to 2 minutes before removing from cookie sheet. Store tightly covered.

2 cups sugar

2 cups butter or margarine, softened

1 cup flaked coconut

1 teaspoon vanilla

3 cups all-purpose flour

1 teaspoon baking soda

1/2 teaspoon salt

Sugar

Heat oven to 350°. Beat 2 cups sugar, the butter, coconut and vanilla in large bowl with electric mixer on medium speed, or mix with spoon. Stir in flour, baking soda and salt.

Shape dough by rounded teaspoonfuls into balls. Place about 3 inches apart on ungreased cookie sheet. Press bottom of glass into dough to grease, then dip into sugar; press on shaped dough to flatten slightly. Bake 8 to 10 minutes or until edges are golden brown. Remove from cookie sheet to wire rack.

1 Cookie: Calories 70 (Calories from Fat 35); Fat 4g (Saturated 1g); Cholesterol 0mg; Sodium 70mg; Carbohydrate 8g (Dietary Fiber 0g); Protein 0g.
Diet Exchanges: 1/2 starch, 1 fat.

No-Roll Coconut-Sugar Cookies

Ginger-Almond Cookies

CHILL: 3 hr ● BAKE: 9 min per sheet ● YIELD: About 7 dozen cookies

Cookie Tips

Here's another eggless recipe to add to your reportoire!

A straight-edged knife blade makes it easier to cut even slices of refrigerated dough. Another tip is to cut straight down through the dough; don't use a sawing motion.

1 1/2 cups sugar

1 1/2 cups shortening

3/4 cup molasses

4 cups all-purpose flour

1 tablespoon plus 1 teaspoon ground ginger

1 tablespoon ground cinnamon

1 tablespoon ground cloves

1 1/2 teaspoons baking soda

1 1/2 teaspoons salt

1 1/2 cups finely chopped almonds

Beat sugar, shortening and molasses in large bowl with electric mixer on medium speed, or mix with spoon. Stir in remaining ingredients except almonds. Stir in almonds. Divide dough in half. Shape each half into roll, about 2 inches in diameter. Wrap and refrigerate at least 3 hours.

Heat oven to 350°. Cut dough into 1/4-inch slices. Place 2 inches apart on ungreased cookie sheet. Bake about 9 minutes or until almost no indentation remains when touched lightly in center. Cool 2 minutes; remove from cookie sheet to wire rack.

1 Cookie: Calories 95 (Calories from Fat 45); Fat 5g (Saturated 1g); Cholesterol 0mg; Sodium 65mg; Carbohydrate 11g (Dietary Fiber 0g); Protein 1g.
Diet Exchanges: 1/2 starch, 1 fat..

Glazed Lemon Bars

BAKE: 35 min per pan ● YIELD: 24 bars

1 cup Bisquick Original baking mix

2 tablespoons powdered sugar

2 tablespoons butter or margarine

3/4 cup granulated sugar

1/4 cup flaked coconut, if desired

1 tablespoon Bisquick Original baking mix

2 teaspoons grated lemon peel

2 tablespoons lemon juice

2 eggs

Lemon Glaze (below)

Heat oven to 350°. Mix 1 cup baking mix and the powdered sugar in small bowl. Cut in butter, using pastry blender or crisscrossing 2 knives, until crumbly. Press in ungreased square pan, 8 × 8 × 2 inches. Bake about 10 minutes or until light brown.

Mix remaining ingredients except Lemon Glaze. Pour over baked layer. Bake about 25 minutes or until set and golden brown. Loosen edges from sides of pan while warm. Spread with Lemon Glaze; cool completely. Cut into 6 rows by 4 rows.

Lemon Glaze

1/2 cup powdered sugar

1 tablespoon lemon juice

Mix ingredients until smooth.

1 Bar: Calories 75 (Calories from Fat 20); Fat 2g (Saturated 1g); Cholesterol 20mg; Sodium 90mg; Carbohydrate 13g (Dietary Fiber 0g); Protein 1g.
Diet Exchanges: 1 starch.

Cookie Tips

The strong flavor of lemon provides lots of flavor, so you don't miss the fat as much. This version of lemon bars has half the fat of a traditional recipe.

Make It Your Way

Cut into diamonds or triangles and arrange on a doily-lined serving platter. See our bar-cutting diagram on pages 58–59.

Raspberry-Chocolate Bars

BAKE: 30 min per pan ● YIELD: 48 bars

1 1/2 cups all-purpose flour

3/4 cup sugar

3/4 cup butter or margarine, softened

1 package (10 ounces) frozen sweetened raspberries, thawed and undrained

1/4 cup orange juice

1 tablespoon cornstarch

3/4 cup miniature semisweet chocolate chips

Heat oven to 350°. Beat flour, sugar and butter with electric mixer on medium speed, or mix with spoon. Press in bottom of ungreased rectangular pan, 13×9×2 inches. Bake 15 minutes.

Mix raspberries, orange juice and cornstarch in 1-quart saucepan. Heat to boiling, stirring constantly. Boil and stir 1 minute. Cool 10 minutes. Sprinkle chocolate chips over baked layer. Spoon raspberry mixture over chocolate chips; spread carefully.

Bake about 20 minutes or until raspberry mixture is set. Refrigerate until chocolate is firm. Cut into 8 rows by 6 rows.

1 Bar: Calories 80 (Calories from Fat 35); Fat 4g (Saturated 1g); Cholesterol 0mg; Sodium 35mg; Carbohydrate 10g (Dietary Fiber 0g); Protein 1g.
Diet Exchanges: 1/2 starch, 1 fat.

Raspberry-Chocolate Bars, Cardamon-Cashew Bars (page 308)

Chocolate-Pecan Squares

BAKE: 20 to 22 min per pan ● YIELD: 36 squares

Cookie Tips

These rich little bars will remind you of pecan pie, but they are cholesterol-free!

Make It Your Way

How about **Butterscotch Chocolate-Pecan Squares**? Get there by using 1/4 cup butterscotch-flavored chips and 1/4 cup semisweet chocolate chips instead of all chocolate chips.

1 cup all-purpose flour

1/2 cup packed brown sugar

3 tablespoons butter or margarine, softened

1/2 cup packed brown sugar

1/2 cup butter or margarine

1 cup chopped pecans

1 teaspoon vanilla

1/2 cup semisweet chocolate chips

Heat oven to 350°. Beat flour, 1/2 cup brown sugar and 3 tablespoons butter with electric mixer on low speed until blended. Beat on medium speed 1 to 2 minutes or until crumbly. Press evenly in bottom of ungreased square pan, 9×9×2 or 8×8×2 inches.

Cook 1/2 cup brown sugar and 1/2 cup butter over medium heat, stirring constantly, until mixture begins to boil. Boil and stir 1 minute. Stir in pecans and vanilla. Pour over layer in pan.

Bake 18 to 20 minutes or until topping is bubbly. Sprinkle evenly with chocolate chips. Bake 2 minutes longer to soften chocolate (do not spread). Cool 10 minutes; loosen edges with knife. Cool completely. Cut into 6 rows by 6 rows. Store covered in the refrigerator.

1 Square: Calories 80 (Calories from Fat 45); Fat 5g (Saturated 1g); Cholesterol 0mg; Sodium 35mg; Carbohydrate 8g (Dietary Fiber 0g); Protein 1g.
Diet Exchanges: 1/2 starch, 1 fat.

Chocolate-Pecan Squares

Cardamom-Cashew Bars

BAKE: 34 to 42 min per pan ● YIELD: 48 bars

Cookie Tips

This is the bar to make when you're entertaining friends who are watching their waistline. These bars are not only low-fat but also rich and delicious tasting.

Cashews

This kidney-shape nut grows out of the bottom of the cashew apple. Cashews have a wonderful sweet, buttery flavor.

Crust (below)

1 1/2 cups packed brown sugar

1/2 cup fat-free, cholesterol-free egg product or 2 eggs

3 tablespoons all-purpose flour

2 teaspoons vanilla

1/2 teaspoon ground cardamom or cinnamon

1/4 teaspoon salt

1 cup cashews, pieces and halves

Orange Drizzle (below)

Heat oven to 350°. Grease rectangular pan, 13×9×2 inches. Prepare Crust; press dough evenly in pan. Bake 15 to 20 minutes or until very light brown.

Beat remaining ingredients except cashews and Orange Drizzle in medium bowl with electric mixer on medium speed about 2 minutes or until thick and light colored. Stir in cashews. Spread over baked crust.

Bake 19 to 22 minutes or until top is golden brown and bars are set around edges. Cool completely. Spread with Orange Drizzle. Cut into 8 rows by 6 rows.

Crust

1/2 package (8-ounce size) reduced-fat cream cheese (Neufchâtel)

1/2 cup powdered sugar

1/4 cup packed brown sugar

2 teaspoons vanilla

1 egg yolk

1 1/4 cups all-purpose flour

Beat cream cheese and sugars in medium bowl with electric mixer on medium speed until fluffy. Beat in vanilla and egg yolk. Gradually stir in flour to make a soft dough.

Orange Drizzle

3/4 cup powdered sugar

1 tablespoon orange juice

Mix ingredients until smooth and spreadable.

1 Bar: Calories 100 (Calories from Fat 25); Fat 3g (Saturated 1g); Cholesterol 10mg; Sodium 55mg; Carbohydrate 16g (Dietary Fiber 0g); Protein 2g.
Diet Exchanges: 1 starch, 1/2 fat.

Golden Cereal-Nut Clusters

STAND: 1 to 2 hr • YIELD: About 2 dozen cookies

1/2 pound vanilla-flavored candy coating

3 cups Golden Grahams® cereal

1/2 cup salted peanuts

1/2 cup miniature marshmallows

Chop candy coating into small pieces; place in heavy 10-inch skillet. Cover and heat over low heat about 5 minutes or until coating is soft; remove from heat. Stir until smooth and creamy.

Stir in cereal until well coated. Stir in peanuts and marshmallows. Drop mixture by rounded tablespoonfuls onto waxed paper, or spread mixture evenly on waxed paper or aluminum foil. Let stand 1 to 2 hours or until completely set.

1 Cookie: Calories 95 (Calories from Fat 45); Fat 5g (Saturated 2g); Cholesterol 5mg; Sodium 60mg; Carbohydrate 11g (Dietary Fiber 0g); Protein 2g.
Diet Exchanges: 1/2 starch, 1 fat.

Cookie Tips

For gift-giving or for a pretty cookie tray presentation, drop the mixture into decorative miniature muffin liners.

Make It Your Way

Oh, **Chocolate Cereal-Nut Clusters** would taste good! All you need to do is substitute chocolate-flavored candy coating for the vanilla coating.

Butter Crunch Clusters

PREP: 10 min ● YIELD: About 2 dozen cookies

Cookie Tips

If you would like to reduce the fat, look for reduced-fat peanuts in the nut or snacks section of the supermarket.

Make It Your Way

To make **Apple-Cinnamon Butter Crunch Clusters**, use Apple Cinnamon Cheerios®.

1/2 cup butter or margarine

2/3 cup packed brown sugar

1 tablespoon corn syrup

2 cups Cheerios® cereal

1 cup salted cocktail peanuts or Spanish peanuts

Heat butter in 3-quart saucepan over low heat until melted. Stir in brown sugar and corn syrup. Heat to boiling over medium heat, stirring constantly. Boil and stir 1 minute; remove from heat.

Stir in cereal and peanuts until well coated. Drop mixture by tablespoonfuls onto waxed paper; cool.

1 Cookie: Calories 105 (Calories from Fat 65); Fat 7g (Saturated 1g); Cholesterol 0mg; Sodium 95mg; Carbohydrate 9g (Dietary Fiber 0g); Protein 2g.
Diet Exchanges: 1/2 starch, 1 fat.

Butter Crunch Clusters, Golden Cereal Nut Clusters (page 309)

Helpful Nutrition and Cooking Information

Nutrition Guidelines:

We provide nutrition information for each recipe that includes calories, fat, cholesterol, sodium, carbohydrate, fiber and protein. Individual food choices can be based on this information

Recommended intake for a daily diet of 2,000 calories as set by the Food and Drug Organization

Total Fat	Less than 65g
Saturated Fat	Less than 20g
Cholesterol	Less than 300mg
Sodium	Less than 2,400mg
Total Carbohydrate	300g
Dietary Fiber	25g

Criteria Used for Calculating Nutrition Information:

- The first ingredient was used wherever a choice is given (such as 1/3 cup sour cream or plain yogurt).

- The first ingredient amount was used wherever a range is given (such as 3 to 3 1/2 pound cut-up broiler-fryer chicken).

- The first serving number was used wherever a range is given (such as 4 to 6 servings).

- "If desired" ingredients (such as sprinkle with brown sugar if desired) and recipe variations were *not* included.

- Only the amount of a marinade or frying oil that is estimated to be absorbed by the food during preparation or cooking was calculated.

Ingredients Used in Recipe Testing and Nutrition Calculations:

- Ingredients used for testing represent those that the majority of consumers use in their homes: large eggs, 2% milk, 80% lean ground beef, canned ready-to-use chicken broth, and vegetable oil spread containing *not less than 65% fat*.

- Fat-free, low-fat or low-sodium products are not used, unless otherwise indicated.

- Solid vegetable shortening (not butter, margarine, nonstick cooking sprays or vegetable oil spread as they can cause sticking problems) is used to grease pans, unless otherwise indicated.

Equipment Used in Recipe Testing:

We use equipment for testing that the majority of consumers use in their homes. If a specific piece of equipment (such as a wire whisk) is necessary for recipe success, it will be listed in the recipe.

- Cookware and bakeware **without** nonstick coatings were used, unless otherwise indicated.

- No dark colored, black or insulated bakeware was used.

- When a baking *pan* is specified in a recipe, a *metal* pan was used; a baking *dish* or pie *plate* means oven-proof glass was used.

- An electric hand mixer was used for mixing *only when mixer speeds are specified* in the recipe directions. When a mixer speed is not given, a spoon or fork was used.

Metric Conversion Guide

Volume

U.S. Units	Canadian Metric	Australian Metric
1/4 teaspoon	1 mL	1 ml
1/2 teaspoon	2 mL	2 ml
1 teaspoon	5 mL	5 ml
1 tablespoon	15 mL	20 ml
1/4 cup	50 mL	60 ml
1/3 cup	75 mL	80 ml
1/2 cup	125 mL	125 ml
2/3 cup	150 mL	170 ml
3/4 cup	175 mL	190 ml
1 cup	250 mL	250 ml
1 quart	1 liter	1 liter
1 1/2 quarts	1.5 liters	1.5 liters
2 quarts	2 liters	2 liters
2 1/2 quarts	2.5 liters	2.5 liters
3 quarts	3 liters	3 liters
4 quarts	4 liters	4 liters

Weight

U.S. Units	Canadian Metric	Australian Metric
1 ounce	30 grams	30 grams
2 ounces	55 grams	60 grams
3 ounces	85 grams	90 grams
4 ounces (1/4 pound)	115 grams	125 grams
8 ounces (1/2 pound)	225 grams	225 grams
16 ounces (1 pound)	455 grams	500 grams
1 pound	455 grams	1/2 kilogram

Measurements

Inches	Centimeters
1	2.5
2	5.0
3	7.5
4	10.0
5	12.5
6	15.0
7	17.5
8	20.5
9	23.0
10	25.5
11	28.0
12	30.5
13	33.0

Temperatures

Fahrenheit	Celsius
32°	0°
212°	100°
250°	120°
275°	140°
300°	150°
325°	160°
350°	180°
375°	190°
400°	200°
425°	220°
450°	230°
475°	240°
500°	260°

Note: The recipes in this cookbook have not been developed or tested using metric measures. When converting recipes to metric, some variations in quality may be noted.

Index

A

Almond(s)
  Bars, 154
  Bars, Cherry-, 76
  Biscotti, Orange-, 205
  Blanched, about, 135
  Bonbons, 186
  -Coconut Topping, 87
  Cookies, Ginger-, 302
  Cookies, Meringue-
    Topped, 192
  Crisps, 230
  -Filled Crescents, 239
  Glaze, 186
  Macaroons, 250
  Macaroons, Coconut-, 290
  Paste, about, 192
  Pillows, Orange-, 267
  Pinwheels, Cherry-, 232
  Tea Cakes, Chocolate-, 181
  Topping, 154
Amaretto Brownies, 64
Amaretto Frosting, 64
Animal Cookies, 133
Anise Biscotti, 204
Apple
  Balls, No-Bake, 197
  Bars, Double, 80
  -Cinnamon Butter Crunch
    Clusters, 310
  Cookies, Oatmeal-
Applesauce
  –Brown Sugar Drops, 36
  Cookies, 38
  Cookies, Spicy Iced, 104
  -Granola Cookies, 46
Apricot
  Balls, No-Bake, 197
  Bars, 199

Bars, Date-, 72
-Cherry Bars, 157
Filling, 275
Linzer Bars, 74
Pockets, Glazed
    Chocolate, 236

B

Baked-On Frosting, 115
Baking pans
  For bars, xxi
  Greasing, xxv
  Lining with foil, xxiv, 85
Baking powder, in recipes, xii
Baking soda, in recipes, xii
Banana
  Bars, Frosted, 291
  -Cornmeal Cookies, 193
  -Ginger Jumbles, 47
  -Nut Bars, 78
  Oaties, Frosted, 21
Bars
  Almond, 154
  Apricot-Cherry, 157
  Baking pans for, xxi
  Baking tips for, xxiv
  Banana-Nut, 78
  Caramel Candy, 90
  Caramel Fudge, 153
  Cardamom-Cashew, 308
  Carrot-Raisin, 158
  Cherry-Almond, 76
  Chocolate Chip–Pecan, 152
  Chocolate-Raspberry
    Cheesecake, 164
  Cinnamon-Coffee, 82
  Coconut Macaroon, 97
  Cutting, tips for, xxvi, xxviii

Cutting guide for, 58–59
Double Apple, 80
Dream, 87
Easy-Yet-Elegant
    Raspberry, 160
Frosted Banana, 291
German Chocolate, 150
Glazed Lemon, 303
Lemon, 161
Lemon Cheesecake, 166
Lemon Cream Oat, 88
Linzer Torte, 74
Luscious Lemon-
    Raspberry, 162
Mixed Nut, 91
Mousse, 85
No-Bake Honey-Oat, 96
Peanut Butter and Jam, 126
Peanut Butter and Jelly, 159
Peanut Butter–Toffee, 156
Pumpkin-Spice, 81
Raspberry-Chocolate, 304
Rocky Road, 149
Tiramisu Cheesecake, 86
Toffee, 84
Triple Chocolate-
    Cherry, 158
Tuxedo Cheesecake, 167
The Ultimate Date, 72
Zucchini, 77
Baseballs, Cinnamon, 135
Berry Cups, Chocolate, 260
Berry Madeleines, 257
Bird's Nest Cookies, 216
Biscotti
  Anise, 204
  Orange-Almond, 205
  Walnut, 296
Black-Eyed Susans, 116
Bloom, on chocolate, xv

Blueberry Cheesecake Bars,
    Lemon-, 166
Bonbons, Almond, 186
Bourbon Balls, Chocolate-, 198
Brandied Fruit Drops, 42
Brandy Snap Cups, 260
Brooms, Witches', 112
Browned Butter Glaze, 38
Brownie Crinkles, 294
Brownie Drop Cookies, 143
Brownie(s)
    Amaretto, 64
    Baking tips for, xxiv
    Cocoa, 62
    Cream Cheese, 70
    Cutting guide for, 58–59
    Cutting tips for, xxvi
    Fudgy Saucepan, 60
    German Chocolate, 68
    Milk Chocolate–Malt, 61
    Mocha, 66
    Peanut Butter Swirl, 71
    The Ultimate, 56
    Vanilla, 65
Brown Sugar, in recipes,
    xi, 182
Brown Sugar Drops, 36
Brown Sugar Maple No-Roll
    Sugar Cookies, 177
Bumblebees, 118
Butter, in recipes, ix–x
Butter Crunch Clusters, 310
Butter Glaze, Browned, 38
Butterscotch
    Chocolate-Pecan Squares, 306
    Mousse Bars, 85
    -Oatmeal Crinkles, 182
    Shortbread, 222

C

Candy Cookies, Giant
    Colorful, 100
Candy Corn Shortbread, 110
Cappuccino-Pistachio
    Shortbread, 202
Caramel

Apple Cookies, 120
Candy Bars, 90
Frosting, 226
Fudge Bars, 153
Glaze, 120
-Pecan Brownies, 62
-Pecan Cookies, 122
Cardamom, about, 282
Cardamom-Cashew Bars, 308
"Carrot" cookie press, 190
Carrot-Molasses Cookies, 146
Carrot-Raisin Bars, 158
Cashew Bars, Cardamom-, 308
Cashew Biscotti, Orange-, 205
Celebrations, listing of cookie
    recipes for, 243
Cereal-Nut Clusters,
    Golden, 309
Cheesecake Bars
    Chocolate-Raspberry, 164
    Lemon, 166
    Tiramisu, 86
    Tuxedo, 167
Cherry
    -Almond Bars, 76
    -Almond Pinwheels, 232
    Bars, Apricot-, 157
    Bars, Triple Chocolate-, 158
    –Brown Sugar Drops, 36
    Cream Cheese Brownies, 70
    Glaze, 157
    Madeleines, 257
    Ravioli Cookies, 233
    Sand Tarts, Chocolate-, 259
    Triangles, 240
Chocolate. *See also* Chocolate
    Chip; Fudge; Fudgy
    -Almond Tea Cakes, 181
    Bars, German, 150
    Bars, Raspberry-, 304
    Berry Cups, 260
    -Bourbon Balls, 198
    Brownies, German, 68
    Brownies, Triple, 56
    -Caramel Fudge Bars, 153
    Cereal-Nut Clusters, 309
    Checkers, Pistachio-, 200
    -Cherry Bars, Triple, 158

-Cherry Sand Tarts, 259
Chocolaty Meringue Stars, 298
Cookies, 138
Curls, 212
-Dipped Ladyfingers, 248
Drizzle, 259
Drop Cookies, 25
Frosting, 25
Glaze, 66, 122
-Glazed Graham Crackers, 224
Grating, 212
Linzer Hearts, 266
Malted Milk Cookies, 101
–Peanut Butter No-Bakes,
    28, 128
–Peanut Windmills, 129
–White Chocolate Chunk
    Cookies, Outrageous
    Double, 15
Melted, dipping, 212
Melted, drizzling, 211
Melting, procedure for, xiii–xiv
Milk, –Malt Brownies, 61
Mini-Chippers, 299
-Mint Cookies, 26
-Oatmeal Chewies, 24
Oatmeal Lacies, 20
-Orange–Chocolate Chip
    Cookies, 178
Peanut Bars, 90
and Peanut Butter-Dipped
    Elephant Ears, 105
Peanut Butter Squares,
    No-Bake, 94
-Pecan Squares, 306
-Peppermint Refrigerator
    Cookies, 174
Pockets, Glazed, 236
-Raspberry Cheesecake
    Bars, 164
Seized, preventing, xiv
Shortbread, 221
Spritz, 244
Storage of, xv
Substitutes for, xviii
Topping, 85
Types of, xiii

Chocolate, White. *See* White
    Chocolate
Chocolate Chip. *See also*
    Chocolate Chip Cookie(s)
  Cream Squares, 220
  –Pecan Bars, 152
  -Raspberry Cheesecake
    Dessert, 164
  Rocky Road Bars, 149
Chocolate Chip Cookie(s), 140
  Chocolate, 138
  Chocolate-Covered
    Peanut-, 14
  Chocolate-Orange–, 178
  Deluxe, 6
  Double Chocolate–, 12
  Fresh Mint–, 10
  Giant Toffee–, 5
  Inside-Out, 12
  Oatmeal–, 2
  Peanut Butter–, 141
  Sandwich, 8
  Sour Cream–Milk, 9
  The Ultimate, 4
Chocolaty Meringue Stars, 298
Christmas Bars, 77
Christmas Cookie Slices, 214
Christmas Magic Window
    Cookies, 109
Cinnamon
  Baseballs, 135
  -Coffee Bars, 82
  Cookies, Honey-, 32
  Espresso Cookies, 180
  Footballs, 135
  Knots, 194
  -Mocha Cookies, Frosted, 29
  -Nut Crisps, 231
  Twists, 194
Clock, Ginger Cookie, 108
Clove-Spiced Frosting, 77
Coating, Espresso, 180
Cobweb Cookies, 113
Cocoa Brownies, 62
Coconut
  -Almond Macaroons, 290
  Bars, Carrot-Raisin, 158
  Brownies, 66

-Fudge Cups, 195
-Fudge Filling, 195
Macaroon Bars, 97
Meringue Cookies, 49
-Pecan Frosting, 68
Pineapple Puffs, 43
–Sour Cream Cookies, 38
-Sugar Cookies, No-Roll, 300
Teacakes, Toasted, 179
Tinted, 212
Toasted, 212
Topping, Almond-, 87
Coffee Bars, Cinnamon-, 82
Coffee Bean Mocha Squares, 220
Coffee Frosting, 66
Coffee Liqueur Brownie
    Drops, 143
Colored Sugar, 212–13
Confectioners' sugar, in
    recipes, xii
Cookie cutters, substitutes
    for, 216
Cookie dough
  Measuring, xxii
  Mixing tips, xxii
  Refrigerating and freezing, xxvi
  Soft or sticky, cure for, xxviii
Cookie-Mold Cookies, 258
Cookie Pizza, 119
Cookie(s)
  Baking tips for, xxv–xxvi
  "Cures", xxvii–xxix
  Equipment for making,
    xx–xxii
  Ingredient equivalents, xvi–xvii
  Mailing tips, xxvii
  Painting, 211
  Problems and solutions,
    xxvii–xxix
  Storing, xxvii, 298
Cookie sheets
  Cooling, xxv
  Greasing, xxv
  Liners for, xx
  Types of, xx
Cooling racks, xxii
Cornmeal Cookies,
    Banana-, 193

Cornmeal Crispies, 52
Corn syrup, in recipes, xi
Cranberry-Filled Spritz, 246
Cranberry-Orange Cookies, 278
Cran-Raspberry-Chocolate
    Bars, 304
Cream Cheese
  Brownies, 70
  Filling, 70
  Frosting, 78
  Softening, in microwave, 162
  Spread, 216
Cream Squares, 220
Cream Wafers, 218
Creamy
  Filling, 218
  Frosting, 221
  Frosting, Easy, 225, 227
  White Frosting, 114
Curls, Chocolate, 212
Currants, about, 42

D

Date
  Bars, The Ultimate, 72
  Cookies, Spicy Pumpkin-, 39
  Cookies, Whole Wheat–, 34
  Drop Cookies,
    Old-Fashioned, 40
  -Filled Spritz, 246
  Filling, 72
  -Nut Pinwheels, 232
Decorated Gingerbread
    Cookies, Easy, 148
Decorating Glaze, 135
Decorating ideas, easy, 210–13
Decorator Cookies, Lemon, 190
Decorator's Frosting or
    Glaze, 210
Deluxe Chocolate Chip
    Cookies, 6
Dipping into chocolate, 212
Double Apple Bars, 80
Double Banana-Nut Dessert, 78
Double Chocolate–Chocolate
    Chip Cookies, 12
Double Chocolate Drops, 143

Double Chocolate–White Chocolate Chunk Cookies, Outrageous, 15
Double Lemon Cookies, 142
Double–Peanut Butter No-Bakes, 28, 128
Double Oat Cookies, 18
Double Peanut Cookies, 30
Dough. *See* Cookie dough
Dream Bars, 87
Drizzling melted chocolate, 211
Drop cookies
  listing of recipes, 1
  Measuring dough for, xxii

E

Easy Creamy Frosting, 225, 227
Easy Decorated Gingerbread Cookies, 148
Easy decorating ideas, 210–13
Easy Glaze, 239
Easy Pink Frosting, 124
Easy-Yet-Elegant Raspberry Bars, 160
Eggs, in recipes, xii, 143, 192
Egg Yolk Paint, 106, 210
Elephant Ears, Mini, 105
Equipment, cookie-making, xx–xxii
Espresso Coating, 180
Espresso Cookies, Cinnamon, 180
Esther's Bracelets, 276

F

Fats, types of, ix–xi
Fig-Filled Whole Wheat Cookies, 199
Fig Filling, 199
Filling. *See also* Frosting
  Apricot, 275
  Coconut-Fudge, 195
  Cream Cheese, 70
  Creamy, 218
  Date, 72
  Fig, 199
  Peach, 240

Pecan, 92
Plum, 275
Poppy Seed, 234, 275
Prune, 274
"Flocking", on cookies, 211
Florentines, Miniature, 269
Flour
  Measuring, viii
  Storing, viii
  Types of, vi–vii
Food coloring
  Paint, 210
  Stains, 213
  Types of, 124
Food processors, xxi, 296
Footballs, Cinnamon, 135
Four Chip Cookies, 4
Freezing cookie dough, xxvi
Fresh Mint–Chocolate Chip Cookies, 10
Frosted
  Banana Bars, 291
  Banana Oaties, 21
  Cinnamon-Mocha Cookies, 29
  Jumbo Molasses Cookies, 288
  Pumpkin-Pecan Cookies, 279
  Soft Molasses Cookies, 37
  Spice Cookies, 226
Frosting, 285. *See also* Filling; Glaze; Topping
  Amaretto, 64
  Baked-On, 115
  Caramel, 226
  Chocolate, 25
  Clove-Spiced, 77
  Coconut-Pecan, 68
  Coffee, 66
  Cream Cheese, 78
  Creamy, 221
  Creamy Vanilla, 65
  Creamy White, 114, 227
  Decorator's, 210
  Easy Creamy, 225
  Easy Pink, 124
  Gingerbread, 272
  Lemon-Lime, 44
  Malted Milk, 101

Mocha, 29
Orange, 278
Peppermint, 26
Rum, 176
Spiced, 279
Vanilla, 21
White, 291
Yogurt, 215
Fruit. *See also specific fruits*
  Drops, Brandied, 42
  Drops, Whole Wheat–, 34
  -Flavored Sugar Cookies, 208
Fudge
  Bars, Caramel, 153
  Cups, Coconut-, 195
  Filling, Coconut-, 195
Fudgy
  Layer Squares, 83
  Macadamia Cookies, 27
  Saucepan Brownies, 60

G

German Chocolate Bars, 150
German Chocolate Brownies, 68
Ghost Cookies, 114
Giant Colorful Candy Cookies, 100
Giant Honey and Oat Cookies, 22
Giant Pizza Cookie Slices, 108
Giant Toffee–Chocolate Chip Cookies, 5
Ginger
  -Almond Cookies, 302
  Cookie Clock, 108
  Cookies, Moravian, 225
  Crystallized, about, 196
  Jumbles, Banana-, 47
  -Pecan Chews, 50
  Shortbread Wedges, 196
Gingerbread
  Cookies, 227
  Cookies, Easy Decorated, 148
  Frosting, 272
  Village, 272
Gingerpop Cookies, 124

Glaze, 276. *See also* Frosting;
    Topping
  Almond, 186
  Browned Butter, 38
  Caramel, 120
  Cherry, 157
  Chocolate, 122
  Chocolate Drizzle, 259
  Decorating, 135
  Decorator's, 210
  Easy, 239
  Easy Chocolate, 66
  Key Lime, 247
  Lemon, 303
  Light Brown, 36
  Orange, 267
  Orange Drizzle, 308
  Pink, 76
  Poppy Seed, 53
  Rosette, 262
  Tart Lemon, 281
  Thin, 282
  Thin Cookie, 270
  Two-Way, 237
  Vanilla, 43
  Vanilla Drizzle, 126
  White, 82
Glazed Chocolate
    Pockets, 236
Glazed Lemon Bars, 303
Glazing Icing, 268
Golden Cereal-Nut
    Clusters, 309
Goldfish Drops, 131
Graham Crackers, Chocolate-
    Glazed, 224
Granola Cookies, 143
Granola Cookies,
    Applesauce-, 46
Granulated colored sugar, 144
Granulated white sugar, in
    recipes, xi
Grating chocolate, 212
Greasing cookie sheets and
    pans, xxv
Green Cherry-Almond Bars, 76
Grinding oats, viii–ix

H

Half-Moon Cookies,
    Swedish, 251
Halloween Cutout Cookies, 106
Hamantaschen, 274
Hand-shaped cookies, listing of
    recipes, 169
Hats, Witches', 113
Hazelnut
  Meringue Sticks, 241
  -Oatmeal Lacies, 24
  Sablés, 280
Honey
  Cookies, Whole Wheat–, 32
  -Graham Cracker
      Cookies, 224
  -Oat Bars, No-Bake, 96
  and Oat Cookies, Giant, 22
  -Oat Sandwich Cookies, 189
  in recipes, xi
Hungarian Poppy Seed
    Cookies, 234

I

Ice-Cream Sandwiches, 130
Icing, 104
Icing, Glazing, 268
Ingredient(s)
  Equivalents, xvi–xvii
  in recipes, vi–xiii
  Substitutions, xviii–xix
Inside-Out Chocolate Chip
    Cookies, 12

J

Jam Bars, Peanut Butter
    and, 126
Jelly Bars, Peanut Butter
    and, 159
Joe Froggers, 228
Jumbo Molasses Cookies, 288

K

Key Lime Coolers, 247
Key Lime Glaze, 247

Kid cookies, listing of
    recipes, 99
Kringla, 196
Krumkake, 256

L

Ladyfingers, 248
Leaf Cookies, 120
Leavening agents, in recipes, xii
Lebkuchen, 268
Lemon
  Bars, 161
  Bars, Glazed, 303
  Cheesecake Bars, 166
  Cookies, 142
  Cream Oat Bars, 88
  Decorator Cookies, 190
  Glaze, 281, 303
  -Lime Cookies, 44
  -Lime Frosting, 44
  -Raspberry Bars, Luscious, 162
  Slices, 285
  Squares, 75
  Tea Biscuits, 281
Letter and Number
    Cookies, 133
Light Brown Glaze, 36
Lime
  Cookies, Lemon-, 44
  Coolers, Key, 247
  Frosting, Lemon-, 44
  Glaze, Key, 247
  Slices, 285
Linzer Hearts, Chocolate, 266
Linzer Torte Bars, 74
Liquids, in recipes, xii
Low-fat butter or margarine, x
Luscious Lemon-Raspberry
    Bars, 162

M

Macadamia Cookies, Fudgy, 27
Macadamia Cookies, White
    Chocolate Chunk-, 16
Macaroon Bars, Coconut, 97
Macaroons, Almond, 250

Macaroons, Coconut-
    Almond, 290
Madeleines, Orange, 257
Magic Window Cookies, 109
Mailing cookies, xxvii
Malt Brownies, Milk
    Chocolate–, 61
Malted Milk
    Cookies, 101
    Frosting, 101
    Powder, about, 61, 101
Maple No-Roll Sugar Cookies,
    Brown Sugar, 177
Maple-Nut Refrigerator
    Cookies, 172
Maraschino cherries, about, 76
Marbled look, creating, 211
Margarine, in recipes, x
Marshmallow Treats, Peanut
    Butter–, 292
Mary's Sugar Cookies, 208
Measuring cups, xxi
Measuring spoons, xxi
Melting chocolate, procedure
    for, xiii–xiv
Meringue
    Cookies, Coconut, 49
    Stars, Chocolaty, 298
    Sticks, Toffee, 241
    -Topped Almond
        Cookies, 192
Metric conversion guide, 313
Milk paint, 210
Miniature Florentines, 269
Mini Cookie Pizzas, 102
Mini Elephant Ears, 105
Mint
    Cookies, Chocolate-, 26
    Cream Cheese Brownies, 70
    Drops, Pastel, 48
    –Chocolate Chip Cookies,
        Fresh, 10
    Ravioli Cookies, 233
Mixed Nut Bars, 91
Mixers, hand or stand, xxi
Mixes, listing of cookie recipes
    using, 137

Mixing dough, procedure
    for, xxii
Mocha
    Brownies, 66
    Cookies, Frosted
        Cinnamon-, 29
    Frosting, 29, 66
    Squares, Coffee Bean, 220
Molasses
    Cookies, Carrot-, 146
    Cookies, Jumbo, 288
    Cookies, Soft, 37
    in recipes, xi–xii, 225
Molding cookies, procedure for,
    xxiii–xxiv
Moravian Ginger Cookies, 225
Mousse Bars, 85
Multigrain Cutouts, 115

N

No-Bake(s)
    Apricot Balls, 197
    Chocolate–Peanut Butter,
        28, 128
    Honey-Oat Bars, 96
    Peanut Butter Squares, 94
No-Roll Coconut-Sugar
    Cookies, 300
No-Roll Sugar Cookies, 177
Number and Letter
    Cookies, 133
Nutmeg, about, 39
Nutrition information, 312
Nut(s). See also specific nuts
    Bars, Banana-, 78
    Bars, Mixed, 91
    Clusters, Golden Cereal-, 309
    Crisps, Cinnamon-, 231
    Cups, Fudge, 195
    Decorating with, 213
    Meringue Cookies, 49
    Pinwheels, Date-, 232
    Refrigerator Cookies,
        Maple-, 172
    Storing, xv
    Toasting, 64

O

Oat bran, about, 18
Oat(meal)
    Bars, Lemon Cream, 88
    Bars, No-Bake Honey-, 96
    Chewies, Chocolate-, 24
    Cookie, The Ultimate, 2
    Cookies, 142
    Cookies, Double, 18
    Cookies, Giant Honey and, 22
    Cookies, Toasted, 17
    Crinkles, Butterscotch, 182
    Lacies, 20
    Oaties, Frosted Banana, 21
    -Raisin Cookies, 293
    Sandwich Cookies,
        Honey-, 189
Oats
    Grinding, viii–ix
    Toasting, viii
    Types of, for recipes, viii, 88
Oils, types of, ix–xi
Old-Fashioned Date Drop
    Cookies, 40
Old-Fashioned Rum-Raisin
    Cookies, 41
Orange
    -Almond Biscotti, 205
    Almond Macaroons, 250
    -Almond Pillows, 267
    Biscotti, 204
    Cookies, 44
    Cookies, Chocolate-, 26
    Cookies, Cranberry-, 278
    Drizzle, 308
    Frosting, 278
    Glaze, 267, 308
    Madeleines, 257
    –Chocolate Chip Cookies,
        Chocolate-, 178
    Ravioli Cookies, 233
    Slices, 285
Outrageous Double
    Chocolate–White
    Chocolate Chunk
    Cookies, 15

P

Packaged mixes, listing of
   recipes using, 137
Paint (cookie)
   Designs, 211
   Egg Yolk, 106, 210
   Food color, 210
   Milk, 210
Palmiers, 252
Pancake turners, xxi
Pastel Mint Drops, 48
Pastry blenders, 152
Peach Filling, 240
Peach Triangles, 240
Peanut Butter
   and Chocolate-Dipped
      Elephant Ears, 105
   Cookies, 170
   Hidden Middles, 188
   and Jam Bars, 126
   and Jelly Bars, 159
   –Toffee Bars, 156
   –Chocolate Chip Cookies, 141
   –Marshmallow Treats, 292
   No-Bakes, Chocolate–,
      28, 128
   Squares, No-Bake, 94
   Swirl Brownies, 71
Peanut(s)
   Bars, Chocolate, 90
   -Chocolate Chip Cookies,
      Chocolate-Covered, 14
   Cookies, Double, 30
   Drops, Goldfish, 130
   Golden Cereal-Nut
      Clusters, 309
   and Oat Cookies, Giant
      Honey-Roasted, 22
   –Sour Cream Cookies,
      Salted, 38
   Storing, xv
   Windmills, Chocolate–, 129
Pear Bars, Double, 80
Pecan(s)
   Bars, Chocolate Chip–, 152
   Brownies, Caramel-, 62

Chews, Ginger-, 50
Cookies, Caramel-, 122
Cookies, Frosted
   Pumpkin-, 279
Crisps, 230
Filling, 92
Frosting, Coconut-, 68
Maple-Nut Refrigerator
   Cookies, 172
Pie Squares, 92
Squares, Chocolate-, 306
Peppermint
   Coconut-Almond
      Macaroons, 290
   Frosting, 26
   Pinwheels, 214
   Refrigerator Cookies,
      Chocolate-, 174
Pineapple Puffs, 43
Pink Frosting, Easy, 124
Pink Glaze, 76
Pinwheels
   Cherry-Almond, 232
   Date-Nut, 232
   Peppermint, 214
Pistachio-Chocolate
   Checkers, 200
Pistachio Shortbread,
   Cappuccino-, 202
Pizza, Cookie, 119
Pizza Cookie Slices, Giant, 108
Pizzas, Mini Cookie, 102
Pizzelles, 254
Plum Filling, 275
Poppy Drop Cookies, 53
Poppy Seed
   Cookies, Hungarian, 234
   -Filled Crescents, 239
   Filling, 275
   Glaze, 53
Potato flour, about, 251
Powdered sugar, in recipes, xii
Pressed cookies
   Listing of recipes, 169
   Procedure for making, xxiv
Prune Filling, 274
Puff pastry, about, 252

Pumpkin
   -Date Cookies, Spicy, 39
   -Pecan Cookies, Frosted, 279
   -Spice Bars, 81

R

Raisin
   Bars, Carrot-, 158
   Cake Mix Cookies,
      Oatmeal, 142
   -Chocolate Chip Cookies,
      Chocolate-Covered, 14
   Cookies, Banana-, 47
   Cookies, Oatmeal, 293
   Cookies, Old-Fashioned
      Rum-, 41
   -Filled Chocolate Drops, 25
   Sandwich Cookies, Rum-, 176
Raspberry
   Bars, Easy-Yet-Elegant, 160
   Bars, Luscious Lemon-, 162
   Brownies, 66
   Cheesecake Bars,
      Chocolate-, 164
   -Chocolate Bars, 304
   Logs, 229
Ravioli Cookies, Mint, 233
Reduced-calorie butter or
   margarine, x
Refrigerating cookie dough, xxvi
Refrigerator Cookies
   Chocolate-Peppermint, 174
   Maple-Nut, 172
   Tips for, xxiv
   The Ultimate, 171
Rich Peanut Butter Chip
   Cookies, 170
Rocky Road Bars, 149
Rocky Road Cookies, 125
Rolled cookies
   Listing of recipes, 207
   Procedure for making,
      xxii–xxiii
Rolled Sugar Cookies, 144
Rolling pins, xxiii
Rosette Glaze, 262

Rosettes, 262
Rum
   –Chunk and Macadamia
      Cookies, White
      Chocolate, 16
   Frosting, 176
   -Raisin Cookies, Old-
      Fashioned, 41
   -Raisin Sandwich Cookies, 176
   Types of, 41
Russian Tea Cakes, 179

S

Sablés, Hazelnut, 280
Salted Peanut–Sour Cream
   Cookies, 38
Sandbakelse mold, 259
Sandwich Cookies
   Banana-Cornmeal, 193
   Chocolate Chip, 8
   Honey-Oat, 189
   Maple-Nut, 172
   Rum-Raisin, 176
Sandwiches, Ice-Cream, 130
Scoops, cookie or ice-cream,
   xvii, 100
Seascape Cookies, Spicy, 282
Seizing, preventing, xiv
Shortbread
   Butterscotch, 222
   Candy Corn, 110
   Cappuccino-Pistachio, 202
   Chocolate, 221
   Wedges, Ginger, 196
Shortening, in recipes, xi
Snickerdoodles, 183
Snowflakes, 261
Softening butter, ix
Soft Molasses Cookies, 37
Soft No-Roll Sugar
   Cookies, 300
Sour Cream
   Cookies, 38
   –Milk Chocolate Chip
      Cookies, 9
   –Sugar Cookies, 209

Special diets, listing of cookie
      recipes for, 287
Spice
   Bars, Pumpkin-, 81
   Cookies, Frosted, 226
   –Sour Cream Cookies, 38
   Spritz, 244
Spiced Frosting, 279
Spicy Iced Applesauce
      Cookies, 104
Spicy Pumpkin-Date
      Cookies, 39
Spicy Seascape Cookies, 282
Spoons, wooden, xxi
Spread, Cream Cheese, 216
Spring Blossoms, 116
Springerle, 254
Spritz, Date-Filled, 246
Spritz, The Ultimate, 244
Squares
   Chocolate-Pecan, 306
   Cream, 220
   Fudgy Layer, 83
   Lemon, 75
   No-Bake Peanut Butter, 94
   Pecan Pie, 92
Stains, food color, 213
Stockings, Sugar Cookie, 270
Storing cookie dough, xxvi
Storing cookies, xxvii, 298
Strawberry Bars, Triple
      Chocolate-, 158
Substitutions, ingredient,
      xviii–xix
Sugar
   Colored, 212–13
   Granulated colored, 144
   Granulated white, xi
   Powdered, xii
   "Sanding", 285
   Vanilla, 65
Sugar Cookie(s)
   Mary's, 208
   No-Roll, 177
   No-Roll Coconut-, 300

Rolled, 144
Sour Cream–, 209
Stockings, 270
Tarts, 216
Sunflower Cookies, 203
Sunshine Cookies, 238
Swedish Half-Moon
      Cookies, 251
Sweeteners, in recipes, xi–xii

T

"Thimble" Cookies, 185
Thin Cookie Glaze, 270
Thin Glaze, 282
Three-Leaf Clover, 184
Thumbprint Cookies, 185
Tinted Coconut, 212
Tiramisu Cheesecake Bars, 86
Toasted Coconut Teacakes, 179
Toasted Oatmeal Cookies, 17
Toasting procedure for
   Coconut, 212
   Nuts, 64
   Oats, viii
Toffee
   Bars, 84
   -Chocolate Chip Cookies,
      Giant, 5
   Toffee Bars, Peanut Butter,
      156
   Meringue Sticks, 241
Topping
   Almond, 154
   Almond-Coconut, 87
   Chocolate, 85

Triple Chocolate Brownies, 56
Triple Chocolate-Cherry
    Bars, 158
Tuxedo Cheesecake Bars, 167
Two-Way Glaze, 237

U

The Ultimate
    Brownie, 56
    Chocolate Chip Cookie, 4
    Date Bars, 72
    Oatmeal Cookie, 2
    Refrigerator Cookies, 171
    Spritz, 244
    Valentine's Day Cookie, 264

V

Valentine's Day Cookie, The
    Ultimate, 264
Vanilla
    Bourbon Balls, 198
    Brownies, 65
    Drizzle, 126

-Frosted Toasted Oatmeal
    Cookies, 17
Frosting, 21, 65
Glaze, 43
Milk Chip Cookies, Sour
    Cream-, 9
Milk Chips, about, 65
Sugar, 65
Vegetable oil
    Spreads, in recipes, x
    Types of, ix–xi

W

Walnut Biscotti, 296
Walnut Pie Squares, 92
Wheat germ, about, 115
White Chocolate
    About, xiii
    Chunk Cookies, Outrageous
        Double Chocolate–, 15
    Chunk–Macadamia
        Cookies, 16
    Melting, xiv
White Frosting, 114, 227, 291

White Glaze, 82
Whole Wheat
    –Banana-Ginger Cookies, 47
    –Brown Sugar Drops, 36
    Cookies, Fig-Filled, 199
    –Fruit Drops, 34
    –Honey Cookies, 32
    Rounds, 35
Windmills,
    Chocolate–Peanut, 129
Wintergreen Refrigerator
    Cookies, Chocolate-, 174
Wire cooling racks, xxii
Witches' Brooms, 112
Witches' Hats, 113

Y

Yogurt Frosting, 215
Yogurt Stack Cookies, 215

Z

Zucchini Bars, 77